John Brocklebank

Continental and Oriental Travels

Being Excursions in France, Italy, Egypt, Sinai ...

John Brocklebank

Continental and Oriental Travels
Being Excursions in France, Italy, Egypt, Sinai ...

ISBN/EAN: 9783337209612

Printed in Europe, USA, Canada, Australia, Japan

Cover: Foto ©Andreas Hilbeck / pixelio.de

More available books at **www.hansebooks.com**

CONTINENTAL AND ORIENTAL TRAVELS:

BEING

EXCURSIONS

IN

FRANCE, ITALY, EGYPT, SINAI, PALESTINE, AND SYRIA.

WITH

BIBLICAL ELUCIDATIONS AND HISTORICAL NOTES.

BY

JOHN BROCKLEBANK.

LONDON:
HAMILTON, ADAMS, & Co., PATERNOSTER ROW;
SIMPKIN, MARSHALL, & Co., STATIONERS'-HALL-COURT.
LEEDS: H. W. WALKER, 37, BRIGGATE.
MDCCCLXV.

PREFACE.

It may have surprised my Friends that, having spent the principal part of my life in a rural retreat, I should be induced to wander from my native country, and face the perils of a journey by land and sea, extending over thousands of miles. And as I presume none but Friends will interest themselves in my adventures, I can have no hesitation in revealing the motives by which I was influenced. I travelled that I might gain a more comprehensive and particular knowledge of the World, especially respecting the Religious Condition of its Inhabitants.

When it pleased God to convert my soul, I began to "Search the Scriptures" for the "Words of Eternal Life," and as my experience became enlarged, I directed attention to the study of Human Nature. My faith in the Sacred Writings was thus confirmed, for I observed that the Character and Conduct of men improved in proportion as they yielded to their guidance. After studying Religion and Humanity at home for about five and twenty years, I conceived a desire personally to know something of the Manners, Customs and Religions of Foreigners. I set out accordingly in the Spring of 1862, on a Tour upon the European Continent, passing through France, and visiting Italy. And so much was I interested with what I had seen, that I afterwards resolved, the Lord permitting, to visit Egypt, the Desert of Sinai, and the Holy Land. Mr. Plummer, of Leeds, proposed that two of his sons should accompany me in the latter journey, which I regarded as a favourable circumstance, since in the former, I had felt the inconvenience of being alone.

It may be useful here to remark, that we obtained Circular Notes on application to Messrs. Coutts & Co., Bankers, London, who have Representatives throughout the Civilised World. We found these convenient as being at once portable and safe. Passports can be procured from the Foreign Office through the recommendation of a friendly Banker. These are *viséd* by authorised Officials of the Countries specified in them.

In the present Work, which is my first attempt at Authorship, I invite my Friends more to regard the *matter* furnished than the *manner* in which it is presented. I have not scrupled to avail myself of every aid within reach, often adopting the language of my Authors, and not always deeming it necessary to mention their names. I therefore here apprise the Reader that he is not perusing a History exclusively of *my* Travels and Researches, but a Narrative into which the Experience and Information of others are interwoven. He may, however, rest assured that whatever he finds in the following pages is Authentic, or at least generally reported as such. What I have not personally witnessed, I have spared no pains to verify.

CONTENTS.

CHAPTER I.—FRANCE.

Departure—BOULOGNE—PARIS—Tuileries—Louvre—Triumphal Arch—Port Maillot—Bois de Boulogne—Chapel Marbœuf—La Madeleine—Palais Royal—Louvre—Notre Dame de Lorette—Notre Dame—St. Roche—Luxembourg—St. Genevieve—St. Germain L' Auxrios—St. Germain Des Pres—Invalides—St. Sulpice—Ecole des Beaux Arts—Etienne du Mont—Pera La Chaise—Hotel de Cluny—St. Clotilde—Greek Church—Wesleyan Chapel—American Church—Fountains—Protestantism—Population—ST. DENIS—VERSAILLES—FONTAINBLEAU—LYONS—Peter Waldo—MARSEILLES—Aspect of the Country
Pages 1-20

CHAPTER II.—ITALY.

Mesageries Imperials—NAPLES—Theatre of San Carlo—St. Gennario—St. Severus—Museum—Villa Reale—Markets—Population—Religion—VESUVIUS—Eruptions—Crater—Accident at the Observatory—POMPEII—HERCULANEUM—CIVITA VECCHIA—ROME—Lodgings—Seven Hills—Colosseum—Nero's Tower—Prison of the Apostles—Site of St. Peter's Crucifixion—Castle of St. Angelo—Vatican—ST. PETER'S—History—Cost—Measurements—Admission—Visit of the Prince of Wales—View from the Balcony—Interior—Confessional—Dialogue—RELIGIOUS CEREMONIES—Palm Sunday—Ash Wednesday—Holy Thursday—Washing the Disciples' Feet—Good Friday—Easter Sunday—Benediction—ILLUMINATIONS—FIREWORKS—CHURCHES—Basilica San Paolo—Santa Maria Maggiore—San Giovanni in Laterano—Marble Stairs—Walls—Anglican Chapel—Population—Streets—Reminiscences ... ... Pages 21-65

CHAPTER III.—EGYPT.

VOYAGE—Irish Channel—Atlantic—GIBRALTAR—Convicts—Fortifications—Markets—Mediterranean Coasts—MALTA—Harbour of Valletta—Town—Population—Markets—Garrison—*Sirocco*—Harbour of Alexandria—ORIGIN OF THE EGYPTIANS—Historical Sources—Mizraim—Saracens—Turks—Arabs—Rahab—EARLY HISTORY—Patriarchal Age—Ancient Dynasties—Political Relations to Israel—Cape Rounded by Necho—Decay—Prophecies—MAHOMET—Early History—Koran—Visions—First Converts—Entertainment of Koreish—Preaching—Night Journeys—Year of Mourning—Hegira—Successes—Pilgrimage of the Valediction—Death—Person—Mahometan Superstition—MODERN HISTORY—Christianity—Mahometanism—Changes of Dynasty—Mamelukes—Turks—Mehomet Ali—Massacre of Mamelukes—Prosperity under Mehemet—Ibraham—Greek Expedition—Abbas—Law of Succession—PEOPLE—Physique—Painting—Ophthalmia—Beautiful Teeth—Hair—Education—Serfdom of Women—Hospitality—COSTUME—*Of Men*—Prohibition of Silk—Girding up the Loins—Turban—Sandals—*Of Women*—Ornaments—Veils—*Dress of the Poor*—DOMESTIC RELATIONS—Courtship—Betrothals—Marriage Feasts—Wedding Garment—Divorce—Mahomet's Advice to Husbands—Polygamy—Slaves—FUNERALS—Processions—Wailers—Interments—Coffins—SLAVERY—Dealers—Masters—Brand—Bastinado—Manumission ... ... Pages 66-116

CHAPTER IV.—EGYPT—CONTINUED.

ALEXANDRIA—Great Square—Pompey's Pillar—Cleopatra's Needles—Pasha's Gardens—Catacombs—Ruins—St. Mark—Apollos—JOURNEY TO CAIRO—CAIRO—Donkeys—Citadel—Mosque of Mehemet Ali—Joseph's Well—Joseph's Granaries—Tombs—Shoobra—Mosques—Moueddin—Esbekiah Gardens—Squares—Christian Churches—Said Pasha—Streets—Watermen—Santons—Hairy Garments—Runners—*Houses*—Fountains—Divans—Pillows—Furniture—Windows—Inscriptions—Lattices—Secret Doors—Gates—Population—VISIT TO THE PYRAMIDS—Artificial Hatching—Pyramids in Sight—Pyramid of Cheops—Ascent—Summit—Descent—Entrances—SPHYNX—Description—Conjecture of Dr. Stanley—Monuments—NILE—Source—Reminiscences—Inundations—Irrigation of Land—Biblical Allusions—Agriculture—Fruitfulness—Thrashing—Climate—PETRIFIED FOREST—EXCURSION TO HELIOPOLIS—Arab Village—Goshen—Heliopolis—Refuge of Joseph and Mary—Remarks
Pages 117-157

CHAPTER V.—THE DESERT OF SINAI.

JOURNEY FROM CAIRO—Preparations—Contract with Dragoman—Caravan—Suez—Overland Route to India—Suez Canal—Wells of Moses—Red Sea—Passage of the Children of Israel—LIFE IN THE DESERT—Camel—Pitching Tents—Encampment—Baking—WATERS OF MARAH — WADY GHURUNDEL — Wells and Palms of Elim—WILDERNESS—ENCAMPMENT BY THE SEA—STAIR-ROCK—VALLEY OF WRITING—WADY FEIRAN—Traditional Rephidim - PLAIN OF RAHAH—CONVENT OF ST. CATHERINE—Church of the Transfiguration—Chapel of Helena —Charnel House— Mosque — SINAI— Ascent—Relation of Sinai to Horeb—*Way through Petra*—Flight of Cranes—RETURN TO ALEXANDRIA—Reflections ...   ... Pages 153–186

CHAPTER VI.—PALESTINE—JERUSALEM.

ALEXANDRIA TO JERUSALEM—Joppa from the Bay—Landing—Town—*Grave of Dorcas—House of Simon the Tanner—Vision of Peter*—Plain of Sharon—Rose—Mirage—Lydda—Sepulchre of Dorcas—St. George — Ramleh — Arabian Steed — Approach to Jerusalem — Prussian Hospice—JERUSALEM—Dragoman—VIEW OF THE CITY FROM THE MOUNT OF OLIVES—HILLS OF JERUSALEM—Mount Zion—Moriah—Calvary—Akra—Bezetha—MOUNTAINS AROUND JERUSALEM— Olivet—Galilee Hill—Hill of Ascension—Hill of Offence—Scopus—Hill of Evil Counsel—RAVINES—Valley of Hinnom—Potter's Field—Valley of Jehoshaphat—Gethsemane—Tyropœan—POOLS—Pools of Gihon—Siloam—Fountain of the Virgin—En-Rogel—Bethesda—Pool of Bathsheba—BUILDINGS—Mosque of Omar—El-Aksa—Harem—Church of the Holy Sepulchre—*Tomb of Our Lord—Angel's Chapel—Chapel of the Apparition—Stone of Unction, &c.—Chapel of Helena—Manger, &c.*—Biblical Estimate of Holy Places—Convent of St. James—Dialogue with a Pervert— Tower of David—Cœnaculum—STREETS—Via Doloroso—Place of Wailing—Lepers' Quarter—Population—TOMBS—of Zacharias—of Absalom—of Jehoshaphat—of the Prophets—of the Kings—of the Judges—Grotto of Jeremiah—Tomb of Stephen—PROTESTANT MISSION—Bishop Alexander—Bishop Gobat—Hospital—Schools, &c.—Reflections ...   ... Pages 187–236

CHAPTER VII.—PALESTINE—CONTINUED,

Agreement with Dragoman—Roads to Bethany—BETHANY—Castle of Lazarus –Tomb—House of Simon the Leper—BETHPHAGE—Scene of the Ascension—Fountain of the Apostles—Wayside Inn—WILDER-

NESS OF TEMPTATION—Maniacs—Wady el Kelt—Plain of Jericho—
JERICHO — Jericho of the Canaanites — Of Hiel — Modern City —
QUARANTANIA—Fountain of Elisha—JORDAN—Pilgrims—DEAD SEA
Vale of Siddim — Submerged Cities — Greek Convent — DETOUR
THROUGH THE WILDERNESS—Triumphal Way—Village "overagainst"
Bethany—JERUSALEM TO HEBRON—Plain of Rephaim—Mar Elias—
Sepulchre of Rachel—Solomon's Pools—HEBRON—Encampment—
Reminiscences—Town—Cave of Machpelah—Tomb of Esau—Population—HEBRON TO BETHLEHEM—Eshcol—Abraham's Oak—BETHLEHEM—Church of the Nativity—Grotto—Grotto of St. Jerome—Convents — Well of Bethlehem — Population — Return to Jerusalem
Pages 237-270

CHAPTER VIII.—PALESTINE—CONTINUED.

Adieu to the Sacred Capital—Ramah of Benjamin—Rachel's Wailing—
BEEROTH — BETHEL — Reminiscences — *Beitin* — SHILOH — SHECHEM—
Reminiscences—Gerizim and Ebal—Joseph's Tomb—Jacob's Well—
Population of Nabulus—Samaritans—SAMARIA — Reminiscences—
Gibeah—Dothan - Jenin—PLAIN OF ESDRAELON—Jezreel—Shunem
—Nain—Endor—Mount of Precipitation—NAZARETH—Reminiscences
—Beautiful Town—Latin Convent—Holy Grotto—Joseph's Workshop—Synagogue—Fountain of the Virgin—Population—Women of
Nazareth—TABOR—Ascent—Ruins—Grotto of the Transfiguration—
TIBERIAS—SEA OF GALILEE—MOUNT OF BEATITUDES—CANA OF
GALILEE—BETHLEHEM OF ZEBULUN—Brook Kishon—CARMEL—Caves
— Convent — Grotto of Elisha — Hanna Habesh — Elijah's Altar—
Ancient fruitfulness and Present desolation of Palestine
Pages 271-311

CHAPTER IX.—SYRIA AND THE MEDITERRANEAN.

HHAIFA —'Embarkation — ACRE — TYRE — Fulfilment of Prophecy —
Reflections of M. Lamartine—SIDON—BEYROUT—Picturesque Situation—Filth of the Streets—Port—Trade—Population—LEBANON—
French Road—Cultivated Terraces—Cedars—Snow-fall—Quarters for
the Night—Ride to DAMASCUS—Reminiscences of Damascus—Admirable Situation—Permanence of the City—Bazaars—Antiquities—
"*Street called Straight*," &c.—Population—RETURN TO ALEXANDRIA—
MESSINA — STROMBOLI — ETNA — SYRACUSE — CORSICA — Napoleon—
Straits of Bonifaccio—Arrival in England—Conclusion Pages 312-339

Continental and Oriental Travels.

CHAPTER I.

FRANCE.

On the 15th of February, 1862, I left Whitley-Bridge station *en route* for the Continent, and after passing through seven counties, viz., York, Derby, Stafford, Warwick, Worcester, Gloucester, and Somerset, I arrived at Bath.

In this city, so famous for its Hot Water Springs, which issue from the earth at a temperature of 117°, I remained with a friend for eight days, occasionally visiting Bristol, Clifton, and other places of interest in the neighbourhood. It numbers a population of 60,000, is beautifully situated in a salubrious vale, surrounded and protected by hills luxuriantly verdant, and is adorned with many stately buildings. There are ten churches, of which the "Abbey," a fine ancient cathedral-like edifice, standing in the centre of the city, and from being lighted with fifty-two windows, styled "The Lantern of England," is the principal attraction. There are also several Dissenting places of worship, and two Wesleyan chapels, one situate in New King Street, the foundation stone of which was laid by John Wesley in 1780.

On the 25th, I left Bath, and passed through Wiltshire, Berkshire, Buckinghamshire, and Middlesex to London, where I remained a week, but the metropolis being no novelty to me, I spent my time there principally in visiting friends. On the Sunday I heard Mr. Spurgeon and Mr. Punshon, and at the hands of the latter received the memorials of the Redeemer's passion. I thought them both incomparable preachers and very great and good men. On the Tuesday morning following, I left London by the South Eastern for Folkestone, whence I crossed over to Boulogne.

BOULOGNE.

This town contains from thirty to forty thousand inhabitants, about a fourth of whom are English, by whose wealth it is principally sustained. It is also warmed and lighted by English coal. Here are upwards of one hundred and twenty Boarding Schools, chiefly devoted to the education of English youth; but in my opinion the religious interests of Britannia's sons would be far better conserved at home.

PARIS.

At Boulogne I dined with a very agreeable gentleman from London, with whom, in the afternoon, I took my seat in the train for Paris, and reached that city at 11 P.M. My luggage was examined before I was permitted to leave the Station. I took up quarters with my new companion while he remained, but after his departure, the rest of the company being foreigners, I removed to the Hotel de lille et D'Albion, Rue St. Honore, which I found to be quite a continental home.

THE PALACE OF THE TUILERIES—the official residence of the Emperor Napoleon III., is a very stately and majestic pile, exhibiting various styles of architecture, as portions of it were built at different periods. The Private Gardens are accessible only when the Court is absent; but there are Public Gardens open in summer from seven in the morning till nine at night, and in winter from seven till dusk. They comprise an extensive arrangement of ornamental flower-beds interspersed with fountains and colossal marble statues, two groves of fine chesnuts, elms, planes, and limes, skirting a grand avenue. This forms a delightful and highly fashionable Promenade, particularly on Sunday afternoons, when every variety of colour and dress prescribed by the fashion of the hour, is displayed.

THE LOUVRE is connected with the Tuileries, and

covers and encloses a space of about sixty acres English, including two octagonal Gardens, somewhat in the fashion of the London Squares, enclosed with elegant iron railings. The interior of the Palace is principally devoted to Museums, Galleries of Pictures and Sculptures, which are open to the public (Mondays excepted), from 10 A.M. to 4 P.M. Here also are the Imperial Stables, one of which furnishes forty-four stalls for saddle horses, and another contains ten boxes, and a place for washing, besides apartments for carriages.

THE TRIUMPHAL ARCH (*Arc de Triomph*), is a monument of the pride of the Great Napoleon who conceived it, and decreed its erection in 1806, in which year, on the 15th of August, the foundation stone was accordingly laid. Around the base is a circular area enclosed with blocks of granite and cable chains, interspersed with handsome bronze lamp posts. From the platform on the summit, which is gained by ascending two hundred and sixty-one steps, and the payment of a small fee, there is a magnificent view of Paris and its environs. The day was beautifully clear when I ascended, and the whole city was very distinctly seen. On the entry into the capital of Maria Louisa, upon her marriage to Napoleon, an immense wood-and-canvas model of this arch was temporarily erected and brilliantly illuminated.

THE PORT MAILLOT.—Inside the fortifications, on the left, is the Port Maillot, one of the chief entrances to the Bois de Boulogne, and opening to some of the choicest wood scenery that can well be conceived in the neighbourhood of a great capital, with beautiful lakes and carriage drives in every direction. As in Hyde Park, London, the Parisian aristocracy take their daily drives in this lovely place.

THE CHAPEL MARBŒUF.—Returning from the Bois de Boulogne, on the right of the Champs Elysees is the neat small English church called the Chapel Marbœuf.

THE CHURCH OF LA MADELEINE stands on an elevated platform, approached at each end by a flight of twenty-eight steps, at the western end of the Boulevards. It is a Grecian building, and without a spire or tower. In the walls there are niches containing statues representing thirty-two saints. In the front, in basso relievo, there is a representation of Christ as the Judge with Magdalen at his feet; to his right are the Angels of Mercy, Innocence, Faith, Hope, and Charity; in the corner an angel is represented greeting a happy spirit rising from the tomb; on the left the Angel of Vengeance repels the vices, Hatred, &c.; and the group is completed by a demon and a damned spirit falling into the abyss of perdition. Above this is another scene in which Moses, holding the Tables of the Law, commands obedience, while on each side are depicted the

Stoning of the Blasphemer, and the Prohibition of Idolatry. Entering the church a splendid organ with a case richly carved in the Corinthian style, strikes the vision; and the edifice is everywhere adorned with sculptures and paintings. The principal picture represents Magdalen in a divine rapture, borne to Paradise on the wings of angels. The roof of this vast building is constructed of iron and copper; it is warmed by hot water; and, concealed from view, there is a peal of fixed bells. On Sundays and Holidays High Mass is celebrated in this church at 11 A.M.

The Palais Royal, for seventeen years the residence of the Duke of Orleans (Louis Philippe), until 1830, when it was seized by the Republican mob and made the meeting place of the Constituent Assembly, is consequently a place of interest, but visitors are not permitted to view the interior. The Gardens, however, are open to the public, which are beautiful and rendered further attractive by rows of lime trees extending from one end to the other. The ground floor of the Palace is now converted into shops which are amongst the most splendid in Paris.

The Hotel du Louvre, which is an immense building, borders on the eastern side of the Palais Royal. It occupies nearly two English acres of land, and is the most fashionable hotel in the city. Throughout this establishment there are bracket-clocks which are corrected to the true time by an electrical connection with a great clock in the Cour d'Honneur. Travelling baggage is conveyed by machinery from storey to storey as required. Dishes, smoking hot from the kitchen, run along subterranean railways, and at the proper place are lifted by a mechanical contrivance to the dining room. The waiters are summoned by electric bells, and speaking tubes, which communicate with the offices. The linen is washed and dried by steam. Like the basement of the Palais Royal, the ground floor of this immense building is also converted into magnificent shops.

THE CHURCH OF NOTRE DAME DE LORETTE, which was built in 1823, is a beautiful structure. The portico is supported by four Corinthian columns, and contains a sculptured representation of the Virgin with the infant Saviour receiving the adoration of angels.

THE CATHEDRAL CHURCH OF NOTRE DAME is a regular cruciform edifice, the eastern end of which terminates in eight facets, and at the western end there are two lofty square towers, apparently intended to support spires. Behind these is a new spire surmounted by a gilt cross which is elevated 135 feet from the roof and 280 from the floor. I ascended one of the towers whence I had a noble view of Paris, but not equal to that from the Triumphal Arch. The paintings and decorations of this grand old church are numerous and costly, and the Priests exhibit there, richly set in diamonds, what they call "a piece of the true cross on which Jesus was crucified." Strange infatuation!

THE CHURCH OF ST. ROCHE, famous as the theatre of many stirring events during the Revolutions, is entered by a flight of steps extending the whole breadth of the front, which displays two ranges of Doric and Corinthian columns supporting a pediment surmounted by a cross. This edifice, which is very beautiful, has recently received considerable adornments, conspicuous amongst which is an elegant Tribune fitted up for the use of the Empress. This is considered to be the most richly embellished Church in Paris, and is also celebrated for the excellence of its choir.

THE PALACE OF THE LUXEMBOURG in 1583 was purchased and enlarged by the Duke d'Epinay; in 1795 the Directorate held their sittings there; when Buonaparte was in the ascendant it exchanged its name for the Palais du Consulate; it was devoted to the sittings of the Consuls until 1814, when the Chamber of Peers was created; and now it rejoices in the name of the Palais du Senate. Entering the apartments at present occupied by the Government, the first room is that in which the Senators meet, and is adorned with statues of great beauty. The chamber adjoining is very tastefully decorated. There you are introduced to the Throne Room *(Salle du Trone)*, which is superb beyond description. I saw nothing in Paris comparable to it. The Throne, where Napoleon I. was crowned, fronts the side wall to the right, and is decorated with the greatest affluence. Here also are valuable pictures representing scenes of deep historical interest, such as The Imperial Election of Napoleon; The Signing of the Concordat; The Return of the Pope to Rome in 1849; Napoleon Visiting the Works of the New Louvre; The Senate Proclaiming the Emperor; and The Marriage of the same illustrious personage. There are also the Library, the Chapel, the Gallery of Modern Art, &c., all of which are very grand.

THE CHURCH OF ST. GENEVIEVE, called after a saint of that name said to be buried there, famous as "The Pantheon" in the days of the Revolution, but now again used as an ecclesiastical building, is a noble pile. The interior is richly adorned with sculptures and paintings. Underneath it is a vast series of vaults containing monuments and funeral urns disposed somewhat after the fashion of the tombs at Pompeii. The tombs of Voltaire and Rousseau are here, and there is here also a fine marble statue of the former. In the centre there are two concentric passages where the softest sound is repeated in a loud echo.

THE CHURCH OF ST. GERMAIN L'AUXRIOS — the

parish church of the Tuileries, is cruciform, with an octagonal east end, a tower rising at the intersection of the nave and transept, and the principal, or west front, consisting of a well sculptured porch and five rich gothic arches. The ground in front is planted with chesnut trees, now full grown and luxuriant.

THE CHURCH OF ST. GERMAIN DES PRES is remarkable as being the oldest in Paris, and also as containing the monument of Casimu, King of Poland.

THE HOTEL DES INVALIDES has a most magnificent dome, from the summit of which rises a lantern with a gilt spire, globe, and cross, attaining an altitude of 323 feet. The interior of the church is splendid. It is a circular area with branches of a great cross extending in the directions of the four cardinal points. Between these are four circular chapels, each having three lofty arched entrances, one of which, flanked with fluted Corinthian columns, faces the middle of the church, where there is now erected a circular parapet surrounding the crypt which contains the Tomb of Napoleon I. This tomb, together with the church exterior and interior, is the most complete thing in Paris. Here also is an Hotel or Hospital for invalid soldiers disabled by wounds, or who have remained in the army for thirty years. All answering these descriptions are entitled to the privileges of the Institution. When I visited the Hotel the number of invalids, including officers, who are all boarded, lodged, clothed, &c., was 3,300. The table service of the officers is plate, and the gift of the Empress Maria Louisa. The soldiers breakfast upon soup, beef, and vegetables, and dine upon meat or eggs and vegetables. On Fridays they have cheese. Each man is daily served with about a quarter of a pound of meat, some wine, and a pound and a half of white bread. The wine and bread are the same quality for officers and men; the officers are privileged with the allowance of an extra dish. Each individual has a separate bed, straw mattress, wool mattress, bolster, and press for his clothes. These buildings cover sixteen acres.

THE CHURCH OF ST. SULPICE is a splendid cruciform structure. The pulpit rests upon a platform approached by two flights of steps, and is ornamented with figures representing Faith, Hope, and Charity. The organ gallery is supported by twelve magnificent composite columns. There is also an aperture in a metal plate in the window of the southern transept so arranged that the sunbeam passing through it forms a luminous circle upon the pavement about 10 inches in diameter. This passes over a line by which at noon it is bisected.

THE SCHOOL OF FINE ARTS *(Ecole des Beaux Arts)* is an institution under the control of the Minister of the Interior. It is divided into two sections, viz., (1) that of Painting and (2) that of Sculpture and Architecture. Lectures on every subject connected with the Arts are gratuitously given by twenty Professors. Prizes are also annually distributed, the first of which entitles the winner to study at Rome, and spend four months at Athens, at the expense of the State.

THE CHURCH OF ETIENNE DU MONT is cruciform, with an octagonal eastern end, and an aisle, with chapels in each arcade, goes round the whole. The works of art in this edifice are magnificent, and the richness and singularity of the architecture, its pictures, and other decorations, constitute it one of the most interesting in the capital. It is now being enlarged and repaired at a cost of two millions of francs.

THE CEMETERY OF PERE LA CHAISE covers about 212 acres, upon the slope of a hill to the north-east of Paris, celebrated for the beauty of its position as early as the fourteenth century. Pera la Chaise once resided here, and for one hundred and fifty years it was a country retreat of the Jesuits. In 1804 it was converted into a cemetery, and is now the principal place of sepulture to the capital. The most distinguished persons choose it as the place of interment for their relatives, so that it stands unrivalled in the number and costliness of its monuments—some representing Temples, some sepulchral Chapels, some Mausoleums, Pyramids, and Obelisks. It is a great curiosity. The Chapel is a plain Doric building, and in front is an open platform whence there is a fine view of Paris. The landscape scenery around is extensive and very beautiful. It is not surprising therefore that, in summer particularly, it should be a favourite resort alike to Parisians and strangers.

The Hotel de Cluny is one of the oldest and finest remnants of the ancient French metropolis. It also possesses peculiar interest from its history, as it was in 1515 the résidence of Mary, the sister of Henry VIII. of England, and widow of Louis XII. of France. It was subsequently used as a Nunnery. And finally it came into the possession of an enthusiastic and learned antiquarian, M. du Sommerand, who has deposited there, arranged in chronological order, a valuable collection of Mediæval Reliques, sacred, civil, and military.

The Church of St. Clotilde faces a square which is tastefully laid out as a garden and open to the public. There are three entrances to this building in the front; it has two beautiful spires, and is remarkable for a Peal of Bells comprising the whole octave, which is the most musical in Paris.

The Greek Church, which has been recently built, is small, but of a very expensive style of architecture, and so richly gilded within and without as to invest it with a gorgeous appearance. For its size, it is perhaps the most costly edifice in the capital. I mingled with the congregation worshipping there on Sunday, the 16th March.

The Wesleyan Chapel is an humble place, where from eighty to a hundred persons statedly worship. There is, however, another very superior building in course of erection, together with School-room, Library, and two Ministers' Houses in the same place. These erections are to cost about £15,000, the principal part of which will be raised in England to supplement a grant from the Wesleyan Missionary Society.*

The American Episcopal Church, which is under the pastoral care of the Rev. Dr. Mc Clintock, is a neat plain building, nearly new. I had the pleasure to attend Divine Service there.

Fountains, &c.—Paris is everywhere adorned with beautiful Fountains, thirty-five of which are monumental; and there are many other stately erections which enhance the attractions of the city. The Obelisk in the Place de la Concorde, brought from Thebes by the First Napoleon, is particularly imposing and interesting.

Before the revolution of 1789, there were no less than one hundred and sixty Romish Churches in the French capital, together with fifty-six Monasteries and fifty-two Nunneries. Many of these were de-

---

* This Chapel has since been completed and opened for Divine Worship. It is situate in the Rue Roquépine Prolongée, adjoining the Boulevard Malesherbes, near the Madeleine.

stroyed by the Republicans, and the power of the Priests received a shock from which it will never recover.

William Farel and John Calvin were educated in the University of this metropolis. Protestants were first called "Calvinists" in France, and "Calvinist" is still the synonym for "Protestant" in that country. But, with few exceptions, the people are votaries of Rome. There are three small Anglican Churches—not "Steeple Houses," for Protestant places of worship on the Continent are seldom adorned with spires, but Rooms consecrated for the accommodation of a few persons—mere glimmering lights amid the gloom of Popish superstition. Protestantism in its varied forms barely maintains an existence. The consequence is, that the most beautiful city in the world is alarmingly profane. Here virtually is no Sabbath. With few exceptions, shops are open from morning until night. So are the Theatres, and other places of amusement, and Sunday is even preferred for steeple chases and other races. So much for the religion of his Holiness!

The Population of Paris is estimated at a million-and-a-half, which is about half that of London. In the variety and taste of their manufactures the Parisians are not surpassed by any people upon earth, but their productions, however elegant, are by no means as substantial as those of England.

They excel in making jewellery, clocks, watches, trinkets, musical instruments, philosophical apparatus, mathematical instruments, lace, and embroidery.

The French metropolis is divided by the course of the Seine, as the English is by the Thames, and the views from the bridges are imposing.

ST. DENIS.

This is a very ancient town. We are informed that it received its name from one St. Denis who was beheaded there, respecting whom the Monkish legend adds, that he picked up his own head and, placing it under his arm, walked with it to Paris, a distance of about four miles! It is celebrated for its Abbey, where the Kings of France were buried,—a church of great beauty, highly ornamented, and rich in sculptures and paintings. Here also Napoleon Buonaparte founded an Institution for the gratuitous education of five hundred girls, relatives of members of the Legion of Honour. When there I saw a military funeral. The music was rendered exceedingly solemn by the muffled drums.

VERSAILLES.

This town is distant from Paris about ten miles. The Palace here, with the two Trianons, Park, and Gardens, are very magnificent, excelling any thing even in the capital. In the Private Park, which covers about 100 acres, there are one hundred and sixty statues, forty different basins and fountains, some of which are highly ornamental. These play during the summer on the first Sunday in the month. The Palace and Palace-yard extend over 20 acres. The rooms of the Palace are tastefully decorated, and adorned with a splendid collection of paintings, mostly at the personal expense of Louis Philippe. Outside the Private Park there are about 50,000 acres of forest, all tastefully arranged and beautifully ornamental. The two Trianons, or Minor Palaces, which were severally built for their mistresses, by Louis XIV. and Louis XV., are within this forest. In connection with these pretty little structures the State Carriages are kept, two of which were used by Napoleon I., but the most magnificent is one bought by Louis Philippe for the occasion of his coronation at a cost of £40,000. There is also a very small one presented by the Sultan of Turkey to the young Prince Imperial, which, the first time he used it, was drawn by a goat. Moreover, there are here in the occupation of the Emperor about 10,000 acres of arable, meadow, and pasture land, so that in all there will be about 60,000 acres of state property connected with the Palace of Versailles. The population of the town is about 30,000, and there are three Catholic Churches, one French Protestant Church, one Anglican Church, and a Jewish Synagogue.

FONTAINBLEAU.

On Monday, 24th March, I left Paris, and after a run of 37 miles arrived at Fontainbleau, where the Emperor resides during the hunting season. The next day I visited the Palace, which is a noble building. The rooms are spacious and richly hung with costly paintings. The Throne-Room is superb. There are here also a variety of curious articles presented to the Emperor by the King of Siam when on a visit at this Palace, and amongst the number several idols worshipped by the Siamese. The population of Fontainbleau is 8,200.

LYONS.

On Wednesday morning I was on the rails again, and after travelling 280 miles reached Lyons at 10.55 P.M. On the following day I rambled through the city. It is certainly an extraordinary town, and admirably situated for mercantile purposes, traversed, as it is, by two great rivers, viz., the Saone, crossed by nine bridges, and the Rhone, which is spanned by eight. It is probably the chief silk manufacturing city in Europe, containing within the walls upwards of 7,000 mills in which are nearly 20,000 looms. The population, including the suburbs, amounts to 275,000 souls. Here are many public squares, the finest of which is that of Louis le Grand. This square contains an equestrian statue of Louis XIV., and is ornamented with fountains and beautiful lime trees. Near the Church of Notre Dame stands a Tower about 630 feet high, from which there is a magnificent view of rivers, plains, hills, country seats, gardens, and orchards; and to crown the whole, of the snow-capped peak of the famous Mont Blanc distant nearly 100 miles.

This city must be ever interesting to Protestants as the residence of the celebrated Peter Waldo, under whom as early as the twelfth century a great reformation was inaugurated, and who also was the first to translate the Scriptures into a modern tongue. It is related of him, that being at a supper party when one of the company fell dead upon the floor, his soul was alarmed and his conscience awakened. In these circumstances he had recourse to the Bible for instruction and consolation, and was thus conducted to the possession of the "one thing needful" through faith in the blood of atonement. He now desired to communicate to others the happiness he experienced, abandoned his mercantile pursuits, distributed his wealth to the poor, set about the translation of the oracles of God, and otherwise devoted himself to the work of evangelization.

MARSEILLES.

On Friday morning I started off again, and reached Marseilles, which is distant from Paris, by a direct line of rails, 535 miles. This is a fine improving city, though in extent and beauty scarcely equal to Lyons. It is the chief port of the Mediterranean and Steam Packet Station for Italy, the Peninsula, and the East. On the outskirts of the city there are many eminences, the loftiest of which is crowned by the Church of Notre Dame. Upon another commanding site stands the New Royal Palace built for the Emperor by the municipality.

To an English eye, passing through France, the country has a barren appearance, though exceedingly rich in agricultural productions. This arises from the fact that the fields are not divided by hedge-rows, nor is there half the quantity of timber that is grown in Britain, so that the country in general looks like a vast plain. On my return at the end of April, however, everything looked truly lovely. Chesnuts, lilacs, and other trees were almost in full bloom, anticipating the same appearances in England by about six weeks. The French vines grow in the open air—not against the sides of houses as in the south of England, but after the fashion of the hop gardens in Kent and Sussex. They are planted in rows about as far apart as gooseberry bushes, and are trained upon poles about three feet high. It is scarcely necessary to say that the French wines and brandies are made from the fruit of these vines.

CHAPTER II.

ITALY.

AFTER spending three days at Marseilles, on Monday, 31st March, I took ship in one of the French Imperials for Italy, but on account of the roughness of the sea we did not sail until next morning. There being still a heavy swell on the water, most of the ship's company were sick, myself amongst the number. I remarked the curious circumstance that upon awaking out of sleep the sickness was gone, but, quick as thought, returned the instant I became conscious of the rolling motion of the ship. At midnight, however, after sailing nineteen hours, the proud waves subsided, and I had no more sickness during the remainder of the voyage.

For the benefit of Tourists, I may here remark that the Mesageries Imperials are by far the best steamers. The second class accommodation in them is equal to the first in the ordinary French boats, or of the Austrian or Liverpool vessels. And, however excellent the accommodation for first-class passengers on board the Peninsular and Oriental Company's ships, their second cabins are wretched. But in the packet in which I sailed, the second class cabin and berths were beautifully clean, and were occupied by respectable passengers; and the table was tastefully spread with a clean cloth and napkins, and supplied with a variety of choice dishes, served, of course, in the French style. A decanter of wine is placed between two persons, and replenished, if required. The table is sumptuously spread with all kinds of dessert. The waiters, also, are highly respectable and very attentive.

NAPLES.

After a sail of from 400 to 500 miles, only touching at Civita Vecchia, we ran into the Bay of Naples, from which the capital of the Two Sicilies had the appearance of a very splendid city. When I got to the Hotel de l'Univers, I was right glad to find the landlady an Englishwoman. Before leaving England I took the precaution of noting down the hotels recommended by my friends who had travelled, and accordingly found a first-class house in every place. Lighting upon respectable hotels, and people blessed with common sense, greatly enhances the comfort of travelling. Early next morning I commenced my rambles, when I encountered streets so narrow and dirty, that the illusion from the Bay was speedily dissipated. The suburbs, however, are surpassingly beautiful.

THE THEATRE OF SAN CARLO.—This was once reputed the largest in the world, but is now exceeded by one in America.

THE CHURCH OF ST. GENNARO is notorious as the depository of some of the blood of St. Januarius, the patron saint of Naples, which, upon a certain day annually, the Bishop makes to liquify for the edification of the faithful. As the story goes, when Januarius was martyred by the Pagans, his blood was carried into the city by the Bishop, whereupon four evils ceased, viz., war, pestilence, hypocrisy, and famine. But, unfortunately, the miraculous blood has not succeeded in preventing their revival. When Murat was King of Naples, the blood of Januarius would not liquify; but he planted two cannons against the church, and assured the Bishop that if he did not perform the miracle, the edifice should be blown down. The ecclesiastic protested that it was impossible, but at length, seeing that Murat was in earnest, complied. Some years since, Dr. Cumming exposed the trick at Exeter Hall, by means of a chemical mixture, which is thrown into ebullition by the heat of the hand. So have the Neapolitans been duped! The success of the cheat takes a palpable shape in forty-five statues of solid silver, some large as life, exhibited in the vestry of the church.

THE CHURCH OF ST. SEVERUS. — Here are two statues beautifully cut out of a solid block of white marble, one veiled, representing "Modesty"; the other "Deceit," throwing off a network covering.

THE MUSEUM is one of the richest in the world. It contains a large number of ancient bronzes, vases, mosaics, ornaments, instruments, pans, and other household goods, dug out of the ruins of ancient Herculaneum and Pompeii. The Library and Picture Gallery also attract the attention of visitors, but we shall not attempt to describe these.

THE ROYAL PROMENADE (*Villa Reale*) is incomparably beautiful, and is the principal resort of fashion in Naples. It opens upon the Bay with the Town rising in the rear. It is 2,000 yards in length, and the walks are adorned with parterres, fountains, and orange trees.

MARKETS.—The town is abundantly supplied with provisions of every kind; fish and shell-fish are plentiful, as also vegetables and fruit. A great quantity of snow, brought from the Castellamare Mountain, is kept in vast reservoirs, and used for ices and cooling drinks. Many of the houses are seven storeys high, so the people often spare their locomotive muscles by drawing up their meat, vegetables, &c., in baskets, and letting down their money in the same way.

The great street of Toledo is thronged with people and carriages at all times of the day, and until late at night, or rather until two or three in the morning, when fashionable persons retire to rest.

THE POPULATION of Naples amounts to 350,000. It would have been more had not the cholera swept away 16,000 in 1836-7, and 10,000 in 1854. No one who passes through the streets can wonder at this, for they are filthy beyond description. The lower classes, formerly called Lazzaroni, numbering at least 40,000, literally lived from hand to mouth, and slept in the open air; but in this respect the city is much improved, though thousands of poverty-stricken wretches still prowl about who scarcely know how to subsist. Hence Naples, more than any city in Europe, swarms with pickpockets.

RELIGION.—Popery is evermore the mother of poverty. But hope is dawning even in Naples. God has employed Garibaldi to secure to the people a measure of religious liberty. That extraordinary man presented an eligible site for the erection of a new English Church. When I was there, an appeal was made to the liberality of Protestants—visitors as well as residents, in support of this project,—and I suppose by this time it is completed. On the Sabbath I worshipped with a very attentive congregation in a small Scotch Chapel. Having long groaned beneath the Papal yoke, Naples is now "stretching out her hands unto God," and determined to be free. The Lord has seen the affliction of his people, and heard their cry, by reason of Priestly oppression and Kingly despotism. The Tyrant has been deposed, and his kingdom transferred to better hands. The reign of terror is over. Everywhere liberty of conscience and an open Bible are respected, and a great and effectual door is opened to the Evangelist. "The harvest truly is plenteous, but the labourers are few." O that "the Lord of the harvest would send forth more labourers into his harvest"!

VESUVIUS.

Like other continental travellers, of course, I also must see the Burning Mountain. Accordingly I joined a party, in which the German, French, Italian, and English nations were represented; a learned young lady acting as general Interpreter. For four or five miles our journey was by rail. We then walked about a mile to a place where donkeys and mules are kept for the use of excursionists. Each of our party here mounted a mule, and was furnished with a staff; then, following our guide, who also was mounted, with the volcano rearing its fiery summit amid the clouds full in view, we rode through fields of lava to the highest terrace practicable to the quadrupeds. Now commenced our arduous task in good earnest. Upward we toiled, and after a full hour's hard, tough climbing, we attained the summit, with a profound conviction that the ascent of Vesuvius is a daring adventure. The top of the mountain was all on a smoke, and the crater in the centre forcibly reminded me of a huge empty lime pit. Snow is often seen resting upon the parts which are not burning, and the region was so chilling that I literally shivered, probably through the reaction after the heated state into which I was thrown through the effort of ascending.

The last eruption occurred in 1859. In 1850 there was one, when the lava which issued from the crater extended like a fiery flood over a distance of seven miles, and rushing into the sea, filled up a large portion of the Bay. It is estimated that in 1737 a mass of matter passed from the mountain to the sea equal to 33 million cubic feet; and in 1794 the still greater quantity of about 46 million, — an accumulation that would form a mountain even greater than Vesuvius. This of course is incomprehensible upon the supposition that Vesuvius furnishes the supply, but assuming that it is only the vent through which the matter flows from the depths of the earth, the difficulty disappears. Were there no such vent who can declare what would have been the fate of Italy? The eruption which involved Herculaneum and Pompeii occurred in the year 79. Six years earlier the inhabitants were premonished by a most destructive Earthquake; and the relics recently discovered shew that they had been living in detestable crimes. At length the black smoke belched from the crater of the volcano, attended by portentous rumbling noises; then came the showers of ashes, cinders, and stones. In two short hours all was over. Herculaneum, Stabiæ, and Pompeii were no more. Stones weighing eight pounds fell upon Pompeii, while Stabiæ was overwhelmed with fragments of about an ounce weight. What became of the people is uncertain, for comparatively few human bodies or bones have been exhumed.

An adventurous Frenchman once threw himself into the crater of this mountain when it was active, and shortly after his body was seen hurled into the air. The volcano was now silent, and some of our party descended with the guide a short distance into the vortex.

On our return we came to an Observatory, a portion of which is occupied, and dismounted to take some refreshment. As I was alighting, with one foot yet in the stirrup and the other on the ground, a mule leaped upon mine, and before I had time to release myself, away they both went, kicking, and galloping, and dragging me along the ground. My companions could not render me any assistance; but as a good Providence ordered, my foot was liberated, and I got up without injury further than that of a severe shock, though my coat was torn in pieces.

Our fair Interpreter manifested a tender sympathy with me in this misfortune. While on the ground that kind Christian lady came to ascertain the amount of injury I had sustained, and recommended that I should lie down in the house, assuring me that the party would not leave me. This I declined, not deeming it necessary. She then urged me to take some brandy which she and her sister had brought with them, by which I was so revived as to be able to proceed with the party. What a remarkable Providence that the only individual who could speak with me should possess so much of the spirit of the Good Samaritan! What a striking proof of the love and guardian care of Deity who numbereth the hairs of our heads!

From Naples to the summit of Vesuvius and back occupied eight hours, and was a hard day's work.

POMPEII.

Seen from the summit of Vesuvius, Pompeii appears close to its base, though really six miles distant. With a guide and an interpreter I visited this buried city. Not more than a third of it has been excavated. I was filled with admiration and awe. Here is the Theatre, capable of seating 5,000 persons; there is the Forum; around are pillars, pedestals, ruins of arches, temples, and various buildings. Now we come upon the Court of Justice, an edifice 200 feet long and 80 feet wide; and now a kind of Exchange, 130 feet by 65, with a double gallery and portico in front. Yonder is the Amphitheatre, 430 feet long and 335 broad; near to which also are the Public Baths, still in excellent preservation. The solemnity of Pompeii, however, is not due to its individual buildings, but to its general aspect. Passing along narrow, roughly-paved streets, which, having been cleared of the ashes, retain the appearance they had 1,800 years ago, we find on either side about one hundred houses with numerous shops and fountains. Here was a money-changer's establishment, and there stand the jars in which he kept his cash; on the other side was an oil shop, and also the offices of a baker and a wine-vender. These, and houses of worse character, are readily recognised by inscriptions cut in stone. The rooms in the houses are small, but neat, and many of the walls are covered with frescos in excellent preservation. The upper stories and roofs appear to have consisted of wood, and these were all destroyed. In one of the gardens, said to have belonged to a theatrical gentleman, are numerous little marble statues, and a miniature stage, also of marble; and there is likewise a fountain, supplied by means of lead pipes with brass taps, soldered together in precisely the same manner as the work is done now. In a vault under the Governor's house were found the skeletons of seventeen persons, including that of the Governor's daughter, distinguished by her jewels. They were leaning against the walls, and the marks of their bodies are still visible. This subterranean gallery extends a considerable distance, and the victims probably retreated there to escape the fiery shower. The jewels and other relics are treasured in the Museum at Naples. The ancient walls of the city have also been traced, and prove it to have been about two miles in circumference, having six gates and twelve watch towers. Outside the north-western gate stands the Cemetery or Street of Tombs,—for they range there in such order as to make this death-like city still more deathly. Part only of the Cemetery has been cleared. It is said that the British Government offered the late King of Naples £200,000 to be allowed to excavate the remainder, but, though extremely necessitous, he refused.

HERCULANEUM.

Herculaneum was accidentally discovered nearly 1,600 years after the eruption of A.D. 79, by a man, who, when sinking a well, fell into an open space which proved to be the Theatre. The steps and seats of this building are said to remain perfect to this day. Unlike those of Pompeii, the excavations of Herculaneum are all underground, and can be viewed only by torchlight. My curiosity was not sufficient to surmount a repugnance I have to subterranean explorations. Travellers, however, report that a whole street has been cleared, and that a prison was discovered in which the skeletons of several captives were found in irons. The prison windows are secured with iron bars, and there is a stone on which, probably, criminals had been beheaded. Ten years since, a house was opened in which there were a variety of kitchen utensils and two skeletons. A small heathen Temple was also exposed which contained the bodies of two priests. How terrible is the curse of God!

CIVITA VECCHIA.

On Tuesday the 8th, we embarked on board the steamer for Civita Vecchia. We had a beautiful passage, and arrived at our destination about nine next morning, though it was eleven before we were permitted to land, two hours being required by the police to examine our passports and the captain's bill of health. Being released from the police, we had a scramble to get into the boats waiting to land us. At Civita Vecchia, which is the port of Rome, though thirty-six miles distant from the city, our baggage underwent examination at the Custom's-house, where a small fine was laid upon every package. Such was the consumption of time in this operation that many of us were too late for the noon train. Another train started about four in the afternoon, and trailed us to

Rome in two hours and some minutes. Locomotives in Italy are not so swift as in England or France, yet sluggish as they are, they are the means of diffusing light far too rapidly to suit his Holiness, who is therefore no friend to railways.

ROME.

On leaving the Railway Station at Rome, I took the Omnibus, and ordered the driver to set me down at the Hotel de l'Angleterre, near the Corso. When I entered the house, the landlord informed me that they were quite full; so was every good hotel in the city, and that it was believed there were no less than 50,000 visitors, 20,000 being English, to witness the ceremonies of "Passion Week." He very kindly, however, sent his son with me to seek a private lodging; and after a two hours' search, with great difficulty, for a scudò, or 4s. 3d. of our money, per night, we secured the use of a bed and wash-hand stand, in such a room as I never before occupied. The place was tolerably clean, but all the furniture in it, not excepting my bed, was scarcely worth a sovereign; and withal the hostess could not understand a word of my mother tongue. Probably at another season I might have had my accommodations for two months at the price I paid her for a fortnight. Easter is the Roman harvest.

This marvellous city is nearly thirteen miles in circumference. It is divided into two unequal parts by the Tiber,—a deep sluggish stream, which traverses it in a winding course of about three miles, running generally from north to south. Churches, Palaces, Country-Seats, Hills, Squares, Streets, Fountains, Aqueducts, Ruins, Antiquities,—all bespeak the ancient magnificence of the place. There are here a greater number of Monuments of Art than in any other city upon earth. Merely to inspect its beauties would consume months; and years would be required to become familiarly acquainted with them. The Rome of the Middle Ages, which rose from the ruins of the ancient city, had nearly disappeared at the beginning of the sixteenth century; and scarcely any part of the present Capital is older than the time of Sixtus V., who commenced rebuilding it in its present form.

The Seven Hills upon which the ancient city reposed, viz., the Capitoline, Palatine, Cœlian, Esquiline, Aventine, Quirinal, and Viminal, are the first objects which excite the interest of a Traveller. Nearly the whole of Rome, as it existed before the time of Augustus, rested upon these. Hence some commentators are of opinion that the Angel indicated these to St. John when he described the Seven Heads of the Beast upon which the Scarlet Lady was seated: —" The seven heads are seven mountains, on which the woman sitteth." (Rev. xvii. 9.) It is more probable, however, that the word "mountains" here must be taken figuratively, as denoting *seven forms of power*. The Forum still stands on the slope of the Palatine, once the seat of an inconsiderable village when ancient Rome arose, and was the Cradle of the greatness of succeeding ages. It is now covered with the ruins of the Palace of the Cæsars, which are surrounded with vineyards and gardens. The Triumphal Arches of Titus, Constantine, &c., and the ruins of Palaces, Baths, Temples, Bridges, and other relics which we cannot enumerate, distributed over these elevations, remain to attest the grandeur of days for ever gone.

THE COLOSSEUM is one of the most stupendous ruins in existence. That superb building was commenced by the Emperor Flavius Vespasian, in the year 72 of the Christian era. It was composed of Travertine marble. Three rows of arches, supported by half columns, surrounded it, each row numbering eighty arches, and the edifice terminated by four rows of pillars—the first Doric, the second Ionic, and the third and fourth Corinthian. This immense amphitheatre has a circumference of 1,702 English feet, and is 163 feet high. The Arena or central space was surrounded by the Podium, on which seats were placed for the Emperor, the Senators, and other magnates, while the space above was occupied by the various classes of citizens. There was accommodation for 107,000 spectators, there being seats in the amphitheatre for 87,000, while the piazzas above would contain 20,000 more. Imagine that immense congregation collected to witness the contortions and agonies of Gladiators and Wrestlers, Bull-fights, and similar savage scenes! The arena of the Colosseum was the scene of fearful tragedies during the Ten Persecutions. Ignatius was brought from Antioch in the reign of Trajan to be torn by wild beasts here, and the traditions of the church abound in names of Martyrs who perished under the inspection of its crowds.

In the year 1750, Benedict XIV. consecrated the Colosseum to the memory of the Heroes who suffered there, "for the word of God and for the testimony of Jesus Christ." Accordingly over the main entrance to the Amphitheatre there is a Tablet announcing that the building had been purged from all heathen practices and idolatrous defilements. Yet on one side of the gateway there is a cross carved in marble, with the following inscription:—"BACIANDO LA SANTA CROCE SI AQUISTA UN' ANNO E XL GIORNI D' INDULGENZA"—*If you kiss the Sacred Cross, you shall have one year and forty days Indulgence!* The cross is blackened with the kisses of the credulous. Again, in a small chapel in one of the archways inside the building are these words:—"INDULGENZA PLENARIA

Perpetua"— *Plenary Perpetual Indulgence!* But over the door of the Pantheon is an inscription still more extravagant — "Indulgentia Plenaria Quotidiana Perpetua pro Vivis et Defunctis "—*A Daily Perpetual Plenary Indulgence for the Living and the Dead!* Strange reformation of Idolatry! What could there have been more shocking in the superseded worship of Jupiter, Juno, and Minerva?

Nero's Tower,—where that Monster amused himself with his lyre while his capital was in flames. It is related of his insatiable cruelty that he ordered a number of Christians to be covered with combustibles, and so distributed as to light up his Gardens in their martyrdom. But there is a God of Vengeance. Haunted by his conscience, that Incarnation of Wickedness vainly attempted to kill himself, and then besought his attendant to rid him of an intolerable existence. A suicide may change the form of his being; he cannot annihilate himself. He may precipitate himself into hell; he has no power to expel himself from damnation.

The Prison of the Apostles is situated under the Church of St. Guiseppe de' Falegnami, and consists of two chambers, one over the other, excavated in the tufa rock. In the centre of the vault there is a circular aperture, through which it is supposed the prisoners were let down. A more horrible place at this side eternity it is scarcely possible to imagine.

Tradition says that Peter and Paul were incarcerated here by order of Nero; and the Guides show a Font which they say is supplied by a spring miraculously produced by the Apostles to enable them to baptise the Jailor and their fellow-prisoners.

THE SITE OF ST. PETER'S CRUCIFIXION is shown near the Church of St. Pietro in Montorio. But whether this apostle was ever in Rome has been gravely doubted by the learned. No mention is made of him in the Acts of the Apostles after he was at the Council of Jerusalem; but from Gal. ii. 11, it appears that he was subsequently at Antioch, where he was reproved by Paul; and it is generally believed that from Antioch he returned to Jerusalem. Eusebius, however, informs us that Origin wrote to this purpose:—"St. Peter is supposed to have preached to the Jews of the Dispersion in Pontus, Galatia, Bithynia, Cappadocia, and Asia; and at length coming to Rome, was crucified with his head downwards." Dr. Lardner has argued ingeniously in support of this supposition, and after reviewing the reasoning of that able person, Adam Clarke has the following note:—"I commend Dr. Lardner for his candour, and thank him for his advice; but there is danger in believing too much as well as in believing too little. To me there is not the slightest evidence that Peter ever saw Rome, much less that he was first Bishop of that city. Those who mention his having been there adduce no fact of history to vouch their belief, but a sort of uncertain report. The New Testament, by direct inference, is altogether against the tradition."

THE CASTLE OF ST. ANGELO, now the celebrated Papal Fortress, was originally erected by Hadrian, about A.D. 130, and for a considerable period was known as the Mausoleum of that Emperor. After the time of Hadrian, it became the Sepulchre of Lucius Verus, the Antonines, and many of their successors, down to the time of Septimius Severus, who was buried there in 211. It is a massive circular Tower, 987 feet in circumference, cased on the outside with huge rectangular courses of peperino, and standing on a square basement, each side of which is 247 feet in length. It was converted into a Fortress in the time of Honorius, about A.D. 423, and in the wars of Justinian was successively held by the Goths and Greeks, and at length passed into the hands of the Exarchs. At the close of the sixth century, according to Church tradition, while Pope Gregory the Great was engaged in a procession to St. Peter's for the purpose of offering up a solemn service to avert the pestilence which followed the inundation of 589, Michael the Archangel appeared to him standing on the summit of the fortress, in the act of sheathing his sword, to signify that the plague was stayed. In commemoration of this event, the

Pope erected a Chapel on the summit, which was subsequently superseded by a Statue of Michael. Thus, in process of time, the ancient name of this building sank into comparative disuse, and it is now commonly styled the "Castle of St. Angelo," or the Castle of the Holy Angel. Boniface IX. repaired the Fortress, and Alexander VI., about the year 1500, raised the upper part, strengthened the base by erecting the bulwark of travertine, and completed the covered gallery which leads from the castle to the Vatican, begun by John XXIII. on the foundation of the Leonine walls. In 1644, the outworks of the Fortress were constructed by Urban VIII., and furnished with cannon made of bronze stripped from the roof of the Pantheon.

THE VATICAN is the winter residence of the Popes; and as St. Peter's stands first amongst the Churches of Christendom, so is the Vatican first amongst the Palaces. This is true, notwithstanding, that it consists of a pile of buildings irregular in their plan, because composed of parts constructed at different times. There seems to have been a Palace attached to the Basilica of St. Peter probably as early as the time of Constantine. It certainly existed in the eighth century, for Charlemagne resided in it at his coronation by Leo III. In the twelfth century, Innocent III. rebuilt the palace: in the following age it was enlarged by Nicholas III.. For upwards of a thousand years the Popes had inhabited the Lateran Palace, and did not make the Vatican their permanent residence until after their return from Avignon, in 1377. From that time they seem to have vied with each other in the extent and variety of their additions, so that at present the Vatican and Church of St. Peter's, with the Colonnade and Fountains all adjoining, cover a space of 20 acres. In the Palace there are eight grand Staircases and two hundred smaller ones; twenty Courts and 4,422 Rooms. The Picture Galleries in the Private Chapels, the Frescos, the Museums, the Libraries, and Galleries of Sculptures, are most extensive and valuable.

ST. PETER'S.

St. Peter's is incomparably the most magnificent building in the world. The old Church is under the present one, and is highly curious, being rich in ancient monuments. As early as the year 90 we are informed that Anacletus, Bishop of Rome, who received ordination from Peter, erected an Oratory on the site, to mark the Burial Place of that Apostle. In 306, Constantine founded a Basilica, on the same spot, which, from that time, became the great attraction of Christendom. The foundations of the present majestic pile were laid in 1450, and the erection was in progress during three centuries and a half following, extending through the reigns of no less than forty-three Popes. So enormous were the expenses incurred, that Julius II. and Leo X. resorted to the public sale of Indulgences to raise the necessary funds; and it is well known that this abomination roused the indignation of Luther and provoked the Reformation. At the close of the seventeenth century, Carlo Fontana estimated the cost at 46,800,498 scudi, or £10,000,000, exclusive of 900,000 scudi expended in the Sacristi, and also of the cost of the Bell-Towers, Models, Mosaics, and sundry other little matters. The space covered by this Cathedral is said to be 350,000 square feet, or eight acres, English. On the central pavement of the Nave are marked the measurements of St. Peter's as compared with those of the other principal Ecclesiastical Structures. It is there stated that this Church is 837 palms in length within the walls, and 862·8 without, which, calculating the palm at 8·795 English inches, gives $613\frac{1}{2}$ feet as its extreme length. St. Paul's, in London, is 710 palms, or $520\frac{1}{2}$ feet; the Cathedral at Milan is 606 palms, or 443 feet; St. Paul's, in Rome, is 572 palms, or $419\frac{1}{4}$ feet; St. Sophia, in Constantinople, is 492 palms, or $360\frac{1}{2}$ feet. The height of the Nave of St. Peter's, near the door, is $152\frac{1}{2}$ feet, and the width $87\frac{1}{2}$; while the side Aisles measure $33\frac{3}{4}$ feet in width; so that, including the thickness of the Pilasters that separate the Aisles and the Nave, the breadth of the whole area is $197\frac{3}{4}$

feet. The extreme length of the Transepts is 446½ feet. The height of the Baldacchino, or grand canopy, covering the High Altar, is 95 feet. The circumference of the four great Pilasters that support the Dome is 253 feet. The diameter of the Cupola, including the outer walls, is 195½ feet; the width in the walls 139 feet, three feet less than that of the Dome of the Pantheon. The height of this Dome, from the pavement to the base of the Lantern, is 405 feet, and to the top of the Cross outside, the height is 448 feet. Thus, St. Peter's, at Rome, exceeds St. Paul's, in London, by 93½ feet in length, by 64 in height, and by 50 in the diameter of the Cupola, including the thickness of the walls. The amount annually expended in keeping this wonderful structure in repair, together with other minor items, is 30,000 scudi, or £6,300.

Visitors are not admitted to ascend the Dome of this world-renowned Cathedral after twelve o'clock, though they may remain till one. Permission is granted by order of the Directors of the Fabrica of St. Peter's, obtained through an application signed by the Consul; but I procured the privilege on Good Friday, by handing a small fee to the doorkeeper. This ascent is the best means of forming an idea of the magnitude of the edifice. A horse might be ridden up the broad spiral Staircase which leads to the roof, so gradual and gentle is the ascent; and on

the walls are inscribed the names of the members
of the reigning houses of Europe who have been up.
One of the latest is that of the Prince of Wales,
who ascended into the Ball on the 10th February,
1859. He is the only British Prince whose name
appears. A series of Passages and Staircases conduct from the roof to the various stages of the
Dome, winding between the double walls of the Drum,
and opening on the great circular Galleries within,
from which we can look down into the Church, and
appreciate the stupendous proportions of the building.
The people moving on the Pavement, seen from these
Galleries, scarcely appear like human beings, while
the Mosaics, which, viewed from below, had the
effect of the most minute and delicate work, are now
discovered to be remarkably bold and coarse. The
stairs lead between the walls of the Dome to the base
of the Lantern, from which another flight rises to the
top, on which the Ball reposes. This may be safely
entered by a ladder placed in an almost vertical
position. But fashionable ladies, who might succeed
in squeezing themselves through the entrance, will
certainly be under the necessity of doffing the crinoline to accomplish the retreat. The Ball is copper,
eight feet in diameter, and large enough to contain
sixteen persons. A small iron ladder winds round
the exterior to the Cross, which is sixteen feet in
height.

From the Balcony leading to the Ball, the whole of Rome, with her desolate Campagna, spreads out like a map before the spectator, on one side bounded by the chain of the Apennines and the Alban Hills, and on the other by the Mediterranean. There is scarcely any prominent object of interest in the modern city which may not be readily distinguished from this commanding station, and nowhere are the Apennines and other surrounding mountains seen to greater advantage.

In the interior of St. Peter's there is a display of magnificence which defies description; it must be inspected to be appreciated. There are no stained windows nor paintings, but the ceilings are a tissue of Mosaics, so exquisitely executed as to require a tolerably close inspection to be distinguished from the finest pictures. It contains nearly one hundred polished marble Pillars, one hundred and thirty-five Statues, twenty-nine Altar-pieces, and eighteen superb Monuments, and the very floor is laid with marble. The High Altar is placed under the centre of the great Dome, and stands immediately over the Relics of St. Peter. This is used upon the great Festival occasions, and is approached for the celebration of Mass by the Pope alone, or by a Cardinal authorized by special Apostolic Brief. The space before the Confessional is surrounded by a circular Balustrade of marble, on which are suspended ninety-three lamps that burn night and day. A double flight of steps leads down to the Shrine of St. Peter, where the first object that attracts attention is the Kneeling-Statue of Pius VI., designed by himself during his captivity, and representing him as praying before the Tomb of the Apostle. On the right side of the Nave against the last Pier, is the well known bronze Statue of St. Peter, on a marble chair, with his foot extended, and which, Devotees entering the Basilica, kiss, and after each salutation press with their foreheads. When St. Peter's was built, Niches were made in the columns, to be occupied in after days by Colossal Statues of Popes and Patron Saints, and it is observable that these niches are all filled save *one*, which is in the most prominent part of the Church, nearest to St. Peter's Tomb, and above the Statue of that Apostle. This circumstance is remarkable, if not ominous, for it seems probable that the Temporal Power of the Popes will become extinct with Pio Nono.

Numerous objects of interest are, for obvious reasons, necessarily passed over without notice in the present account. I must, however, observe, that in one part of the Church there are Confessionals, apparently designed for the use of the various European nations, so that Pilgrims might confess in their own languages. My attention was one day directed to a number of Penitents in these, when I said to an Irish gentleman with whom I had formed a slight acquaintance—

"Do those Priests ever confess?"

"Yes," was his reply.

"To whom?"

"To the Cardinals."

"Do the Cardinals confess?"

"Yes."

"To whom?"

"To the Pope."

"And does the Pope confess?"

"Yes."

"The Pope confesses! Marvellous! And pray to whom does his Holiness confess?"

"To his Chaplain, once a month."

"Then what becomes of his Infallibility?"

"The Holy Father does not profess to be infallible as a man, but as the Vicar of Christ. It is to the Holy Catholic Apostolic Church that Infallibility is ascribed, of which the Pope is the Infallible Head."

Strange incongruity! And yet more strange that absurdities so monstrous should be accepted by a reasoning creature.

RELIGIOUS CEREMONIES.

It may be proper here to give some account of the principal religious Ceremonies performed in the Cathedral in Passion Week.

PALM SUNDAY.—At 9 A.M. the French soldiers, with fixed bayonets, enter the Church, followed by the soldiers of State or Body-Guard of the Pope, who form a line for the Procession through the Nave. Half an hour after, the Bishops, Archbishops, and Cardinals; together with the Canons of St. Peter's and the Heads of the various religious Orders, in sacerdotal robes; and last of all the Sovereign Pontiff, seated on a portable Throne, carried by twelve men in scarlet attire, move in grand procession. The Holy Father assuming the attitude of dispensing blessings to the countless multitude of spectators, while the soldiers and all good Catholics fall upon their knees before him. On arriving in the Pontifical Chapel behind the High Altar, he receives the homage of the Cardinals, habited in violet. Immediately afterwards his Holiness consecrates the Palms which they bear in their hands, and then, assisted by a Cardinal Deacon, distributes them, first to their Eminences, and then to the inferior dignitaries of the Church. The distribution ended, the Pope is carried round the Cathedral in procession, followed by the Palm-bearers. On returning to the Pontifical Chapel, the Cardinals exchange their violet for scarlet robes, and High Mass is performed by a Cardinal Priest, which lasts from 11.15 to about 1 o'clock. This terminated, the Pope is carried to his Robing-Room, in the Chapel of the Madonna della Pieta, from which he returns to his Apartments, passing through the Chapel of the Sacrament and the private way into the Palace. The ceremonies on this day are very imposing. Gentlemen in uniform are admitted into the Pontifical Chapel, and ladies have places assigned to them on either side of the altar.

ASH WEDNESDAY.—At 4.30 P.M., the "First Miserere" is chanted in the presence of the Pope in the Sixtine Chapel. To secure seats, it is necessary to go at two o'clock. A Triangle, furnished with lighted candles, is arranged previous to the service, and at the conclusion of the different Psalms, these candles are extinguished in succession till a solitary light remains. This is at length removed behind the altar, during the singing of the Miserere, and brought forth again at its conclusion, when a general knocking with a stick takes place. This absurd pantomine is intended to denote the Light on earth during the Saviour's presence, His descent into the Tomb, His resurrection, and the attendant circumstances.

HOLY THURSDAY.—On this day, High Mass is celebrated in the Sixtine Chapel by a Cardinal—generally the Dean of the Sacred College—and, at the close, a Procession is formed, which proceeds to the Capella Paolina, the Pontiff carrying the Host, which he places on the altar. The Capella Paolina this day represents the Holy Sepulchre! Weather favouring, his Holiness appears then upon the Balcony in front of St. Peter's, a few minutes after twelve, and pronounces his Benediction upon the multitude assembled below; but, should rain fall, the Benediction is given within the Church. This part of the ceremony concluded, the Pope appears in the northern Transept, at about 12.45, and proceeds to wash the feet of thirteen Priests, assumed to represent the twelve Apostles, together with the Angel who miraculously appeared to St. Gregory the Great on a similar occasion! The feet washing concluded, the Pope waits upon the same thirteen individuals at table, in the gallery of the Portico, at 1.15, and gives them the Last Supper. These impersonations of the Apostles and the Angel are representatives of various countries. Thus the Diplomatic Agents of France, Austria, Spain, and Portugal, have the right of presentation; three Italians are chosen by the Pope's Majordomo; a Swiss is selected by the Captain of the Swiss Guard, and two Oriental Catholics by the Heads of the United Armenian and Greek Churches at Rome. Each priest, after his feet have been washed, receives a gold and silver medal, and a nosegay of flowers, and carries away all the viands placed before him, as also the napkin and white dress in which he was attired. The Pope commences by girding on himself an apron richly embroidered, which is afterwards the perquisite of the Grand Chamberlain *(Maestro di Camera);* after which, Prelates kneeling, present him with the plates, which he lays before the Pilgrims. The Supper consists, first, of boiled fish; secondly, broiled fish;

thirdly, a dish of celery prepared with other ingredients; and, finally, two figs and two apples, are assigned to each, with port wine for Dessert. During the repast, the Pope's "Crocifero," or Cross-bearer, reads prayers. At 4.30 P.M., the "Second Miserere" is chanted in the Sixtine Chapel; after which, his Holiness, attended by his household, proceeds to pray in the Capella Paolina. The Cardinal Grand Penitentiary sits for three hours before dark in the Transept of the Cathedral, to give Absolution for mortal sins, which otherwise cannot be remitted! The Pauline Chapel, the various Sepulchres, and the principal Streets of the city, are brilliantly Illuminated on the evening of this day.

GOOD FRIDAY.—The Sacramental elements, which, on the day preceding, were consecrated in the Sixtine Chapel, are, upon the morning of Good Friday, carried back from the Pauline, where they had been deposited in imitation of the Burial of the Saviour. Mass is here celebrated by the Cardinal Grand Penitentiary, at 9.30 A.M.; after which the Pope and the Sacred College hear a sermon from a Friar of the Black Franciscan Order. The "Final Miserere" is then chanted in the Sixtine Chapel, at 4 P.M.; after which the Pope and his Cardinals move in procession through the Cathedral, and appear before the Tomb of the Apostle to pray, while the Relics of the Holy Cross, the "Volto Santo," or Holy Towel, and the Spear which pierced the Saviour's side, are exhibited from the Balcony over the statue of St. Veronica.

EASTER SUNDAY is distinguished by the grandest Ceremony of the Romish Church. The dawn is ushered in by the cannon of the Castle of St. Angelo. At 9.30, High Mass is celebrated by the Pope in person. His Holiness enters the Church in solemn procession, as upon Palm Sunday, all the details of which are symbolical.

He is borne upon a portable Throne to express his Exaltation as the Vicar of Christ.

Two Fans of Ostrich plumes, in which the Eyes of peacock's feathers are inserted, are carried before him, to signify the Vigilance he requires, and that he is regarded by the eyes of humanity.

The lower Circlet of the Triple Crown represents the Pope's Temporal dominion; the Mitre denotes the Spiritual; the second Circlet shows the union of both; and the third, the Imperial power of his Holiness as the Head of Temporal and Spiritual authority.

Seven Candelabras, borne before the Pontiff by Acolytes, represent the seven ecclesiastical "Rioni," or divisions of the city, which answer to the "Seven Candlesticks," amid which the Son of God, in the visions of the Apocalypse, was seen walking; and likewise expresses the seven Gifts of the Holy Spirit.

When the Pope arrives opposite the Chapel of the Holy Sacrament, the procession halts; he descends from his throne to adore the Host exposed upon the illuminated altar of that Chapel. The *cortege* then passes on to a Throne erected for the occasion at the Epistle side of the Tribune, where the Homage is performed; and, after reading to himself the prayers preparatory to saying Mass, whilst the office of Tierce is sung, his Holiness is vested. A procession is then formed, consisting of the Thurifer, Crossbearer, Greek and Latin Deacons, Subdeacons, the Cardinal Bishop, and three Cardinal Deacons, the Pope, with his two Private Chamberlains, and the Auditor of the Rota, bearing his mitre, the Patriarchs and other Prelates assistant at the Throne. This Procession, which is formed at the end of the Tribune, suddenly turns to the right, and faces the High Altar, which it approaches, and is met there by three junior Cardinals who represent the Magi who came to our Saviour. These Cardinals, in succession, pay homage to his Holiness, and then embrace him with a kiss on the cheek and breast. The Epistle and Gospel are sung, first in Latin and then in Greek, to denote the Union between the Eastern and the Western Churches and the Primacy of the latter. His Holiness having retired to the farthest Throne before the Epistle, towards the conclusion of the Creed, the Sacred Vessels are washed at the Credence Tables. At the Offertory the Motette *Christus Resurgens* is sung to the noble music of Felice Anerio, which is considered one of the finest pieces performed by the Papal Choir. Other music follows, concluding with a Chorus, which swells into a glorious strain, after the Confession of Faith in the Resurrection.

Before the Preface, two junior Cardinal Deacons take their station at the Altar, facing each other, to represent the two Angels who appeared at the Sepulchre. Then is sung the form of words in which the praises of the Church are offered up with those of Angels, Archangels, Thrones, and Dominions. After the *Sanctus*, there is a dead silence, which, at the consummation of the Sacrifice, is broken by the sudden burst of silver trumpets, the effect of which can never be forgotten. The Elements are consecrated by the Pope at the High Altar, to set forth the sufferings of the Redeemer in the sight of the multitude; the Altar representing the Table at which the Eucharist was instituted, and the Throne the Mount upon which the Sacrifice was offered. A second elevation of the Host and Chalice is made by the Assistant Cardinals, after the Pontiff has retired from the Altar, and they are then solemnly carried to the Throne, when his Holiness partakes of both, drinking from the Chalice through a golden tube. The Deacon, Sub-Deacon, Roman Princes, Senator of Rome, and the Conservatives, then receive the Elements from the hands of the Pope; and after the conclusion of the Mass, the "Holy Father" assumes the Tiara, reseats himself on the portable Throne, and is presented by the Cardinal Arch-Priest of St. Peter's with a white velvet Purse containing the Offering made to him for singing the Mass in that Basilica. The whole Ceremony within the Church lasts from 9.30 to 11.45; and a little after 12, the Pontiff again appears upon the Balcony, as upon Holy Thursday, to pronounce the Benediction. The following is a translation :—

"May the Holy Apostles Peter and Paul, in whose power and authority we confide, intercede for us with the Lord. Amen. Through the prayers and merits of the Blessed Mary, ever Virgin, of the Blessed Michael, the Archangel, of the Blessed John the Baptist, of the Holy Apostles Peter and Paul, and all Saints ; may the Omnipotent God have mercy upon you, may all your sins be remitted, and Jesus Christ lead you to eternal life. Amen. Indulgence, absolution, and remission of all your sins, space for true and faithful repentance, and amendment of life, may the Omnipotent God afford you. Amen. And may the blessing of the Omnipotent God, Father, Son, and Holy Ghost, descend upon you and remain with you ever. Amen."

In uttering the Sacred Names, the Pope rises and makes the "sign of the cross" in front, and on each side, over the people; and at the word "descend," he stretches his arms towards heaven and then folds them over his breast.

The Benediction concluded, a Cardinal Deacon reads in Latin and Italian, the Bull of the Plenary Indulgence, to all who, in the spirit of true repentance, have attended the Sacrament; whose hearts are purified from the malignity of sin, and who are, therefore, in a state of reconciliation with the Church. Copies of this document are then thrown amongst the people, when shouts are raised by the concourse, accompanied by waving of hats and handkerchiefs, and vociferations of "Ponte Max," "Ponte Max"—The Great Pontiff, The Great Pontiff.

The Ceremonies at Whitsuntide and Christmas are not so imposing as those of Easter, now described. During the Passion week, ladies must procure tickets of admission from the Pope's Majordomo, at the Sixtine Chapel; but the ceremonies at other seasons are accessible without them. Those wishing to obtain seats must appear in black, without bonnets, and covered with veils. Gentlemen also, if not in uniform, will not be permitted to enter the Sixtine and Pontifical Chapels, unless they wear a black evening dress.

ILLUMINATIONS.—The Illuminations of St. Peter's on Easter Sunday are too well known to require a detailed description. Every column, cornice, and frieze, the bands of the dome, and all the details of the building to the summit of the Cross, are lit up with lines of lamps, when its gigantic proportions stand out against the dark sky as a complete mass of fire. The "Silver Illumination" commences at dusk, and is supplied by 5,900 paper lanterns; then at eight, when the first stroke of the clock gives the signal, the

"Golden Illumination" commences. Now 900 lamps, or iron cups, filled with tallow and turpentine, are lighted so simultaneously by three hundred and eighty-two men, that it seems like a work of enchantment. In about eight seconds—before the clock has finished striking the hour, every lamp is on fire; and now there are no less than 6,800 centres of illumination burning upon the pile.

FIREWORKS.—The night following—Easter Monday, the celebrated Fireworks are displayed upon the Pincian Hill, commencing between the hours of eight and nine. These baffle description. Let it be sufficient to say, that they are considered the most complete exhibition of the kind in the world.

THE CHURCHES OF ROME.

The Churches of Rome are, I believe, upwards of Forty in number, every one of which, is worthy of a visit; while some are beyond description, gorgeous. Marble pillars in endless variety and size support the roofs of some, while others are sustained by columns of porphyry and granite. The floors of several are inlaid with gems so richly polished, as to require care in treading upon them; others are inlaid in diamond shaped marbles and mosaics. The altars groan under the weight of gold, silver, diamonds, rubies, emeralds, and jaspers. The ceilings are highly ornamented, and the entablatures tastefully hung with drapery. I shall only remark upon a few of these buildings, and shall not attempt a particular description of the architecture even of these.

The Basilica San Paola, or Church of St. Paul, next to St. Peter's, most forcibly struck my admiration. It is situate about two miles from the city, on the road which is graced by the Temple of Vesta, the Roman Pyramid, and the English Cemetery. It displays from one hundred and fifty to two hundred pillars of granite, marble, and alabaster; and in the floor of one of the side Chapels, there are no less than sixty different kinds of marble, inlaid in highly polished hexagonal blocks. The walls are faced with lapis lazuli, alabaster, &c. In 1824 this Church was burnt down; but it is now completely restored. It is said to be erected over the Tomb of the Apostle whose name it bears, and who was beheaded by order of Nero.

When brought the second time before that Tyrant, aware of his condemnation, the venerable Apostle wrote his Second Epistle to Timothy, which was probably his last. This consideration makes every word increasingly impressive and affecting. He writes, "I am now ready to be offered, and the time of my departure is at hand. . . . At my *first* answer [viz., before Nero] no man stood with me. . . . I was delivered out of the mouth of the lion." (2 Tim. iv. 6, 16, 17.) Writing to the Philippians, he says, "The things which have happened to me, have fallen out rather to the furtherance of the Gospel, so that my bonds in [for] Christ are manifest in all the Palace." (Phil. i. 12, 13.) This extension of the Gospel into the very Palace of Cæsar, it is said, provoked him to put Paul to death.

BASILICA SANTA MARIA MAGGIORE, or Church of Mary the Virgin, stands upon the ruins of the Temple of Juno Lucina on the crown of Mount Esquiline. The roof is supported by thirty-six Ionic marble columns, besides four granite pillars under the arches of the Nave. The Ceiling was gilded with the first sample from the Peruvian mines. The Grand Altar is composed of an antique porphyry Sarcophagus, supported by four Angels of gilded bronze, and covered with a superb canopy, which rests upon four Corinthian columns, also of porphyry; over which are six Angels sculptured by Bracci. The Chapel of the Holy Sacrament was erected by Sixtus V., and contains the Tomb of that Pope, richly adorned by variegated marbles, paintings, frescos, and basso-relievos. The Borghese Chapel, erected by Paul V., is very magnificent, and contains the Tombs of Paul V. and Clement VIII., both of which are ornamented with basso-relievos. The Altar of the Virgin is splendid, and is adorned with an image of the "Queen of Heaven" resting upon lapis lazuli, and surrounded with jewels. The Paintings above the Tombs, and on the arches over the windows, are the works of Guido. This Church also contains several curious Mosaics, various handsome Tombs; and in the square fronting it, there is a marble Column of the Corinthian order, which is considered a model of elegance.

BASILICA SAN GIOVANNI IN LATERANO, or Lateran Church, occupies the site of the residence of the Senator Plantius Lateranus, from whom it derives its name. The Chapter of the Lateran, still takes precedence of that of St. Peter's. Here the Popes are crowned; and after the election of a new Pope one of the first ceremonies observed is that of taking possession of this Basilica. For 1,500 years it has preserved its rank and privileges. In this Church there are Statues of the Twelve Apostles, several Columns of granite, verd-antique, and gilt-bronze, together with an inexhaustible store of Relics. Amongst these is a Portrait of our Saviour when he was twelve years old; the Table at which the Disciples partook of the Last Supper; and a variety of things, which, but for the solemnity of the subjects to which they refer, would cause considerable amusement; they excite the pity of the thoughtful towards those so infatuated as to believe in them.

THE MARBLE STAIRS.—Near this Church is a Chapel, the ascent to which is formed by a Marble Staircase, declared by tradition to be that by which the Redeemer descended when he left the Judgment Hall of Pilate. These steps are held so sacred that no person is permitted to pass over them except upon his hands and knees; but there are parallel flights for the convenience of Heretics, by which I ascended, being unwilling to pass through the ordeal. These were the stairs upon which Luther crawled to obtain Indulgence, when the Divine Voice, in his heart, pronounced the memorable words, "The just shall live by faith," the reverberations of which produced the Reformation.

THE WALLS OF THE CITY, including those of the Trastevere and the Vatican, are from twelve to thirteen miles in circuit, and are generally constructed of brick, with occasional patches of stone. They have no ditch, but are crested with nearly three hundred Towers. There were formerly twenty Gates, seven of which are now blocked up.

THE ANGLICAN CHAPEL is a beautiful building, large enough to accommodate from seven to eight hundred persons, situate outside the walls. It is supported exclusively by voluntary Contributions from Visitors, for whose convenience it is opened during the *Season*, from October to June. There are few Protestants permanently resident at Rome. The times of Service are 11 A.M., and 3 P.M. on Sundays, and 10 A.M. every week-day. Attached to the Chapel there is a lending Library of Religious Books, which are distributed on Sundays to such subscribers as may apply for them. I attended service at the Anglican Chapel, and admired the gentlemanly bearing of the Clergyman, but was sorry to hear that he was of the High School.

The Population of Rome in 1800 was 153,000. From that time it gradually decreased until 1813, when it was 117,900. It has since been advancing, and in 1846, was 175,214. At Easter, 1861, exclusive of Strangers, it was 184,050. The average number of Births, per annum, in the last ten years, has been 5,606, while the Deaths have been 5,975, proving that the increase of population arises from immigration. There are about 4,500 Priests and Friars, and 1,900 Nuns. The resident Jewish Population, according to the returns of the last census, was 4,196. They are still compelled to live in the "Ghetto," or Jews' Quarter—an invidious barbarity now only to be met with in the States of the Church. A relaxation of that rule, however, has recently been made in favour of the more respectable Israelites, who are now permitted to have Shops and Countinghouses beyond the precincts of that filthy quarter.

The Streets are generally narrow and paved with small pyramidal masses of lava raised from neighbouring quarries. The Corso and Via del Borgo, leading to St. Peter's, are the only thoroughfares which have foot-pavements on the sides. For the most part the Streets are lighted with Oil; but of late Gas has been introduced into those in the vicinity of the Piazza del Popolo, the Corso, and other principal thoroughfares. Thanks to an English Company who have erected extensive Works on the site of the Circus Maximus: there is a prospect that the whole city will eventfully be thus lighted. Several of the main lines of Streets are long and handsome, and often broken by open Spaces or Piazzas. The town is also well drained by a network of Sewers, chiefly on the lines of the ancient *Cloacæ*.

Upon the conversion of Constantine, in the early part of the Fourth Century, some Ancient Temples became transformed into places of Christian worship. A still greater number were subsequently destroyed by invading armies and other violent means. In the Seventh and Eighth Centuries Rome suffered fearfully from Earthquakes, Inundations of the Tiber, Famines, and Pestilences. Disputes respecting the Succession to the Papacy, the contests of Popes with German Emperors, and the frequent absence of the Court, further tended to facilitate the decay of the city. All previous invaders were surpassed by the Normans in the extent of their ravages; for they burnt a considerable portion of the town, dismantled the Capitol and the Colosseum, and laid waste the whole of the Esquiline. Many subsequent invasions and massacres are recorded. In 1345, the city was again overflown by the Tiber, insomuch that nothing remained visible but the hills. In 1349, it was desolated by a fearful earthquake. In 1527, it was cruelly pillaged by an invading foe. In 1530, another inundation came, scarcely less calamitous than the preceding. From an early period new Churches were erected, and repairs effected at the expense of the ancient Monuments; and the Lime-kilns of the Middle Ages were supplied from the ruins of Temples and other edifices. These were further despoiled of columns for the benefit of ecclesiastical structures, and in this pious desecration of a venerable antiquity the Popes have been unscrupulous. As early as the Eighth Century Gregory III., took nine columns from a Temple for the Basilica of St. Peter. Adrian I. destroyed the Temple of Ceres and Proserpine to build S. Maria in Cosmedin. Paul II. built the Palace of St. Mark with materials taken from the Colosseum. Thus the destruction of Monuments proceeded until the middle of the Fifteenth Century, when Æneus Sylvius was elected Pope, under the title of Pius II., who issued a Bull to stay the spoliation. But, notwithstanding all the efforts of barbarian hands, and the effects of great physical convulsions, we must not be surprised that a City, which has existed for 2,600 years, should still abound in Relics.

On Wednesday, 23rd April, I bid farewell to the

"Eternal City," and arrived in London on the 29th, in time to spend nearly a week in inspecting the triumphs of Art in the International Exhibition. While there, whether in the Crystal Palace, or in the crowded streets, I oftentimes reflected gratefully upon mercies I had received, and the dangers through which I had been conducted by a gracious Providence.

CHAPTER III.

EGYPT.

THE VOYAGE.

Accompanied by Messrs. Eli and John Plummer, I left Leeds, on Saturday, 8th November, 1862; and arriving in Liverpool, we immediately went to Mr. Papayanni, and paid him Sixteen Guineas each for the Best-Cabin accommodation to Alexandria. The next day we were on board a fine ship, comparatively new, and admirably fitted. We soon cleared the dock. But we found the river so agitated, that the steamer rolled tremendously, and I was sent to my berth in an indescribable condition. There I remained for four-and-twenty hours, after which, I managed tolerably; still, however, lying down and eating sparingly. But on Thursday noon, some nice tender beef, a preserve-pudding, some cheese, and a half-pint of sherry, made me a new man.

Upon the evening of this day, we had considerable excitement on board, occasioned by our overtaking and passing a screw steamer, 2,500 tons, belonging to the same Company, which had started with coals for Malta, the day before we sailed. We saluted each other by firing cannon. Upon this day also, we were astonished while pacing the deck, by the fall of a sail with its gear, which smashed the large compass, by which the others were regulated. Onward we dashed, nevertheless, and after passing out of the Irish Channel, we had a splendid run across the Bay of Biscay, without encountering the rough seas for which it is so celebrated. We sighted Cape Finisterre, on the Spanish coast, which appeared mountainous, but as we were seventeen miles distant, we could not particularly distinguish objects. We were now fully exposed to the roll of the Atlantic, and rising in the morning, greatly enjoyed a splendid climate—the sun and air in these latitudes being like those of June or July in England, and contrasting most favourably with the cold and fog which then surrounded our friends at home. Upon the morning of the 14th, I was particularly struck with the deep leaden colour of the sea, and the long ground swell, which was quite different from what appears upon our shores. At 5 P.M., we descried Cape Spartel on the North-West Coast of Africa, and at 6, the Trafalgar Light-house appeared upon the horizon. It stands on the entrance of the Bay, memorable for the great Naval Engagement in which Nelson fell in the arms of Victory. The Thermometer stood at 78°. At 8.45, the Tarifa Lighthouse came in sight. About five next morning, we anchored in Gibralter Bay, surrounded by ships of various nations, together with the "Warrior," and other English War-Vessels; the Rock magnificently rising before us, and the buff-colour Town appearing as if its houses were piled one over the other. The blue Mountains of Spain to the North and West, and the towns of San Roque and Algesiras in the distance, completed the beauty of the scene.

THE ROCK OF GIBRALTER runs about three miles into the sea, and is the most Southerly point in Europe. It is connected with Spain by an isthmus of low land, the Southern part of which is English, while the Northern is Spanish, and a space intermediate, neutral ground. Convicts, who may escape across the neutral ground are safe, for the Spanish authorities will not resign them. The sentries have orders to fire upon those who may thus attempt to release themselves from penal servitude. British Officers frequently cross the line to hunt and shoot; but are obliged to go well armed, as kidnapping is far from being uncommon. The Straits of Gibralter are but from ten to fifteen miles across. The Fortifications upon this Rock, therefore, command them so completely, that the place has been justly styled "The Key to the Mediterranean." The Fortress is all but impregnable. Every attempt to dislodge the English has signally failed. The last Siege in 1779, conducted by the combined Fleets of France and Spain, lasted between three and four years, during which, the Garrison suffered the greatest privations, but Elliott defended the place until the Fleets of the enemy were destroyed. The Batteries are not visible from the sea, but look terrible to a person walking amongst them. We were assured, that in case of alarm, nine hundred pieces of Ordnance can be brought into action in the course of a few minutes; and many guns can be made to concentrate their fire upon a given point. In the *Almeda*, or Public Gardens, there is a twenty-one-gun Battery, called "The Snake in the Grass," which an Enemy could not discover until its murderous fire had opened upon him. There are also two Galleries tunnelled through the rock from side to side, pierced with Ports, and armed with heavy Cannon, frowning over the neutral ground, so that in case of an attack from that quarter, the enemy might be blown to pieces, while the defenders are completely screened.

The Streets and Buildings of the town are inferior, but it is free from beggars. The Markets are well supplied with fish, fowl, fruit, and vegetables; and oranges may be purchased at a shilling a hundred. Bread is as dear as in England; meat is cheaper. The Butchers and Bakers are licensed by Government. There are here sometimes nearly a thousand Convicts; who, as compared with our Agricultural Labourers, live in idleness and luxury. Their labour is by no means so exhausting as that of an English "Hedger and Ditcher," and yet they have, as their weekly rations, seven pounds of bread, two of salt pork, two and a quarter of fresh beef, two of peas, one and a half of vegetables, seven ounces of cocoa, seven of sugar, three of salt, and nearly a pint of rum.

It would have been very agreeable to have remained longer at this interesting place, but the time allotted having expired, we were obliged to return to our Ship, which, however, did not sail for several hours. Running out of the Bay, we had a noble view of the Rock. We had also a good view of the Town of Algesiras, where there is a Bull-Fight every Sunday, to which the people flock in crowds from Gibralter. We had likewise splendid views of the African and Spanish Coasts, the latter being about twenty miles distant; yet the atmosphere was so clear, that the small towns sleeping upon the sides of the hills, were distinctly visible. About midnight we passed Malaga, celebrated for its raisins; the next day Cape de Gatta; after which, with the disappearance of the cloud-capped mountains behind the Cape, we lost sight of Spain. Still we ran along the African coast, and were much amused with the singing of the Sailors while hoisting the mainsail, and with gazing upon the Porpoises tumbling in the sea. On the 18th we came abreast of Algiers, when the Captain assured us that it would be dangerous to haul close to land, as the coast was infested with Pirates. The day following rain descended in torrents, and we were confined to the saloon. At 6 A.M. on the 20th, we passed Cape Bon, a magnificent Promontory, and the loftiest point on the African coast. About twelve, we were opposite to the town of Pantillario, on the Island of that name, formerly used as a Convict Station by the Neapolitans; and the morning following we were up early to enjoy the entrance into the Harbour of Valetta.

MALTA is an immense Rock, of about fifty miles in circumference, distant from Sicily also about fifty miles, having several good Harbours and Creeks, and is, with the exception of Gibralter, perhaps the strongest place in the British dominions. The view entering the great Harbour of Valetta, which is the chief town of Malta, is most imposing. The ranges of batteries—the creeks full of shipping with little towns upon the sides—the houses of stone, rising in successive tiers—the public Barraccas or Promenades, with mortars and cannon, and heaps of shot and shell—ships of war, with pennants flying—the busy scenes at the warehouses—gondolas lying at the quays—steamers and yachts riding at anchor—the noble Naval Hospital and other large buildings—the towering craggy rocks—the view of Florianne beyond, and church towers in profusion, all coming at once within the sweep of vision, presents a scene of unusual interest. From the Harbour we passed into the Town, and proceeded over a draw-bridge up a hilly street. The Houses are stone, with flat roofs prepared to receive the rain, and convey it to tanks, or cisterns, hewn in the rock; some of which are very deep. The water thus collected, is that chiefly used for drinking. The rooms are from 15 to 18 feet high, and all the floors are flagged, which, though cold to English ears, this flagging is, nevertheless, the best in that sultry climate. The Streets are straight, generally running at right angles, well paved, and cleaner than those of most towns out of England. Many of those running up against the hill are literally "Streets of Stairs." Tailors, Shoemakers, Tinplate-workers, &c., are commonly seen at work in the streets outside their shops. There are some good Palaces, which formerly belonged to the Knights who governed the Island. Specimens of their Armour, and other curious relics, are preserved in the Palace of the Governor. The Cathedral of St. John, which, before it was stripped of its treasures by Napoleon, was one of the wealthiest in the world, has a floor inlaid with mosaics and costly marbles, and is otherwise beautiful in the interior; but externally presents an humble appearance.

The Population of the Island is about 120,000, of which 3,000 are Ecclesiastics. Valetta numbers about 30,000 persons, and is full of Churches. The Maltese are Romanists of the purest type, they being ignorant and superstitious in the extreme. Everywhere the eye is offended with rude Images of Saints, before which lamps or lanterns are kept burning: and I am assured that in almost every house there is also something of the same sort. In true Popish style, the principal Market is held on *Sunday* morning. The Population overtaxes the natural fruitfulness of the Island, so that quantities of food are imported from Barbary, Sicily, and other parts; consequently Provisions are often dear, and particularly so when the Fleet is in the Harbour. But oranges, figs, pomegranates, prickly pears, peaches, nectarines, caroub or locust, and other fruits of native production, are in such abundance as to be amazingly cheap. In the Governor's Gardens there are no less than twelve hundred orange trees; and, amongst the rest, a particular tree, the fruit of which is always sent to the Queen's table. The people of England pay the Governor £5,000 per annum, £1,500 of which, he is expected to spend in Balls! We have here also a Garrison of one thousand British troops, besides a regiment of Maltese, called the "Fencibles." Every way the Island costs us about £70,000 per annum; but, so long as we must have Fleets, such a Station is invaluable. Ships of all nations are evermore putting in here for Provisions, so that every variety of costume may be seen "alive." This Island is the Melita of the

Acts of the Apostles, where Paul suffered shipwreck. (Acts xxviii. 1.)

After a ramble of five hours in this interesting place, we returned to our Ship, and found six new passengers embarked for Egypt. We had a charming view of the Island, as we put out to sea. The next day being Sunday, the Captain,—a God-fearing man, desired me to conduct a Religious Service; but the ship rolled so tremendously under a heavy sea, that I felt I was not sailor enough to undertake the duty. On Monday, running under a favourable gale, we hoped, in twenty-four hours, to land upon the African shore; and towards evening the Sirocco blowing from the Coast, so heated the atmosphere, and enfeebled our nerves, that we had a foretaste of what we might expect in the lands of the East.

Early in the morning of the 25th, Alexandria came in sight. The land is so flat, that it only becomes visible upon a near approach, the hills being simply composed of sand; but the shore literally bristles with Windmills; from a hundred to a hundred and fifty coming at once within the range of vision. To the left, on the site of the Ancient Palace of the Pharaohs, a Lighthouse stands, and in the distance is Pompey's Pillar—the only Column we could discover. So dangerous are the Reefs protecting the Harbour, that no Captain thinks of venturing in without a Pilot. We took an Arab on board, who, before he brought us to anchor, ran us against the jib-boom of a Turkish Frigate, and rent our rigging in pieces. We had to wait for the Health-Officer until noon; after which, having been sixteen days at Sea, and having travelled over 2,950 miles,[*] through the good Providence of God, we landed in safety. The place of landing was remarkably filthy; and there we were assailed by clouds of donkey-boys; but having transferred our luggage to a bullock-cart, we walked quietly up the main street, to the Hotel Abbatt, near the Great Square, where we established ourselves.

ORIGIN OF THE EGYPTIANS.

There is no Country whose Ancient History is wrapped in greater obscurity than Egypt, if we except the information conveyed in the Sacred Oracles. Learned men, for centuries, have in vain attempted to bring order out of the chaos; but though all agree in certain leading facts, there are others upon which they widely differ, and their discrepancies in dates and minor details, are endless. Respecting the Origin of the People, however, we have information from the Bible.

Moses tells us that, after the dispersion at Babel, the descendants of Ham journeyed Westward, and

---

[*] The journey from England to Alexandria, *via* France, is shorter by 850 miles than that across the Bay of Biscay.

peopled this Country; and David speaks of the First-born of Egypt as "the Chief of their Strength in the Tabernacles of Ham." (Psa. lxxviii. 51.) The Hebrew word, in our Version, rendered "Egypt," is MIZRAIM, whence it is evident that, at least, the major part of that nation sprang from Mizraim, the second son of Ham. From Monumental Remains it appears that Libya, to the West, was colonized by Phut, another son of the Patriarch. Accordingly, the Arabs formerly applied the term, MIZR, exclusively to the people of the Lower Division, but now they use the term, as MIZRAIM was employed by the Hebrews, in synecdoche, for the Egyptians generally.

It may be proper here to state that the Turks, who at present hold the superiority over Egypt, are not only a distinct race from the Egyptians, but also from the Saracens. The resemblance which they bear to the latter, has confused many. The Saracens are Arabs, principally sprung from Shem; while the Turks, like ourselves, are descendants of Japheth.

It is not strictly correct that the Arabs are Ishmaelites, or sprung from Abraham, through the "Son of the Bondwoman." The Bedaween, or "Dwellers in the Wilderness," as contradistinguished from those inhabiting the Towns and Villages, are, in all probability, so descended. They have remarkably preserved the character assigned to the posterity of

Ishmael by the Angel of the Lord. "He will be a wild man; his hand shall be against every man, and every man's hand shall be against him; and he shall dwell in the presence of all his brethren." (Gen. xvi. 12.) They have ever considered the whole of Arabia as belonging to them, and no warrior has been able to expel them. Their dress, food, manners and customs, remain the same as in the days of the Patriarchs. Before the appearance of Mahomet, their Religion was a corruption of the Patriarchal. They practised the Abrahamic rite of Circumcision, and, from time immemorial, they have preserved the Tradition that they were descended from Abraham, through Hagar. They further believe that Adam built the original Temple at Mecca, which, having been destroyed by the Noachian Deluge, was afterwards rebuilt by Abraham and Ishmael. In the present Temple, there is a small Stone, which they hold in great reverence, as having fallen from Adam out of Heaven; and near the same place they show the Tomb of Ishmael, and the Well, which sprang up for his relief. (Gen. xxi. 19.)

It is, however, certain, that the descendants of Cush, the eldest Son of Ham, settled in Southern Arabia, and subsequently spread out into other parts. Then, there were the descendants of Abraham, by Keturah,—the Edomites, those sprung from the brothers of Abraham, who, we are assured, established themselves in the lands of Uz and Buz, besides the Moabites, Amorites, and several others,—all of whom are supposed to have peopled various parts of Arabia. These are generally represented in the Towns and Villages; and from this mixed people came forth those hordes known in modern history by the name of Saracens.

It is interesting to note that Rahab of Jericho, a descendant of Ham, married Salmon, of the line of Shem, and became the mother of Boaz, the great-grandfather of David, of whom Messiah sprang.

EARLY HISTORY.

From the Mosaic Records, it appears, that so early as the days of Abraham, Egypt was a country of considerable importance, if not indeed the first Monarchy upon earth. (Gen. xii.) This fact is also attested by the Marbles and other ancient Monuments. Sir Gardner Wilkinson, who spent twelve years in that country, studying the Antiquities, says that Osirtesin I. was Pharaoh,[*] about the year B.C. 1706, when Joseph was conveyed there. From the Monuments it further appears, that Osirtesin III. was Pharaoh when Joseph died, and that soon after,

---

[*] PHARAOH in the Egyptian, denoted the *Sun*, and also a *King;* for the Sun in all antiquity has been regarded as the natural symbol of Royalty.

the Throne was usurped by an Invader. Hereby light is thrown upon the expression, "Another King arose who knew not Joseph;" for this Foreigner would naturally be without sympathy for the Israelites as the kinsmen of the great Benefactor of a former dynasty. Moses was born B.C. 1571, and eighty years later, when, according to Sir Gardner, Thothmes III., the fourth monarch of the new dynasty, reigned, conducted the Exodus. The Monuments testify, most remarkably, that Thothmes III. was not buried with his ancestors, which was unquestionably true of the Pharaoh who perished in the Red Sea. There is also a drawing in Thebes, represented Amunoph II., his son and successor, as yet very young, and under the tutelage of his mother, when he came to the throne. The more fully the ancient hieroglyphs are deciphered, the more completely they rebuke the impudence of Infidelity.

A dreadful Civil War, predicted by the Prophet Isaiah (chap. xix.), broke out about 720 B.C., upon the death of Sethon, who was contemporary with Hezekiah. The Kingdom was then broken into Twelve Princedoms, which, however, in the course of the century following, appear to have been again reduced under the leadership of a single Monarch. About 610 B.C., Pharaoh Necho,—the "Nechos" of the Monuments, waged war against the Jews, when their King, Josiah, fell in the battle of Megiddo. (2 Kings xxiii. 29—35.) Necho then pushed on to the Euphrates, and reduced Babylon; but upon his return, finding that Jehoahaz had caused himself to be proclaimed King at Jerusalem, he substituted Eliakim in his room, carried Jehoahaz captive to Egypt, where he died, and laid a heavy tax upon the Jews. The history of this warlike Prince, as given by profane writers, remarkably corroborates the Sacred Records. From these we also learn, that he equipped a Fleet in the Mediterranean, and another in the Red Sea, and by means of these was the first to ascertain that ships might pass by the Cape of Good Hope, from one sea to the other. But Necho was eventually conquered by Nebuchadnezzar, and Eliakim, or Jehoiakim, as he was otherwise called, and the Jews became the servants of the Babylonians.

Some years later Zedekiah, King of Judah, made an alliance with Pharaoh Hophra, (Apries,) against the King of Babylon. This Alliance, on the part of Judah, Ezekiel compared to his "resting upon a reed;" but at the same time declared that God would bring the sword upon the Egyptians for their treachery. (Jer. xxxvii. 3—10; Ezek. xxix. 6—12.) So inflated with successes was Apries that, as Herodotus states, he persuaded himself the gods could not dispossess him; or, according to the

Sacred Historian, his language was, "My river is my own, and I have made it for myself." But God said, "I will give Pharaoh Hophra into the hands of them that seek his life." This was strictly fulfilled; for his own troops revolted from him, made him prisoner, and strangled him, though Amasis, whom they had placed at their head, pleaded for his life. Egypt was in the pride of power, when the word of the Lord came to Ezekiel, saying, "I will make the land waste and all that is therein, by the hand of strangers." Joel and Zechariah spoke in the same strain. (Joel iii. 19; Zech. x. 11.) Sixty-four years later, the Persians, under Cambyses, invaded Egypt, and from that day to the present, there has not been "a Prince of the land of Egypt" for Strangers have ruled there. (Ezek. xxx. 13). Through the success of Alexander's arms, the Persian Dynasty in Egypt was subverted in the year 336 B.C. And eighty-three years before the Christian era, this Country fell under the Romans, who remained its masters for seven Centuries.

MAHOMET.

Mahomet, or Mohammed, as the Arabs pronounce his name, was born at Mecca, in the year 571. He was of the tribe of Koreish, one of the noblest among the Arabs, and of the family of Hashem, who had charge of the celebrated Temple of that city. Losing his parents while an infant, and inheriting no larger fortune than five Camels and a female Slave of Ethiopia, he was left to the care of his Grandfather, who, at his death, entrusted the Orphan to his son, Abu-Taleb, on whom the honours and wealth of the family then devolved. The Uncle trained the youth, at a proper age, to the business of a Merchant Traveller, and he continued in that employ till he was twenty-five years old, when he entered the service of Chadijah, a lady of the same tribe, and widow of one of the chief citizens of Mecca, in whose interests he visited the great Fair of Damascus. To this lady he so commended himself by his engaging qualities, that in three years she became his Wife, and thus was raised to a situation becoming his birth and connexions. During his travels he was brought into contact with men of all religions and of various nations; and he obtained that knowledge of opinions, and of the state of the surrounding Governments, of which he availed himself in the solitary meditations of after years.

He now retired to the Cave of Hira, near Mecca, apparently alone in meditation and prayer, but really in conference with a Persian Jew and a Nestorian Christian, who, it is said, he murdered when he had no further need of them. With the aid of these men he composed the KORAN or Book, which he pretended to have received in Parts, at various intervals, from the Angel Gabriel. He declared that his Mission was not to inaugurate a New Religion, but to revive that of Ishmael, their father, which they had corrupted into Idolatry. The fundamental Doctrine of the Koran is "There is but One God and Mahomet is His Prophet." He disclaimed the power of working miracles, assigning, that when God sent Moses and Jesus *with* Miracles, men did not believe, therefore he was now determined that they should believe *without* them.

Every night, when he returned from his Cave, he rehearsed to his wife tales respecting mysterious sights and sounds with which he had been greeted, and in particular that the Angel Gabriel had appeared to him and addressed him as "The Apostle of God." Chadijah was charmed with this intelligence. If she had any doubts, they were removed by her cousin Waraka, who had some acquaintance with the Old and New Testament Scriptures, and declared his conviction that "Mahomet was the 'Prophet' foretold by Moses *Ebn Amram*"—Moses the Son of Amram. Mahomet's first convert was his wife; the next was Zeid, his servant; the third was Ali, son of Abu-Taleb, at that time a boy; the fourth was Abu-Beker, a man of the highest character, and of the greatest influence in Mecca. By Abu-Beker's persuasion, Othman, Abdal-Rahman, Saad, Al-Zobeir, and several leading men of Mecca, were induced to join him. These disciples became the main supporters of his authority, and the bravest of his warriors. For Abu-Beker's help on this occasion, Mahomet styled him "Abd' Alla," *Servant of God;* "Al-Tzeddik," *The righteous;* and "Atik," *The preserved*, viz., from hell-fire. For three years he continued to teach his doctrines privately, only being afraid of the opposition of the Koreish; but at length, confident in the support of Abu-Beker, and in the number of his followers, he directed his cousin Ali, to make ready an entertainment to which all the descendants of Abdol-Motalleb were invited. To an appeal from Mahomet, Ali arose and said, "O Prophet of God! I will be thy *Vizar*, I will beat out the teeth, pull out the eyes, rip open the bellies, and cut off the legs of all who shall dare to oppose thee!" Mahomet embraced Ali with great tenderness, and called upon all present to submit to him, whereupon the Company laughed at him, saying to Abu-Taleb, "Thou must now obey thine own son."

From this period he began to Preach in public, and by his piercing wit, lively imagination, great strength of memory, all which had been improved by travel and solitary thought, the fascination of his addresses was so great, that notwithstanding opposition, his disciples were evermore increasing.

In the twelfth year of his Mission, the Prophet professed to have made his celebrated Night-Journey from Mecca to Jerusalem, and thence to the

Seven Heavens; each of which was five-hundred years' journey above the other! These surprising excursions he made upon a beautiful animal between an ass and a mule, called *Al Borak* or "Lightning," under the guidance of the Angel Gabriel. The First Heaven he described as all of silver with stars hanging from it, each as large as a mountain, and here he met with a decrepit old man who he was informed was Adam, and a multitude of Angels of various shapes. Amongst these was a prodigious Cock, whose crest reached to the Second Heaven, and who crowed so loud every morning, that all the cocks in heaven and earth were awakened, and crowed also. This wonderful story seems to have been suggested by a similar one in the Babylonish Talmud. In the Second Heaven he met Noah; in the Third, Abraham; in the Fourth, Joseph; in the Fifth, Moses; in the Sixth, John the Baptist; and in the Seventh, Jesus. Adam, Noah, Abraham, Joseph, Moses and John the Baptist, commended themselves to the prayers of Mahomet, but it would seem, as a stroke of policy, to please the Christians, Mahomet commended himself to the prayers of Jesus. Besides those particulars here mentioned, the Prophet saw a multitude of things monstrously incredible, to detail which, would require more space than we can afford.

There is no proof that Abu-Taleb ever embraced his Nephew's doctrines, nevertheless he constantly protected him against his enemies; but he at length died at the age of eighty, and soon after Chadijah died in her sixty-fifth year, which period the Mahometans, therefore, marked as "The Year of Mourning." After the death of his Uncle and Wife, Mahomet was exposed to the fury of the Koreish, before which, accompanied by Zeid, his former servant, he first betook himself to *Tajif*. The work of proselyting went on, and the opposition also became more formidable, until at length his enemies at Mecca in Council resolved that one man of each tribe should be chosen to put him to death. Notice of this Conspiracy reached Mahomet, who, in company with his devoted Abu-Beker, escaped to a Cave at Mount Thûr, south-east of Mecca, where he hid himself three days from his pursuers; after which, by a circuitous path through the mountains, the Impostor and his companion arrived safely at Medina. He was met at a short distance from the town by five-hundred inhabitants. Mounted on a camel, shaded by a canopy of palm-leaves, with a turban unfurled before him as a standard, and attended by the bravest of his followers, he made his Public Entry with every demonstration of joy.

This event was called the HEGIRA, or "Flight," from the date of which, answering to the 16th of June, 622, the Mussulmans compute their time.

Mahomet now arrogated the Sacerdotal and Regal

functions, in addition to the Prophetic. He also married Ayesha, daughter of Abu-Beker, gave Fatima, his daughter, in marriage to Ali, and announced his resolution to propagate his doctrines by the Sword. The prospect of booty thus opened, engaged his followers, and after various successes, he wrote letters to Chosru, King of Persia, the Emperor Heraclius, Mokawkas, King of the Copts, and to the King of Ethiopia, requiring them to embrace his faith. These appeals were variously received; and similar letters to others of less note had a like success, which, on the whole, were surprisingly favourable to the designs of the Impostor. He soon made himself master of Mecca, which the Arabs regarded as a Holy City, whereupon multitudes embraced his creed. After a variety of marvellous military exploits, he made his final visit to the Holy City, called the "Pilgrimage of Valediction," and which, to this day, is regarded by his followers as the model of all pilgrimages. Not long after, his end was hastened, through the effects of poisoned meat, and stretching himself upon the carpet in his house at Medina, he expired in the eleventh year of the Hegira, and in the sixty-third of his age. His body was embalmed, and he was buried under the chamber in which he died.

The story about his Iron Coffin being suspended by means of loadstones in the Temple of Mecca was never heard of in the East. The Latin writers seem to have borrowed it from Pliny's description of a Temple at Alexandria. Medina, not Mecca, is the place of his interment, and over his remains a holy Chapel is built, in which the Urn now enclosing them, surrounded with iron trellis-work, is religiously preserved.

The Person of Mahomet is described by the Arabian writers with great minuteness. He was of middle stature, had a large head, his beard was thick, his eyes black and piercing, his nose hooked, his mouth wide, his neck thick, his hair long and flowing; a hairy mole between his shoulders was called "The Seal of his Apostleship." His appearance was beautiful and majestic. Ambition and lust were the passions which divided the empire of his breast.

The Mahometan Delusion arose about the same remarkable period when the Pope of Rome assumed the title of "Universal Bishop." It is also a notable circumstance, that, as Mahomet had predicted that another Prophet should arise after him who would propagate religion by the Sword, the Turks sent Ambassadors to Oliver Cromwell to enquire if he were that Prophet. The Protector was two conscientious to deceive them. But had he taken advantage of their credulity and superstition, who can say what revolutions might have been effected in Mahometan countries.

MODERN HISTORY OF EGYPT.

Under the Ptolemies a prodigious number of Jews settled in Egypt, and the Old Testament was commonly read. Under the Romans the Egyptians had the Gospel very early planted among them, and the Church for some time continued to flourish. The Roman power, however, falling into decay, in the year 640, this Province was conquered by the Sacracens, led by Amer, the Lieutenant of the Caliph Omar. Every Monument of Learning was speedily destroyed, the Mahometan Delusion established, and, notwithstanding the Toleration of the early Caliphs, Christianity fell into a deplorable condition.

About A.D. 970, the Fathemite Caliph of Cyrene, wrested Egypt from the Caliph of Bagdad, and he and his posterity governed it about two-hundred years. In turn this dynasty yielded to Saladin the Kurd, who craftily seized the Reins of Power. His posterity, called Jubites, governed till 1250. About that time the Mamelukes,—slaves brought from Georgia, became formidable, and uniting their energies, usurped the Sceptre. In this Government the Father was not succeeded by his Son, but upon the demise of the Ruler, the Leadership devolved upon a newly imported Slave. During their rule, the Mameluke Slaves chose out of their body twenty-four

Turks and twenty-three Circassians, to fill the Throne.

The Mamelukes were subdued by the Ottoman Turks, under Selim, in 1517, in submission to whose Superiority, however, they continued to rule, under the title of "Pasha." The tribute which the Pasha is obliged to render, in homage to the Sultan, is £400,000 annually, which is more than the amount of our Civil List. The French, under Buonaparte, invaded Egypt, in 1798, and after a dreadful slaughter of the Mamelukes and Turks, seemed to have established themselves. But they were soon driven out by the British, under Abercrombie, and the country was replaced under its old masters. In 1806, however, the rule of the Mamelukes terminated, and the Sultan invested the famous Mehemet Ali with the Government.

Born in 1769, the same remarkable year which gave birth to Napoleon and Wellington, Mehemet Ali, proved one of the most extraordinary characters that appeared in Egypt. For some time after his elevation, the Sultan regarded him with jealousy, and wished to depose him; but he contrived to be popular with his Soldiers, and so engaged the Mamelukes by allowing them to pillage Cairo, that he was able to set the Sultan at defiance. The Turkish Fleet sent to subdue him, came also into his possession. This was effected through the treachery of the Admiral, with the assistance of M. Drovetti, the French Consul. In 1806 he presented the Sultan with 4,000 Purses of Gold, and was admitted into the favour of the Porte. Mehemet's next stroke of policy was the extermination of the Mamelukes, who now became formidable opponents to his ambition. In 1811 he prepared a great Banquet at the Citadel upon the occasion of investing his son Tousoon with the command of an expedition against the Wahabees in Arabia. To this he invited all the Mamelukes. Four hundred, some say six hundred, came, mounted upon their best steeds. When the Guests arose to retire, to their consternation they found the Gates of the Citadel closed. A cry ran through their ranks that they were betrayed; at the same instant the command was given, *Vras, Vras,*—" Kill, Kill," when Greek Soldiers stationed on the roof fired upon the defenceless crowd. One Mameluke alone escaped. He leaped over a precipice through a breach in the wall. The horse was killed but the rider saved. The spot was pointed out to us; and the depth was so great, that were it not well attested, we could scarcely credit the fact.

Horrible as was this murderous act, it has been applauded as a necessary resort of self-defence. Some writers say that the Mamelukes had laid a plot to take Mehemet's life. The Pasha himself affected to believe this.

When Mehemet came to the Viceroyalty, Egypt

was in a melancholy state of anarchy—Bedaween, Mamelukes, Albanians, and Turks, each striving for the mastery. There was no order in any department of the State, life and property were insecure, and agriculture and commerce neglected. Under his administration every thing improved. He tranquilised the country throughout its whole extent, and life became as secure in the Desert as in the Capital. The "wild-ass men" of the desert, (for such is the literal rendering of the Hebrew expression in Gen. xvi. 12,) who had been the terror of the traveller, became now in a great measure submissive to orderly rule. The discipline established in his army exceeded any thing theretofore known in the East. The country rose to an astonishing degree of prosperity; and Mehemet took care that the general regeneration should be subservient to his own coffers.

Some time before his death this great man became incapacitated for the Government, which consequently devolved upon his son Ibrahim, infamous for the barbarities of his Grecian Expedition. He had the heads of the unfortunates piled in heaps, like stones, and sent in ship-loads to Constantinople, as in ancient days of savage rule. (2 Kings x. 7, 8; Judg. vii. 25.) In 1827, England, France, and Russia, signed a Treaty in London, in pursuance of which the Fleets of these Powers appeared in the Bay of Navarino, compelled

Ibraham to conclude an armistice, and finally Greece became an Independent State.*

Upon the death of Ibraham, Abbas Pasha, a grandson of Mehemet Ali, succeeded, notwithstanding that Mehemet had two or three sons surviving. This was in obedience to a peculiarity in the Law of Succession, according to which the *eldest* descendant claims, so that a grandson will take before a son, provided the former be the older man. Abbas was succeeded by Sâid Pasha, a son of Mehemet, and uncle of his predecessor. This person died in the Spring of 1863, while I was in Egypt, and was succeeded by Ismael Pasha, the present Ruler, whose Installation at the Citidel, took place while I was in Cairo, after returning from the Peninsula of Sinai. In honour of this event, the Bazaars and principal Streets were brilliantly illuminated every night. I had also the fortune to run against the new Viceroy. He is a very plain man, apparently unassuming; but he is said to be clever,

---

* England did not support the Greek Revolution until it was evident that the Turks could no longer keep the people down, and it became a question whether Greece should be Independent, or under the "Protection" of Russia. The British Government therefore called the Battle of Navarino "an untoward event," as they foresaw that the Turks, having lost their fleet, would be more than ever at the mercy of the Autocrat. The correctness of this view was proved in 1854.

though not so friendly to England as his predecessor.*

THE PEOPLE.

PHYSIQUE.—The people of Egypt are generally well made. The Arabs are often stout, and, on an average, taller than Europeans. The Bedaween especially, are a noble looking race. The women are short, but exceedingly graceful and upright in their gait. This may arise from their having from girlhood to carry pitchers of water on their heads. From habit, they are able to balance these with the greatest ease and exactness. Their Skin is the colour of dirty brown paper. When only nine or ten years of age they begin to look womanly. When about fifteen or sixteen they have arrived at

---

* When a new Sultan mounted the throne, it was customary to put all his brothers to death, or else have them imprisoned for life, thus to prevent disputes respecting the Right of Succession. The present Sultan, however, has departed from that barbarous usage, and treats his brothers with the utmost kindness. In the days of the Judges " Abimelech hired vain and light persons, which followed him, and went into his father's house at Ophra, and slew his brethren, the sons of Jerubaal, being three score and ten persons, upon one stone." (Judg. ix. 5.) The policy of that dreadful example was identical with that of the Turkish Monarchs. The Persians effect the same purpose in another way. They have a law excluding *blind* persons from the succession. Therefore when the Sha ascends the throne, his brothers and nephews have to submit to the loss of their eyes.

perfection; every step afterwards is downward. At the age of twenty or twenty-two, their faces become shrivelled and wizened.

STAINING AND PAINTING.—The higher, and many of the lower class women, stain their fingers and toes with the juice of a plant called "Henna," which grows plentifully in Egypt. This disfiguration is there so admired as to form one of the recommendations for a husband. They also paint their cheeks, chins, lips, eyebrows, and foreheads. These customs are extremely ancient, being noticed by Moses. (Deut. xxxii. 5.) Jezebel painted her eyelids, and so did the Jewish women in the days of Jeremiah and Ezekiel. (2 Kings ix. 30; Jer. iv. 30; Ezek. xxiii. 40.)

OPHTHALMIA.—A sojourner in Egypt cannot fail to be struck with the immense number of Blind persons there. Various conjectures have been hazarded to explain this fact. Some attribute it to the heat of the climate, some to the night-dews which fall upon them through their custom of sleeping on the house-tops and in the streets. These reasons, however, are insufficient, for the Bedaween, whose habits are similar in these respects, are free from the affliction. It arises more probably from the strange infatuation of the women, who refuse to wash the dirt from their children's faces. They are the victims of a superstition that Evil will befal their offspring should any person regard them with an envious look, to prevent which therefore, they revel in seeing them covered with dirt. I have seen numbers of children whose eyelids were as raw as a piece of beef, and the sore place thickly covered with flies. These insects probably spread the infection by alighting upon the eyelids of healthy persons. The disease may be aggravated by the dust and the arrest of perspiration. If taken in time, I have no doubt, cures might be very generally effected; but so obstinately do the people resign themselves to what they call "the will of God," that they will apply no remedy until it is too late. The blindness remarkable in the population of Egypt, however, is not entirely the result of disease. In Mehemet Ali's time, parents in many instances put out one of the eyes of their sons to prevent their being forced into the army. But the old Pasha was not to be foiled, and so he formed a "One-eyed Regiment!" Many boys had the forefinger of their right hands amputated, that they might escape, as being unable to pull a trigger; but the artful old Ruler made a "Left-handed Regiment." The remnant of these mutilated persons, however, is now fast dying off.

BEAUTIFUL TEETH.—But while Blindness is so common, there are few without Teeth. Everybody in Egypt seemed to have a beautiful white full set of teeth. During a six-weeks' sojourn, I never saw a toothless person, or even one whose teeth appeared to suffer decay. This may be attributed partly to the pureness of the air, and partly to the simplicity of their diet. The labouring classes work for two piastres a day, or fivepence of our money, and mainly live upon bread and water—the bread made of Indian corn, called "Millet" in Ezek. iv. 9. They are perhaps the better for this, at least they appear strong and healthy.

HAIR.—The men generally allow their beards to grow like the Jews and some Englishmen, but not so long, unless in seasons of deep mourning, when they suffer them to grow negligently. The Arabs commonly have their heads shaven, excepting a tuft at the crown. This is spared for the following singular reason. They take it for granted that in case they should be slain in battle, their heads would be piled in heaps. We are hereby reminded that Jehu commanded that the heads of the King's sons should be laid in two heaps at the entering of the gate of Jezreel (2 Kings x. 8). They cannot endure the thought of their heads being carried by the beard, or that the hand of an Infidel should enter their mouth, and therefore grow the tuft that it may serve as a handle for the conveyance of the head. Others say that it is grown for the convenience of the Angel Gabriel, who, they believe, is to pull them into Paradise. It is highly amusing to see a dozen Barbers scraping away at the corner of a street. The "Corners of the

Streets" are used for all purposes, from vermin-hunting up to praying. (Matt. vi. 5.) When a boy's head is shaved the first time, if his father can afford it, he kills a sheep and gives a Feast. This is done with a view to avert evils from the child.

EDUCATION.—Though there are Schools for Boys in every town in Egypt, there are few persons who can either read or write. The Boys in these Schools sit cross-legged upon the mud floor, learning extracts from the Koran, and a few forms of prayer. They all repeat the Lesson aloud and keep swinging their heads and bodies, so as scarcely to allow time to draw their breath. The noise is at once loud and monotonous; but frequently relieved by the smack of the *Koorbaj* on the shoulders of the Scholars, together with the responsive scream. The Schoolmaster in his domain is as arbitrary as the Pasha. From his lash there is no appeal. Should he observe an Englishman looking through the doorway or wooden bars of the windows, the Koorbaj is sure to go smack, smack, crack, crack, over the backs of the Boys, for his amusement. Those who learn to write use small Painted Boards with a smooth surface, from which the ink can be easily rubbed. It was probably such a Board is the "Writing Table" mentioned in Isaiah xxx. 8; Hab. ii. 2; Luke i. 63.

SERFDOM OF WOMEN.—All servile work in the East is done by the women. Men are seen riding comfortably on their donkeys, while their wives run behind, carrying a child and a basket, and spurring on the animal. As in the days of Rebecca and the Woman of Samaria, they still carry water. They go regularly to the wells in the morning, before the heat of the day, and again in the evening, before the sun is down. (Gen. xxiv. 11.) So much are they considered inferior to the men, that they are not allowed to enter a Mosque during the time of prayer. If they pray at all, they must do it at home. Ignorance is called "a woman's jewel." Perhaps there is not a native woman in all Egypt who can read. Some writers relate that when angry with his favourite old wife, Mahomet said, "There will be no *old* woman in Paradise," upon which she wept. Observing this the Prophet comforted her by adding, "They will all become *young* again." Wives are seldom allowed to eat with their Husbands, but wait upon them and their Sons, as Servants, and take their meals afterwards. Rebecca *prepared* the food, and *sent it in* to Isaac and Jacob. Women are never entrusted with the expenditure of their husband's money. Husbands and wives never walk arm in arm; but the man leads, and the wife, as the inferior, is content to follow. If a woman refuses to obey her husband he may take her to the *Kadee* or Chief Judge, when she is denounced as "rebellious," and he is released from all obligation to support her.

HOSPITALITY.—Though an Arab will wrangle a whole day for half a piastre, and though cupidity is stamped in every bargain he makes, yet is he notoriously Hospitable. The feeling which prompted Abraham to kill a calf for the three Strangers, still makes Easterns of every grade willing to divide their last piece of bread with those about them. Abraham sat at the Door of his Tent, not merely to enjoy the cool shade of the overhanging foliage, but also to watch for Travellers that he might invite them to partake of his Bounty. Therefore he ran to meet the Strangers, as soon as he descried them, and, in true Oriental fashion, bowed himself to the ground, and entreated them not to pass away. (See Gen. xviii.; Jud. xix. 17; 2 Sam. xii. 4; Jer. xiv. 8.) What more refreshing to a Traveller, after a wearisome march, barefoot, over a burning wilderness, "in the heat of the day," than a little water to wash his feet? The Orientals still take their Meals at the Doors of their Houses, and, with a genuine welcome, invite any Passenger to join them. And the Bedaween in the desert will "make haste" to kill a lamb or kid, while their wives prepare the bread and milk to set before their guests. The Host also considers his Visitor as under his protection, and would sacrifice his life rather than suffer him to receive injury. Lot offered his Daughters to the wicked men of Sodom, rather than expose his Guests to their fury.

(Gen. xix. 8; see also Judg. xix. 20—24; Job. xxxi. 31, 32.)

COSTUME.

DRESS OF THE MEN.—Men of the higher class wear full Drawers, containing about eighteen yards of muslin,—enough to serve an Englishman for several pairs. These are tied round the body with a cord, the ends of which are embroidered. The Drawers reach just below the knee, where they hang loose, so that the legs are perfectly free. A Tunic, or Shirt, with wide hanging sleeves, is bound round the waist with a Girdle, sometimes of leather, like that of John the Baptist, but generally of cotton or silk. The *leathern* girdles are principally worn, as a mark of humility, by Santons or Dervishes. Those of silk or cotton are gracefully folded and then wrapped round the body so that the fringes may hang. The dresses are so large that a girdle or band of some sort is necessary to hold them together. A Tailor is never required to *fit* them. What served the men of Ashkelon required no alteration to adapt them to those who expounded Samson's riddle.

In winter the men wear a short Vest of striped cotton or silk over the Tunic or Shirt. Some also wear a light Gown of the same fabric, with very long sleeves open from the wrist. These are often like the garment of our Saviour, "without seam." Some wear a kind of Shawl over the head; and some a Burnoose or Cloak with a Hood; while others have a Cloak of Camel's hair as John the Baptist had.

PROHIBITION OF SILK.—Mahomet forbade men to wear silk dresses. But the rich often evade the denunciations of the Prophet, and yet gratify their taste for this luxury, by having a small quantity of cotton mixed with the silk.

GIRDING UP THE LOINS.—When a man is going a journey he tightens his girdle, and tucks up his drawers and tunic, so as to leave every limb at liberty. This is what is in Scripture called "Girding up the Loins." (See Exodus xii. 11; 2 Kings ix. 1; Luke xii. 35; 1 Peter i. 13.) David says "It is God that *girdeth* me with strength," (Psa. xviii. 32.) Deity is also represented as girding Himself with strength. (Psa. xciii. 1.)

THE TURBAN.—The usual head dress in Egypt is first a white cotton Cap, then a Tarboosh, or red cloth cap, and over all a Turban of white muslin about ten feet long coiled round the head. A cashmere shawl is sometimes substituted for the muslin. These Turbans, or "Hats" as they are called in Dan. iii. 21, are of various colours. Immediate descendants of Mahomet wear green; native Christians and Jews wear black or blue; while white is the colour usually worn by the people.

SANDALS.—The legs of the Orientals are generally

bare, though in winter sometimes Socks are worn together with red morocco leather Slippers, turning up at the toes. The Bedaween and some others wear Sandals instead of slippers. These are simple soles of leather or skin, fastened to the feet with straps. Slaves often carry their master's sandals, and this is considered one of the meanest of occupations. John the Baptist regarded himself as unworthy to fulfil this office for his Divine Lord, or even to unloose the straps. (Matt. iii. 11; Mark i. 7.)

THE DRESS OF THE WOMEN is not so varied as that of the men. The higher classes wear the dress which the Americans style the "Bloomer," consisting of very wide Trousers of printed calico or silk tied below the knee, but so long and full that they hang over the bands sometimes to the feet. Over these they wear a Shirt also printed or coloured; a printed Vest which fits close to the body and arms, buttoning down the front; and a loose shawl passed round the body as a Girdle. Few, if any, wear stockings. They have two pairs of red or yellow Slippers however, one fitting inside the other, but without heels. English ladies would find it difficult to shuffle along with these, but the Easterns move in them very gracefully. When dressed for riding, the Bloomer is covered with a large Gown with immense sleeves. Women in Egypt ride astride.

ORNAMENTS.—Eastern women are surpassingly fond

of ornaments, an excellent summary of which may be found in the Prophet Isaiah. (Isa. iii. 18—24.) You may often see suspended from a band upon the forehead a number of counterfeit coins and other trinkets dangling over the nose. These are what Isaiah calls "Ornaments of the face." Some have rings nearly three inches and a half in diameter hanging over the mouth from the right wing of the nose.

VEILS, some white, others black, are usually worn so as to cover the whole face excepting one eye. Rebecca veiled herself when Isaac approached. So particular are the men, that they turn their heads away when they see a lady coming, notwithstanding that she is veiled. Thus, as Job expresses it, they make "a covenant with their eyes." (Job xxxi. 1.) But too often in Egypt this is vile hypocrisy. Sarah was unveiled, and therefore incurred the reproach of Abimalech, who said that Abraham was to her "a covering of the eyes," or veil. (Gen. xx. 16.) But the modesty of the Oriental women of the present day is inexplicable, who feel it more their duty to cover the top and back of their head than their face, and the latter more than other parts of their person. They think nothing of leaving their shirts open at the bosom, and will sometimes uncover the body to conceal the face with the garment.

DRESS OF THE POOR.—The latter remarks apply to the wives and daughters of the poor *Fellaheen* or

Tillers of the Soil, who are obliged to dispense with the Trousers, the Veil, and the Ornaments, and content themselves with a blue Shirt and Scarf. The men of the same class are no less scantily clad. They have nothing more than a blue cotton Shirt and a common Tarboosh. Their shirts are often in a tattered condition through long and constant wear, both night and day. Children are commonly allowed to run about almost naked, in rags and filth; and this is true not only of the families of extremely poor persons, but of those also in better circumstances. The superstition which induces this shameful negligence has been noticed in speaking of the prevalence of Ophthalmia.

DOMESTIC RELATIONS.

COURTSHIP.—When an Egyptian wants a Wife, he is not allowed to visit the Hareems of his friends to select one, for Mahomet forbade men to see the face of any woman they could marry, that is to say any beside their mother or sisters. A man is therefore obliged to employ a *Khatbeh*, or Match-Maker, to find one for him, for which service of course she expects "bucksheesh." The Khatbeh, having found a girl, recommends her to the man as exceedingly beautiful and eminently suitable to him. The Father is then waited upon to ascertain the Dowry he requires; for all wives are purchased, as they were in Patriarchal days. When Jacob had no money to pay for Rachael, he served her father seven years as an equivalent; and, when duped, was obliged to serve a second term to secure his prize. (Gen. xxix.) Fathers still refuse to give a Younger daughter in marriage before an Elder. The people of Armenia in Asiatic Turkey, forbid a younger son to marry before an elder; and this is likewise the law of the Hindoos. The Price of a wife varies from five shillings to three hundred pounds. The girl may not be more than five or six years old, but whatever her age, two-thirds of the Dowry is at once paid to the father in the presence of witnesses. The father then, or his representative, says, "I Betroth to thee my Daughter," and the young man responds, "I accept of such Betrothal." Unless amongst the lower classes, the father expends the Dowry in the purchase of Dress, Ornaments, or Furniture for the Bride, which never become the property of her Husband.

Even when Betrothed, the intercourse of the parties is very restricted. The Arabs will not allow them to see each other; but the Jews are not quite so stringent. The Betrothals often continue for years before the man demands his wife. Thus "Samson went down and talked with the woman," or espoused her, and "*after a time*, he returned to take her." (Judg. xiv. 7, 8. See also 2 Sam. iii. 14.) Girls are demanded at the age of ten, and between that and sixteen years; but after sixteen, few men will seek them, and the Dowry expected is then proportionably low. Girls in Egypt are often mothers at thirteen and grandmothers at twenty-six; and in Persia they are said to be mothers at eleven, grandmothers at twenty-two, and past child-bearing at thirty.

MARRIAGE FEASTS.—When a man demands his Betrothed, a day is fixed for the Nuptials, and for seven nights before, he is expected to give a Feast, which, however, is furnished by the Guests themselves. Thus, one sends coffee, another rice, another sugar, &c. The principal time of this continued Feast is the night before the consummation. The conduct is entrusted to the "Friend of the Bridegroom." (John iii. 29.) About the middle of this day the Bride arrives at the house, and retires to the Hareem where she sits with her mother, sisters, and female friends. At the third or fourth watch of the night,—three or four hours after sunset,—the Bridegroom, who has not yet seen his fair one, goes to the Mosque to pray, accompanied by *meshals*, or torches and lanterns, with music. (Matt. xxv.) Upon his return he is introduced to his Bride, with whom, having given her Attendant a present to retire, he is left alone. He then throws off her veil, and for the first time sees her face. If satisfied he informs the women outside, who immediately express their joy by screaming *Zuggareet*, which is echoed by the women in the house, and then by those in the neighbourhood. (See Psalm xix. 4, 5.)

THE WEDDING GARMENT.—Formerly it was customary for the Bridegrooms to provide their Guests with a kind of loose flowing Mantle, and whoever entered the house without this garment was regarded as one who insulted the Host by tacitly saying, "My dress is quite as good as yours." Hence, in the parable, the man who had not the "wedding garment" was accounted worthy of being cast into "outer darkness," the image being borrowed from the custom of turning such persons into the dark street. The "outer darkness," however, into which those are cast who despise the robe of Christ's righteousness, is the abode of "wailing and gnashing of teeth." To this day the Rich among the Persians furnish their Guests with these Dresses.

The customs in Egypt do not fully agree with those described in Scripture, but in Syria and Persia they correspond to the minutest particular. It is said that the marriage of a Jew will in some cases cost him a whole year's income. We have already noted that the Feast lasts seven days. Perhaps what Laban meant when he said "Fulfil her week" was "Serve seven years to supply the week's Feast." (Gen. xxix. 27; see also Judg. xiv. 12.) As it was in the days of Esther, so still, the men and women feast apart. (Esth. i. 5, 9.)

DIVORCE.—When, upon the last night of the Feast, the Bridegroom lifts the veil of the Bride, if he is not satisfied with her appearance, he has only to say, "I divorce thee," and she must return to her father's house. This is a lasting disgrace to her, and therefore it is not usual to pronounce these words until several days have elapsed. (Comp. Matt. i. 18, 19.) The man, however, if he choses, can change his mind, and make her return; but if he should divorce her a third time, and say, "I *trebly* divorce thee," he cannot recover her without her consent, nor even then, unless in the interval she had been married to another. Formerly it was the custom in Egypt when a man professed himself dissatisfied with his wife, to summon a Jury of Women to consider the case, and if they brought in a verdict against her, the husband was entitled to the return of her dowry, upon which the unfortunate girl was, by her father, tied up in a bag and thrown into the Nile. If the Jury pronounced against the husband, he might still divorce his wife, but was not entitled to the return of her dowry. (See Deut. xxii. 13—21.)

Mahomet advised his followers to keep their wives secluded, saying, "If butter is exposed to the sun it is sure to melt" and "everything in the world is valuable, but the most valuable of all is a virtuous woman." He said he knew but four virtuous women, viz., Asiah the wife of Pharaoh, Mary the mother of Jesus, Kadijah his wife, and Fatima his daughter. The women and children, therefore, reside in a separate part of the house, which is called the Hareem, and are prohibited from seeing even their male cousins. When they can arrange it, men ask their own mothers or sisters to live with their wives, in which case they have more confidence; in company with these they are permitted to visit their friends. But if a wife venture out without these relatives she is almost certain to be greeted with a Bill of Divorcement. This would also follow, if, even by accident, she showed her face to a man. Jealousy in the East is "cruel as the grave."

POLYGAMY.—That God intended man to have *one* wife, is clear from the institution in which he said "I will make him a help-meet for him." (Gen. ii. 18, 24.) Mahomet had *eight*, and allowed his followers each to have *four* if they could maintain them. Some Egyptians have more, though few have as many. It is usual for a man to give his daughter on her wedding day a Slave, as Laban did to Leah and Rachel. These are so completely the property of the wife, that without her consent the husband has no right to interfere with them. It is still common for the wife to give her slave to her husband, as Sarah gave Hagar to Abraham, and as Leah and Rachel gave their slaves to Jacob. The issue of these marriages are regarded as the children of the Mistress, who still holds superiority over her Slave. Thus Abraham had no right to resist the will of Sarah when she desired the expulsion of Hagar and Ishmael. When Bilhah the slave of Rachel gave birth to a son, Rachel accounted it her own, saying, " God hath judged me and given *me* a son." (Gen. xxx. 1—13.)

CONCUBINAGE.—Added to his four Wives, a Mahometan may select from his slaves any number of Concubines he pleases. Not only is this tolerated by law, but the greater number of Concubines he keeps the more reputable does he become.

FUNERALS.

PROCESSIONS.—While in Egypt I witnessed two Funeral Processions. The Corpse wrapped in linen clothes is placed upon a Bier, shaped like a coffin, with two handles at each end, and open at the top. It is simply covered with a cashmere shawl. The procession is headed by men and boys, the latter chanting such sentences as the following:—" I declare the absolute glory of Him who creates whatever has form, and lays low His servants by death." The corpse is then carried head-foremost, and is immediately followed by the principal Mourners. The rear is brought up by professional Wailers, who ever and anon startle the bystander with a sudden frenzied scream. But the voice of *real* grief may also be heard and easily distinguished from the professional noise. I can have no difficulty in believing that the Egyptians at the funeral of Jacob "mourned with a great and sore lamentation." (See Gen. L. 10; Acts viii. 2.) The people sometimes testify their grief by cutting themselves; but this was forbidden to the Hebrews:—"Ye shall not make any cuttings in your flesh for the dead." (Lev. xix. 28; Deut. xiv. 1.)

WAILERS.—All funerals, excepting those of the very poor, are attended by women who hire themselves at so much a day to wail. Those who can make the most horrid shrieks are chiefly in request; and some women are such adepts as to be able to make a living at this dismal trade. These professional Wailers are an old Institution in the East. (Jer. ix. 17—19; Amos v. 16; Mark v. 38.) Some carry tambourines and sing a dirge as they move in the procession. (2 Chron. xxxv. 25; Matt. ix. 23.)

INTERMENTS.—When the cortége reaches the Cemetery, the shawl is removed, and the Corpse is lifted, or rather dragged, from the bier. The men go about their work as roughly as though they were handling the carcase of a pig. The body is wrapped tightly round the neck and ancles in linen clothes, so that the head and the feet are painfully prominent. It is then lowered into the Grave, or placed in the Tomb as the case may be. The graves of the common people are never more than two or three feet deep. The higher classes have raised Tombs with arched roofs, and a large stone at the entrance. We are naturally reminded of the words, "Who shall roll us away the stone from the door of the Sepulchre?" (Mark xvi. 3.) One of the prayers uttered at the grave runs thus:—"O God, he has gone to live with Thee. He stands in need of Thy mercy. If he has done good works, over-reckon his good deeds; if he has done evil, forgive his bad doings. Make his grave wide, and do not let the grave press his sides."

COFFINS.—Such Coffins as those with which we are familiar are not used in the East. That in which the body of Joseph was placed, after it had been embalmed, was such a stone Sarcophagus as may be seen in any of our large Museums. It is evident from the narrative respecting the man cast into the Sepulchre of Elisha, that his body was not in a coffin. (2 Kings xiii. 21.) It is also clear that the body of our blessed Lord was laid in the new tomb of Joseph without one. (Matt. xxvii. 59, 60.) This understood to have been the usage, the account of the raising of Lazarus is more intelligible. And when it is remembered that in funerals the body is carried upon an *open* bier, the history of the raising of the Widow's Son, at Nain, becomes more easily understood.

SLAVERY.

SLAVE DEALERS.—Formerly there was a Slave-Market at Cairo, but Mchemet Ali caused it to be removed, so that Slaves are now purchased at the Offices of the Merchants. The demand is supplied by means of Dealers who are generally men of the most abominable description. Mr. Lane says, that there is scarcely a girl of eight or nine years who has not suffered violence from these wretches, and that many instances occur in which these poor children, during the voyage down the Nile, throw themselves into the stream to escape their cruelty.

SLAVE MASTERS.—As a rule Slaves in Egypt are well treated by their Masters, with whom also they often become favourites, and are raised to stations of influence and power. Joseph was sold into Egypt as a Slave, and became Ruler in the Kingdom; and Daniel was carried into Babylon as a Slave, and was set over the Province. Before the time of Mehemet Ali, Egypt was governed by the Mameluke Kings who were originally Slaves. But however kindly Slaves may be treated, the traffic in flesh and blood must be abhorrent to Christian feeling. The principle, abstractedly, is reprehensible. Some Writers state that after a service of seven years, Slaves can claim their manumission, but this is very doubtful.

THE BRAND OF SLAVERY.—It is still the custom when a Slave is purchased to stamp his hand or some part of his body with a *mark* by which the owner may know his property, just as a Cattle-Dealer stamps his sheep or oxen. Paul apparently alludes to this custom when he says "I bear in my body the *marks* of the Lord Jesus," viz., of the stripes received for His name's sake. (Gal. vi. 17; 2 Cor. vi. 5.)

BASTINADO.—From the earliest times beating was an ordinary punishment. The person accounted "worthy to be beaten" was made to "lie down," and to receive not more than "forty stripes." (Deut. xxv. 2, 3.) The Jews after the Captivity, reduced the number to thirty-nine, lest by miscounting they should exceed forty, and infringe the letter of the law. This explains why Paul received "forty stripes *save one.*" (2 Cor. xi. 24.) The instrument latterly used was a whip with three thongs, so that thirteen strokes made thirty-nine stripes. The greatest number of stripes mentioned by Mahomet was one hundred; but the Turks often inflict five hundred, and indeed lash away until the victim dies. This kind of punishment is in Egypt technically termed the *Bastinado,* and is commonly inflicted upon Slaves.*

MANUMISSION.—It sometimes happens that an Oriental, who has no Children, redeems a Slave, adopts him, and makes him his Heir. This must have been

---

* The Romans treated their Slaves with wanton cruelty, compelling them to carry large Crosses as a sign that their lives were at the disposal of their Masters, while men whipped them round the Theatres for the amusement of spectators, who ridiculed them in their pitiable plight. Thus was the dear Redeemer scourged and mocked and compelled to bear His Cross until He sank under the load, all which He voluntarily endured "despising the shame." Foreseeing the idea entertained by Abraham before the birth of Isaac. (Gen. xv. 3; see also Pro. xxix. 21.) The term *Servant* in the Bible often denotes a Slave. Paul alludes to this redemption and adoption, when he says of the believer in Jesus, that he is "no more a *slave* but a *son*, and if a son, then an *heir* of God through Christ." (Gal. iv. 7.) The same image was present to the mind of David when he said, "O Lord, I am thy *slave*"—"Thou hast loosed my bonds," viz., "redeemed me from the yoke of another master." (Psa. cxvi. 16.) So Christ to his disciples,—"If the Son shall make you *free* ye shall be free indeed." "Take *My yoke* upon you, and learn of Me; for I am meek and lowly in heart: and ye shall find rest unto your souls. For My yoke is easy, and My burden is light." (Matt. xi. 29, 30.)

---

that He would be thus treated as a Slave, He said to His disciples, "Whosoever will come after Me let him take up his Cross"—let him be willing for My sake to suffer as a slave. (Matt. xvi. 24.) The Romans put their slaves to death by crucifixion, as the greatest malefactors, to which Paul alludes when he speaks of Christ as taking upon Himself the "form of a *Slave*" and suffering "the death of the *Cross*." (Phil. ii. 7, 8.)

CHAPTER IV.

EGYPT—CONTINUED.

ALEXANDRIA.

On our arrival in Egypt we did not know a word of Arabic, but no sooner had we engaged our Guide and mounted our Donkeys, than we were made familiar with *Buckshcesh.* In every street through which we rambled, "Bucksheesh," "Bucksheesh"—"A Present," "A Present," greeted us from men, women and children. To purchase the departure of these "Daughters of the Horseleech" was out of the question. They are like the Organ-grinders in our own streets. For if you attempt to fee one of these to cease his strains because they disturb an Invalid, his place is soon occupied by another of his fraternity.

The Great Square in the European quarter of the City is the principal attraction in Alexandria. Here the Foreign Consuls have their Residences or Offices, which are really good buildings, and when the flags of the Nations they respectively represent, float over them in the sunshine against the clear blue sky of that bright climate, the effect is imposing. The New English Church is in this quarter, as also the principal Hotels, and Merchants' Offices. The Greek Christians have erected a neat Temple outside the square; and the Romanists likewise have a Cathedral and a large School. When I returned to Alexandria after an excursion into the Peninsula of Sinai, on Sunday, Feb. 15th, 1863, early in the morning, I heard a Sermon in Arabic in the Catholic Church; at half-past ten I listened to an ethical Discourse in the English Church, and in the afternoon I visited the Greek Place of Worship. How melancholy that this large and populous city should be without a "certain sound" upon the vital truths of the Gospel!

POMPEY'S PILLAR is a round column of red granite 73 feet high, and nearly 30 feet in circumference. This is a single block of stone. Taken together with its Base, Pedestal, and Capital, it is nearly 90 feet high. It is much disfigured by the Names of Travellers daubed upon it in various colours. Though called *Pompey's* Pillar, it is supposed to have been raised in honour of Diocletian.

CLEOPATRA'S NEEDLES lie nearer to the City. These are two Obelisks, of red granite, covered with hieroglyphs. They originally stood at Heliopolis, and bear the *cartouche* or name of Thothmes III., a Pharaoh who oppressed the Israelites. They were transported to Alexandria by one of the Cæsars. Why they were called by their present name is unknown. One of these Obelisks, which now lies half covered with sand, was, many years ago, presented to the English by Mehemet Ali. Our Government, however, did not think it worth the expense of its removal. It is a huge block of dense stone 66 feet in length, and, to transport it to England, would probably cost £15,000. It would certainly be a valuable acquisition to our Antiquarians, but such a sum might be otherwise better appropriated.

THE PASHA'S GARDENS are worthy of a visit, though not equal to those of the Governor at Malta. They abound in fruit-trees—oranges, lemons, pomegranates, &c.,—but the ground is as level as a drawing-room floor.

THE CATACOMBS are upon the Sea Coast, about two miles from the Great Square. They are remarkable Relics of the greatness of ancient Alexandria. One of the Chambers is notable for the elegance of its architecture. My strong aversion to subterranean explorations prevented me from venturing into these.

THE RUINS OF THE ANCIENT CITY.—Under the advice of the French, Mehemet Ali commenced constructing extensive and formidable Fortifications, which remain still incomplete. In digging for the foundations of these the workmen came upon the Ruins of the City which was founded by Alexander B.C. 332. Millions of Brick, Tiles, Blocks of Stone, innumerable marble and granite Columns, some entire, others in a mutilated and fragmentary condition; remains of Houses, Arches, and Walls, all which had been buried to a considerable depth beneath the sand, were brought to light. The Houses appear to have been built upon Arches, which also served to support Aqueducts from the river.

Amongst the Ruins are the Walls of the famous Alexandrian Library, which contained 400,000 volumes, and was the most valuable collection in existence. The original Septuagint—a Translation of the Bible made by order of Ptolemy Philadelphus, and which is said to have cost £200,000, was amongst its treasures. This famous Library was demolished in the time of Julius Cæsar. There was also another most valuable Library in the Serapion, containing 300,000 volumes, which was destroyed by the ruthless hands of the Saracens. When Amru took the City he wrote to the Caliph Omar to enquire what he was to do with the Library, and received the following reply:—"If these Books of the Greeks agree with the Koran, the Koran is sufficient without them, therefore they need not be preserved; if they disagree, they are pernicious, and ought to be destroyed. Let them be burnt." So the Library perished.

History declares that the Ruins of Ancient Alexandria extended for seven miles; nor is this improbable, since, in its pride, it was fifteen miles in circumference, contained 4,000 Palaces, 4,000 Baths, 4,000

Theatres or Public Edifices, 12,000 Shops, and over 600,000 inhabitants, bond and free. It was planned by the Great Alexander who intended it to be at once the Seat of Empire, and the Centre of the Commerce of the World. But the barbarian hands of the Saracens completed its ruin; and the friendly sand from the Desert concealed the shame. Formerly the magnificence of Alexandria was rivalled only by that of Rome. Under the rule of these Fanatics it was revolutionized into a place little better than an Arab Village. The population dropped down to about 6,000 persons, and remained at that figure until the time of Mehemet Ali. Now, however, it has risen to perhaps 140,000. During the last thirty years the value of property has trebled, and commerce is rapidly increasing. All kinds of coin pass current here—the French Franc, the English Shilling, the Austrian Zwanziger, the German Florin, the Sicilian and Spanish Dollar, and the Turkish Ghazi, all have their interchangeable value with Egyptian Piasters. French Napoleons and Five-Franc Pieces, and English Sovereigns are the best for Travellers to take.

The Evangelist, Mark, is said to have suffered martyrdom at Alexandria. The tradition is that during Divine Service he was seized, and for two days in succession, dragged through the streets by the heels, until he sunk under the ordeal. At Alexandria also

Apollos was born, "an eloquent man and mighty in the Scriptures," who "watered" Churches that had been "planted" by Paul. (1 Cor. iii. 6.)

JOURNEY TO CAIRO.

After spending two days at Alexandria, and seeing everything of general interest, early on the morning of the 27th, we started for the Railway Station, a distance of about two miles, and booked for Cairo, a run of about one hundred and thirty. We soon had the extensive Lake Mareotis upon our right. Onward we moved through a flat country intersected by Canals with their Floodgates; but many of these are becoming filled with sand, and the Desert is otherwise fast encroaching upon the once fruitful soil. The Nile itself formerly had *seven* Branches by which it discharged its waters into the Mediterranean, but now it has only *two*. These are the Rosetta and Damietta branches, over both which the railway crosses, in running from Alexandria to Cairo. This filling up of the Mouths of the Nile seems alluded to by Isaiah in the words "The waters shall fail from the sea." (Isa. xix. 5.) The Delta of the Nile is the country lying between these Branches. The line of rails passes through a number of Mud Villages, whose extreme wretchedness is relieved by those towering Palm-trees which contribute so much to the beauty of Eastern scenery. Everything appeared so different from what we had seen, that it seemed like moving in a new world. As we approached Cairo, the Pyramids rising in the distance like geometrical mountains, hove in sight, and at length we ran into the Terminus, after having been seven hours upon the wheels.

CAIRO.

Leaving our baggage at the Station, we went in search of lodgings, and after a long ramble and much inquiry, we were directed to the Hotel d'Orient, one of the most respectable and comfortable houses in the place. In the evening we strolled out, and remarked that the French Cafés were much better at Cairo than at Alexandria.

DONKEYS.—The next morning, as soon as we presented ourselves at the door, a number of Donkeys with their Drivers bore down upon us, every voice at its highest pitch,—" Berry good donkey, Master;" " Berry handsome donkey;" " Dis your donkey, Master;" " Had dis donkey before;" " Donkey fall down? O no, Master!" " Go like Steamer!" The mud or flying dust being particularly inconvenient to Pedestrians, and the heat in the middle of the day being excessive, nobody thinks of walking any distance in Egypt. Having selected our animals, the unsuccessful Candidates quietly retired, while the Victors looked upon them with a jeer, and triumphantly shouted, " Now, den, cut away;" " Here we go;" "Get out o' de way;" "Lick him;" "Dats de ticket for soup;" and other phrases, which they have picked up from English travellers.

The Egyptian donkeys have been appropriately styled, "The Cabs of the country." They are very different creatures from the donkeys of Europe, being well-proportioned, very symmetrical, and uncommonly tractable. Their amblings are exceedingly graceful. Their price is from £8 to £12 each; and they are let out, with a driver, at 2s. per day. They are not only shorn but shaven; certain parts of their legs, however, are, for ornament's sake, left untouched by the scraper. This shaving process is indispensable, as the worst kind of vermin harbour in their hair. They all have stirrups, and a wide stuffed saddle covered with a piece of carpet, which is very easy. The drivers who run with the donkeys are generally boys; and these boys will run thirty miles in a day,—say from Cairo to Sahhara and back. Some are slip-shod; but they are mostly barefoot. They have no covering beyond a small red cap, and a loose blue calico shirt bound round the body with a girdle, and reaching to the knees. They use their bosoms as pockets, and can deposit in them a surprising variety of commodities,—articles purchased at Bazaars by their Hirers, their own food, oranges,—anything.

Having told our boys, on leaving the Hotel, that

we wished to go to the Citadel, off we set full cry, the boys never comprehending that we wished to halt by the way to examine any object of interest. To ride a donkey in Egypt means to gallop, for each attendant is resolved to make his animal show the others the way. Sticks, therefore, are in constant requisition, and the cries of *Yella*—" Quick," are perpetual. Perhaps at the very instant that you are endeavouring to pull up your animal to inspect some novelty, or to save your legs from being bumped against a cart, he deals it a blow and screams out, *Imshee ya Ebne Khanzeer*—"Go along, you Son of a Pig," and you are inevitably foiled. It must not be supposed, however, that the drivers treat their donkeys cruelly; on the contrary, they are very fond of them.

THE CITADEL.—After worming our way for about three-quarters of an hour by Fountains, through Bazaars, and along all sorts of Streets, except paved ones, encountering an unparalleled bustle of Horses, Camels, Donkeys, Dogs, Carriages, Bullock-Carts, Soldiers, Police, Beggars, Santons, Turks, Arabs, Ethiopians, English, Americans, French, Germans, Italians, and of course, Egyptians, we ascended a steep path, passed through two or three strong gates, and were at the Citadel. From this commanding situation the Town below looks like one mass of Balconies, Parapets, Flat-roofs, Domes,

Minarets, Groves, and Gardens. To the right we look out in the direction of On and the Land of Goshen; the Pyramids rise upon the left; the Nile winds its way through a richly cultivated Valley, and the great Deserts of Arabia and Libya are visible to the East and West. The Court-Yard is surrounded by a high wall with strong Gates, and armed with guns. Here the celebrated Pasha, Mehemet Ali, had a Palace; and his Mosque stands close by.

THE MOSQUE OF MEHEMET ALI. — Before the Pasha's death this structure had been six years in course of erection, and had cost nearly a million sterling; but what may have been the total expenditure I am unable to say. Excepting the upper part of the outer walls, the whole building is composed of Egyptian alabaster. The Court is surrounded by a Colonnade, supported by forty-eight massive Columns, and the Fountain in the centre is alabaster. All Mosques have fountains in their courts, for the purpose of washing before prayers. On the East and West sides are Arcades, supported by Pillars; and there are similar Arcades within. The Base, Plinth, and Moulds, like the Pillars, are alabaster, richly carved and ornamented. The interior is about 60 yards by 46, and is gilded and adorned in the most elaborate and florid style. The Tomb of the Pasha is in this Mosque.

JOSEPH'S WELL is situate within the walls of the Citadel. It is 260 feet deep, with a winding Staircase descending into it, and the water, which is supplied from the Nile by an aqueduct, is worked up by bullocks stationed near the bottom. There seems no doubt that it was originally sunk by the ancient Egyptians. Subsequently it became filled with sand. In the time of the Crusades, *Yooseph Salah-e-deen* (Joseph Saladin), ordered it to be cleared out, from which circumstance it came to be called " Joseph's Well." But the Arabs insist that it was constructed by the Patriarch of that name.

Joseph's Granaries, or rather the Site upon which those Granaries once stood, as indicated by tradition, were one day pointed out to me by my Guide. I also went to view the Tombs of the Mameluke Kings, those of the Sultans, and of the Pashas. Some were very ancient. They are all noble Monuments and worth inspecting.

SHOOBRA, the Residence of the Pasha, is approached through an Avenue of mulberries, sycamores, and acacias, extending for three or four miles alongside the course of the Nile. The Palace and Gardens here surpass any thing of the kind in Egypt. The walks are set in mosaics of coloured pebbles in all kinds of fanciful patterns. The Groves, Bowers, and Trelliscovered Paths, with the Fountains and Streams, are delightful. All over the Gardens there are Hedges of box and myrtle; with flowers, cypresses and aromatic plants, in immense variety. The oranges, lemons, citrons, and other fruit trees, seemed as if groaning to be relieved of their burdens. Everywhere the scenery was enchanting, and the fragrance of the air delicious.

MOSQUES.—There are a large number of Mosques in Cairo, some say three hundred, but I should think that an exaggeration. The Mosque of Achmet Taloon is said to be the most ancient. Excepting that of Mehemet Ali, the Mosque of Sultan Hassan may be considered the most attractive. Generally, they are humble, dirty places, unlike "houses of prayer," and unworthy of description. Most of them, however, are open to the Poor when every other door is closed against them.

At the given hours of prayer, the *Moueddin* or Priests, ascend the Minarets, and, often in a melodious and impressive voice, sing, "God is most great! I testify that there is no deity but God, and that Mahomet is His Prophet. Come to prayer! Come to safety! Prayer is better than sleep," &c. There are a few who pray *five* times a day; but all are expected to pray *three* times. The first hour of prayer is very early in the morning. At home or abroad, in the street or by the way-side, in the wilderness or on the ocean, at the appointed hour, the devout Mahometan will prostrate himself, regardless of circumstances.

Who will "limit the Holy One of Israel," and say that there is no mercy for those devotees who sincerely live according to their light?

THE ESBEKIAH GARDENS cover a space of sixty acres, and are luxuriant with sweet-smelling acacia, and flowery walks. They are open to the public, and in the summer evenings are crowded with loungers, smoking, eating confectionery and drinking sherbet. In one part a Juggler will be performing; in another, a Reciter will be telling marvellous tales; Variegated Lamps cover some of the trees; in every direction Tents and Bowers appear; music from various Bands, and the rich dresses of the Turks, all together give the place the air of a fairy scene. The Gardens are surrounded by Avenues of sycamores, palms, and other trees, outside which there is a narrow Canal. This is full of water in summer when the Nile rises, but at other seasons it is coated with filth. The site of these Gardens was formerly a Marshy Lake, from which fevers were bred; but Mehemet Ali had it filled up and planted, and Cairo has been much more healthy since.

Beside these Gardens there are several large Squares which, like the Squares and Parks of London, are the "lungs of the City."

THE CHRISTIAN CHURCHES.—The Romanists and Coptic Christians have each a Church at Cairo. There is also a small English Church or Consecrated Room,

K

where, in the winter season, about thirty or forty fashionable European Visitors worship. This is called a "Mission Station;" but there is no gospel for the Arabs, the service being always conducted in English. The most prosperous cause is that of the American Presbyterians. On Sunday morning Divine Service is conducted here in English, and in the afternoon there is a service in Arabic, which last is by far the best attended. There are thirty-five Copts in communion with this Church, and they have a flourishing School, in which a number of boys are instructed in the "good and right way."

The late Viceroy, Sâid Pasha, issued orders that Missionaries of every denomination should travel on the Railroads in his Kingdom free of charge. When two American Missionaries arrived in Cairo, he presented them with a palace-like building, commodious enough to serve as a Sanctuary, School, and Parsonage. This was saying in effect, " Here you may worship under your own vine and fig tree without fear of molestation." Even the Sultan has such a friendly feeling towards Christians that he has issued a Decree that whosoever should be guilty of murdering or even robbing a European, should be instantly put to death. Throughout the Turkish Empire Christianity is tolerated.

THE STREETS are not more than from nine to eighteen feet wide, Moskie Street excepted, which is about twenty-four. In the middle of these Passages—for they are not worthy of the name of Streets—there is a Channel or Gutter, into which refuse of every kind is swept. The upper stories and eaves of the houses often meet, and many thoroughfares are roofed over with wood. The design of this is to keep off the hot rays of the sun. When recently watered the streets are very slippery, as they are innocent of paving, and consist only of an amalgam of Nile-mud and Desert-sand. The donkeys occasionally fall, but nobody seems hurt. I was twice pitched over their heads, but was up again all right, save the mud contracted by my clothes. When the streets remain several hours unwatered, the moisture evaporates, and the dust becomes intolerable. The crowds throughout these Passages are immense, more especially so in the Bazaars; but the people skip from side to side like goats, and thread their way through each other with wonderful facility. Moving along, you hear the warnings, *Schemalek*,—"Mind the left;" *Emenek*,—"Mind the right;" *O-a*,—"Take care;" *Erguh*,—"Look out;" *Reyleck*,—"Mind your feet." However dull the Pedestrian may be in England, he must learn to be quick in the streets of Cairo. A stupid fellow will infallibly be bumped on one side, or jammed on the other; and even when riding, we must "look out," or have our legs grazed by a Bullock-cart, a Carriage-wheel, the Panniers of a Camel, or some other inflexible obstruction. Animals and Men are evermore in each others way, and Camels and Carriages never stop for anybody.

WATERMEN.—Having mentioned the watering of the streets, it may be well to describe the mode by which that service is accomplished. Men are employed for this purpose, who carry upon their backs Goat-skins filled with water, slung from their left shoulders at one end, and supported by their right hands at the other. In their left hand they hold the neck of the skin, from which, with astonishing expertness, they squirt the water in every direction. Passengers require to "look out," or they come in for a cooling drench. In the same way men go about selling water, and they are so practised that they can fill a cup to the greatest nicety, controlling the vent at the neck as truly as we should control a tap. Donkeys and Camels are also employed to convey water about the City.

SANTONS.—Men dressed in Goat-skins are commonly seen in the streets of Cairo, carrying in their hands long staffs, and crossing from stall to stall asking alms. These Vagrants are called *Santons*, or "Saints." They abound in Egypt, since all persons afflicted with a harmless insanity are there regarded as Saints, and as such, supported by all classes. Designing men, perceiving that this affords an easy method of getting a living, assume the Goat-skin, and impose upon the credulity of the "Faithful."

When Elijah is described as "a hairy man," we are to understand simply that he wore a hairy garment. (2 Kings i. 8.) And it would seem that this was the prophetic dress as it is the badge of the Egyptian Santon, for Zechariah prophesies respecting pure times in which the Prophet should not wear "a rough garment to deceive." (Zech. xiii. 4.) The Margin translates the Hebrew literally, "a garment of hair."

THE ROADS leading into Cairo are tolerably wide, and skirted with sycamores and acacias so as to form Avenues; and they are usually raised a few feet above the level of the surrounding plain, to enable the people to pass and repass during the inundations of the Nile. European Merchants are often seen driving upon these roads, with half naked Arabs running before their horses at an almost incredible speed. Some of these Gentlemen (!) drive at the rate of ten miles an hour, and whip their Runners because they cannot keep ahead. The Turkish Beys have Runners to precede their carriages.

Samuel warned the Israelites that the King whom they desired would cause their sons to run before his chariot. (1 Sam. viii. 11.) We also read that Absalom had fifty men who ran before his chariot. (2 Sam. xv. 1.)

THE HOUSES are of stone, mostly two or three

stories high, and invariably built with flat roofs, protected by battlements or parapets. The people sleep upon these in the Summer, as well as prepare their figs and raisins, and dry their clothes. In contemplating them the Biblical Student is reminded of that most melancholy passage in the history of David. (2 Sam. xi. 2—4.) The parapets are designed for protection, as well as to serve the purposes of privacy, and hence the command, "When thou buildest a new house, then thou shalt make a battlement for thy roof, that thou bring not blood upon thine house, if any man fall from thence." (Deut. xxii. 8. See also Jos. ii. 6; Jer. v. 10.) As many roofs are formed of dried branches covered with mud, grass soon springs up, but is as soon withered under the beams of the sun. The Street Entrances, even to the houses of Europeans, are most forbidding; exactly like the dirty back-yards or narrow passages in the worst parts of our great towns. But after one or two turnings, which are designed to prevent passers from looking in, they open into large Courts, round which the Rooms are arranged. In the centre of the Court there is generally a Well of water. Probably in one similar Jonathan and Ahimaaz hid themselves. (2 Sam. xvii. 18.) The Reception-Room for Strangers is generally paved with red tiles, or square pieces of marble, of various colours, and at the end facing the Entrance the floor is raised a few inches, while in the centre of the room there is a small Fountain playing. The Platform is furnished with a Turkey-Carpet in the centre, which is considered "holy," as the Proprietor of the house is presumed to prostrate himself upon it at his devotions. Visitors, therefore, are expected to take off their shoes before ascending to the Carpet, which custom illustrates various passages of Scripture. (See Exod. iii. 5; Jos. v. 15; Ecc. v. 1; Isa. i. 12.) Around this carpet Divans are arranged, the cushions of which are covered with calico, silk, or any other material according to the taste or means of the owner. (Pro. vii. 16.) Strangers are not permitted to ascend from the basement of the houses, as the upper rooms are devoted to the women and children.

Besides the Court and Fountains, most of the houses have good Gardens and Baths; so that the meanness of their external appearance is compensated by luxury within. The Gardens are not laid out in walks, but are more like Squares filled with orange-trees, sweet-smelling acacias, jasmines, &c., the doors of their private rooms opening into them, so that they can luxuriate in the fragrance while reclining and smoking on their Divans.

Many persons indulge by having soft Pillows under their arm-pits, in addition to those against the wall, "when they stretch upon their Couches." These Pillows are often made by the Women of the Hareem. (Eze. xiii. 18.) From the hours of twelve to two, in summer especially, there is no business transacted, but every one flys to his Divan, or some shaded spot, to escape the scorching sun. Ishbosheth is mentioned as "lying on a bed at noon." (2 Sam. iv. 5.) The term "bed" in Scripture generally means a *Divan*. (Amos vi. 4; 1 Sam. xxviii. 23; Esth. vii. 8, &c.) These Divans, with the carpet, sometimes a long pipe, and perhaps two or three water bottles and perfuming vases, constitute the entire furniture of an Eastern Room. Elisha's Chamber therefore, was well furnished, having a Bed, a Table, a Stool, and a Candlestick! (2 Kings iv. 10.)

In building houses in Egypt, they never study regularity, but aim at making every apartment as secluded as possible, so that they may not overlook each other. Where we read of "windows" in Scripture, the original denotes *Openings:* glass windows were unknown in those days. The "agates" of the "windows," therefore, would be the ornamentation with those gems of the framework of these openings. (Isa. liv. 12.) The better class of houses in Cairo are now being fitted up with glass, stained with representations of birds, flowers, and other devices, instead of the usual lattices. The Doors are generally ornamented, and have the Inscription, in Arabic upon them, "God is the Creator—the Everlasting," which is intended as a charm to keep away the Evil One, and all who have no right there. There is also a small latticed Door in the front of the Balcony, about the size of a boy's face, sometimes a little larger. The inmates see through these lattices all that is passing in the street, without themselves being seen; but if they wish to converse, they open the doors and shew their faces. Thus the Beloved of the Church is represented in the Canticles as first *shewing* Himself through one of these Openings and conversing with His Fair One looking up to Him from below. (Song ii. 9.) There are also staircases outside the houses from the Roof to the Porch or Court, by means of which a person may descend to the street without passing through the house. (Mark xiii. 14, 15.) It was probably by one of these that the Prophet fled from the house of Jehu. (2 Kings ix. 10.) The houses are also provided with a Secret Door by which, in case of danger, the owner might escape, or by which he might dismiss a Friend, or Refugee who would elude pursuit.

THE GATES.—Cairo is surrounded by strong Walls with Gates. These are closed an hour and a half after sunset, and no person is then permitted to enter without the Password, which, however, it is not difficult to obtain. The term "Gates of the City," in Eastern language, means the City itself. (Gen. xxii. 17.) The Gates of Palaces in the East are always the most elaborately ornamented parts of the building. Hence the Palace or Court of the Sultan is styled "The Sublime Porte" or Gate. The expression "Gates of Hell" will now be understood to signify the Power or Resources of Hell. (Matthew xvi. 18.)

THE POPULATION of Cairo has been estimated at 300,000, but that figure is far too low; others state it at 400,000, and there are some who estimate it even at 500,000. The people are mostly Mahometans.

VISIT TO THE PYRAMIDS.

The distance from Cairo to the Pyramids is about eight miles; and a Dragoman charges a *napoleon* each for as many as may employ him, engaging to defray all expenses. We placed ourselves under the guidance of one of these in our first visit to the Pyramids; but the second time we saved seven shillings each by making an agreement with a Donkey Boy. Passing through Old Cairo, we reached the Nile nearly opposite Rhoda Island, where we hired a boat, into which our donkeys were lifted by the legs, and in a few minutes we were at the Libyan side of the stream, about three-quarters of a mile across, from which the people came, called Lubim. (2 Chron. xii. 3.)

ARTIFICIAL HATCHING.—In this place there is an establishment in which some hundreds of chickens every week were hatched by artificial heat. Of late the number has considerably fallen off; but many smaller places have sprung up in other parts. There are thousands of chickens produced in this way all over Egypt. Necessity is the mother of invention. In this warm climate the hens cannot be induced to sit, so that these Ovens have been introduced to supply the lack.

Again upon our Donkeys, with the Pyramids still six miles ahead, we passed through a richly fertile district in a sad state of cultivation, ever and anon encountering Pigsties, miscalled Villages, redeemed from contempt, however, by the graceful Palms surrounding them, and wending our way round small Lakes, left by the retreating waters of the Nile. The objects of our journey, which are visible from a distance of thirty miles, and of which we had glimpses from time to time, at length came full in view. As yet, however, they were miles away. But when we stood at their base, I cast my eyes to the right, to the left, upwards, and was almost struck dumb with wonder. It seemed impossible that works of such magnitude could have been accomplished by man, much less by man 4,000 years ago; but they remain, together with the Ruins of splendid Temples and other Monuments, in different parts of Egypt, indubitable proofs of the high civilization of remote antiquity.

THE PYRAMID OF CHEOPS being the largest, demands a particular description. It has its name from the King by whom it is supposed to have been built. It stands upon an area of 13 acres, or about 550,000 square feet,—a space equal to Lincoln's Inn Fields, in London, including all the buildings around. Let the Reader endeavour to realise a single structure of such a magnitude. The stones composing it are of various sizes; some being 30 feet long, 15 wide, and 4 feet 6 inches deep. Tier after tier, the building becomes regularly smaller, until it approaches a point at the summit, which is 481 feet high—considerably more elevated than the Cross of St. Paul's, London. The steps, formed by the successive tiers, upwards of two hundred in number, vary from two or three feet in width. It is estimated that this Pyramid contains about 7,000,000 tons of stone, and would supply materials to build a wall 10 feet high, and 18 inches broad, which would go three times round England, or once round France. It may then, be easily imagined that 100,000 men required ten years to form the roads for the conveyance of the stones, and twenty years more to complete the building.

We were soon surrounded by clamorous Arabs, urging their services to conduct us to the top, with such intrusive pertinacity as to be very annoying, for neither money nor threats would induce them to leave us. On my first visit I refused to ascend. The second time I started with the intention of accomplishing the feat; but, surveying the height of the Pyramid, and considering the size of some of the steps, I hung fire for some time. At length, gathering courage, I revealed my resolution, when instantly two Arabs seized my wrists as in a vice, two others placed themselves behind me, all shouting, " Now, den, sir, come along. Here we go." And go we did without any mistake; the Arabs skipping up the steps like goats. All I had to do was to place a foot on the edge of the next step; my Arabs raised me, and up we went at a rapid rate, my Motive-Power singing, " Good Gentleman not at all frightened,—not at all frightened !—

> Jack and Jill went up the hill
> To fetch a pail of water ;
> Jack fell down and broke his crown,
> And Jill came tumbling after."

About half way up, we halted to gain breath, when I was lustily plied with the importunate " bucksheesh." During this rest I ventured to look down, and saw the people below like shrimps, but it made me so dizzy that I did not attempt it again. In about fifteen minutes from the time of starting we were at the summit, and after receiving some water from an earthern bottle, I began to look around.

The stones at the top, which compose a platform about twelve yards square, are nearly covered with names and initials of Travellers. The View from this elevation may be better imagined than described. Towards the West the great Libyan Desert stretches interminably—sand, sand, sand,—right away to the horizon one vast glaring Plain, with occasional hills fast crumbling to add their substance to the dreary waste. Towards the East, Cairo, with its lofty Citadel, towering Minarets, and beautiful Gardens, sleeps in the distance. From South to North the Nile rolls its waters, spreading luxuriance in its course, and enriching its banks with myriads of palms and acacias as far as the vision extends. Beneath and around are the other five Pyramids of Ghizeh, two of which are nearly as large as the great one, while the other three are merely models. The gigantic Sphynx is also seen, Tombs innumerable, and the Pyramids of Sahhara, Abouseer and Dashoor, in the distance towards the South.

The descent is much more difficult than the ascent, as the Arabs cannot carry you, but only steady, and keep you from falling. Some years since, an Englishman, who would go up alone, upon returning missed his footing, rolled to the bottom, and was killed. I was dreadfully frightened in jumping from step to step in the descent, some of them being, as already described, four feet six inches deep.

The Entrance to the great Pyramid was first discovered by Sultan Mahmoon, about the year 820, and it is said that the body of Cheops, covered with jewels and gold, was found in a Sarcophagus. The Saracens, true to their instincts, improved this discovery by plunder and spoliation. The ancient Egyptians believed that men would return to life after they had been dead three thousand years, provided their bodies were left undisturbed; and it is said the Pyramids were built by the Kings, and the Entrances concealed, that they might realise the benefit. I did not venture into the dark chambers; but I am assured that in one there is a granite Sarcophagus seven feet four inches long, three feet wide, and three feet one inch deep. How such an immense Stone could have been placed there is mysterious; nor is it less so that the Blocks of Granite which compose the Chamber should have been conveyed to such an altitude.

Some writers think Job alluded to the Pyramids, when he spoke of the Kings of the Earth building desolate places for themselves. (Job iii. 14.)

THE SPHYNX.

From the Pyramids we proceeded to examine the celebrated Sphynx, and found it half buried in the sand. It is a colossal thing, being 143 feet high, and the circumference of its head 192 feet. It has a Human head, the nose of which is broken off; and the body resembles that of a Lion, the claws of which are just visible above the sand. It was cut out of the natural rock. In my Letters, which have been published, I remarked that the Sphynx was an Idol of the ancient Egyptians. This is the opinion of many learned persons; but I am assured that it rests upon tradition unsustained by historical evidence. The following passage from the pen of the Dean of Westminster, may not be out of place here:— "For what purpose was this Sphynx of Sphynxes called into being—as much greater than all other Sphynxes as the Pyramids are greater than all other Temples or Tombs ? If, as it is likely, he lay couched at the Entrance, now deep in sand, of the vast approach to the second, that is, the Central Pyramid, so as to form an essential part of this immense Group: Still more, if, as seems possible there was once intended to be, (according to the usual arrangement which never left a solitary Sphynx any more than a solitary Obelisk,) a brother Sphynx on the Northern side, as this is on the Southern side of the approach, its situation and significance was worthy of its grandeur. And if, further, the Sphynx was the giant representation of Royalty, then it fitly guards the greatest of Royal Sepulchres. (Sinai and Palestine, p. lviii.)

We likewise examined the ancient Tombs with their curious hieroglyphs, the Sarcophagi, the Statues and other Monuments of that wonderful District.

THE NILE.

Under the auspices of the Royal Geographical Society, the late Captain Speke, in 1855, started upon an expedition to settle the long disputed question about the Source of the Nile; and he found in Central Africa, between 32° and 34 East longitude, right upon the line, and about 3,750 feet above the level of the Ocean, a great Lake, called Nyanza, fed from the Mountains of the Moon, on the N.E., and from the Kœnia Mountains on the N.W., whence the "Father of Rivers" flows out. There is a Station of German Missionaries at a place called Gondokora, about 200 miles to the North of this remarkable Lake. Passing through Abyssinia and Nubia, or Upper and Lower Ethiopia, this noble stream advances through Assouan — the Biblical "Syene" (Ezek. xxix. 10), and, after a course of about 1,800 miles, falls into the Mediterranean.

While standing upon the banks of this river, what reflections crowded upon the mind! Like other rivers, indeed, it is simply an accumulation of rain-drops; but its associations are peculiar. This is the stream which laved and fertilised the land of Goshen, upon which the flocks of Israel pastured. This is the stream whose friendly reeds sheltered the infant Moses from "the wrath of the King," and whose waters the same Moses in after years converted into Blood. To the Egyptian it is everything. Not only does he drink its waters, fish in them, transport himself upon them, but they also manure, refresh, and fertilise his fields, and convey the surplus produce to the seaboard for exportation and exchange. Formerly his god; ever his benefactor and his slave.

INUNDATIONS.—In the month of June this River begins to rise, and, swelling over its banks, spreads out like a sea upon the plains. It steadily increases until September, after which it gradually recedes, leaving the deposit of a rich soil. Towards the latter end of November, in running from Alexandria to Cairo, the land was still in a saturated condition, while in many places there were extensive patches of water, suggesting to me the idea of a very boggy country. It has been ascertained that the Vernal rains within the Tropics in the Mountains of Abyssinia are the cause of these overflowings. A heavy shower in Upper Egypt is quite a phenomenon,—indeed rain in any form is infrequent there: in Lower Egypt, near the sea, there are occasional showers. The fertility of the country is so dependent upon the swellings of the Nile, that they are regarded with the utmost solicitude. If the deposit left by the retreating waters is too strong, the people mix sand among it. If they do not rise to a certain height, comparative famine ensues. It is not improbable that the "seven years of famine" in the days of Joseph, resulted from the limited overflowings of the Nile. If they rise to their usual level, there is abundance; a little higher, profusion; but yet higher still, and desolation follows—Villages are swept away, Plantations washed up, and various works demolished. This result is more common than the opposite. Some writers have expressed fear that as the banks are evermore rising above the plain—in some places five inches and in others twelve—in the course of a century, the overflowings must eventually cease, and the hope of Egypt expire. These fears, however, are groundless, for it is ascertained that as the banks are elevated, so also is the bed of the stream.

ARTIFICIAL IRRIGATION.—In crossing the valley, the traveller observes multitudes of narrow Rivulets, not deep enough to drown a rat, but which serve to moisten the earth. These streams draw their supplies from Wells, which are filled when the Nile overflows, and sustained by the filtration through the light soil long after that river has returned to its channel. From these reservoirs it is worked up upon the land by *Shakeyiahs* or Persian water-wheels, turned by bullocks. The humbler people work it up for their own lands by the *Shadoof*, which is simply a Goat-skin Bucket connected with two long poles, after the style of our old fashioned Draw-wells. Frequently four men, one above another, are seen working these Shadoofs. This is required when the banks are high. The first man discharges the contents of his bucket—about two or three gallons of water—into a kind of well, whence it is lifted by the second, who does likewise, so the third, and the fourth raises it to the Channels by which the land is irrigated. This labour is severe, and the men employed at it are almost naked—(Matt. xxiv. 18)—but the result is that the Desert is transformed into a Paradise of fruitfulness. (Gen. xiii. 10 ; Num. xxiv. 6 ; Isa. i. 30, li. 3, lviii. 11; Jer. xxxi. 12; Ezek. xxxvi. 35.) By means of Sluices, the husbandman is able to turn the streams in any direction he pleases. To this there seems to be a reference in such passages as,—"The King's heart is in the hand of the Lord as the rivers of water : He turneth it whithersoever He will." (Prov. xxi. 1.) The term "River" in Scripture often denotes these irrigating *Rills*. (Psa. i. 3, &c.) The ground is formed into squares, from which the water is excluded by elevated ridges until needed. Then the husbandman pushes down the barrier with his foot, when the water flows through the opening and spreads over the enclosure. This is referred to in Psa. lxv. 10, and Ezek. xvii. 7 ; and Job appears to allude to it when he says, "If my land cry against me, or that the *furrows* thereof complain, let thistles grow instead of wheat." (Job xxxi. 38, 40.) Palestine is characterized as a land that "drinketh water," or receives *rain* from the clouds, in contradistinction to Egypt, which is styled a land "watered with the foot." (Deut. xi. 10, 11; 2 Kings xix. 24.)

AGRICULTURE.—As the waters of the Nile recede after the inundation has attained its maximum, they are followed by the Husbandman, who casts in the grain. This custom may have suggested to Isaiah the figure embodied in the words, "Blessed are ye that sow beside all waters, that send forth thither the feet of the ox and the ass." (Isa. xxxii. 20.) Thus, the crops on the high land are ready, almost as soon as the seed is put in nearer to the banks of the stream. Owing to the fertility of the soil and heat of the climate, there is a winter as well as a summer crop; and *three* crops of Indian Corn, or *Doura*. The first harvest is called the "First Fruits," and occurs in March and April. Barley is merely cast upon the surface, and then pressed into the ground by means of a log of wood dragged or rolled over it. Consequently it has to be watered every ten or twelve days. For wheat, small furrows are made with a broad heavy hoe, or with a plough. Wheat does not require much irrigation. Wheat and barley are sown at the same time of the year, and the "Barley Harvest" is consequently reaped the first. (Ruth ii. 23.) Sometimes corn is sown amongst stubble, and irrigated so as to rot the stubble and convert it into manure for the grain. Pigeon's dung* is the only other manure used in Egypt. Rice is usually scattered upon the water, or rather upon the land when very wet, which is referred to in Eccl. xi. 1. The land in Egypt is nearly free from weeds. This is attributable partly to the extreme dryness of the climate, but principally to the fresh soil annually deposited; for weeds do not flourish upon new land.

Returning to Cairo, after visiting the Pyramids, I was struck with the amazing difference between the sandy desolation of the desert, and the fruitfulness of the Valley of the Nile. Wherever there is irrigation there is an unusual power of reproduction in Egypt. They were now reaping the Sugar-cane and Doura. The Cotton, Rice, and other crops, had been long gathered in. On returning from Cairo to Alexandria, after being in the Peninsula of Sinai,—an interval of ten or twelve weeks,—we were struck with the marvellous change upon the face of the land which then seemed a vast swamp. The water had nearly all disappeared, and the corn and other produce were flourishing amazingly.

In reaping, the Sickle is never used, but the corn is

---

* The "Dove's dung" mentioned 2 Kings vi. 25, is a kind of plant, bearing that name, which grows in Egypt, and in other Oriental countries.

plucked up by the roots. Solomon says, "There is a time to plant, and a time to *pluck up* that which is planted." (Eccl. iii. 2.)

There are no Farm-yards in the East. The corn is thrashed out in the open country. A certain writer says, "I once saw twenty-four men thrashing out corn with straight sticks. The corn was laid in a long heap, and the men struck it, keeping time to a tune which the Overseer was bawling." It is usual, however, to thrash by yoking oxen to a log of wood, and making them drag this log over it, so as to rub out the grain from the straw, which is thickly spread in a circle upon the ground. The oxen thus employed are not muzzled, but eat what they please, as they move round. (Deut. xxv. 4.) They have no Winnowing-Machines or instruments with which to dress their grain, but throw it up, so that the wind may carry the chaff away. In hot weather this is done in the night. Naomi said of Boaz, "Behold he winnoweth barley *to-night* in the threshing-floor." (Ruth iii. 2.)

CLIMATE.—The Climate of Egypt is in many respects delightful. The Sky is unclouded generally throughout the year. One morning, during my stay, a kind of misty rain fell, upon which I was assured, that it was the first they had seen for eleven months. This, however, was an exceptional case; usually they have three or four good showers in the course of the year. Frost, snow, or storms of any kind never invade them. I was in Cairo and its neighbourhood during the whole of December, and a great part of January, and found the weather as warm as at Midsummer in England. Trees do not begin to cast their leaves until about the month of March, when, like our evergreens, the old foliage gives place to the new. Being so far Eastward, the sun rises two hours earlier than in England, and the days are two hours longer, owing to its greater proximity to the Line.

THE PETRIFIED FOREST.

About a two hours' Journey to the North-East of Cairo, in the midst of the sandy Desert, there is an extensive tract covered with Trees and Fragments of Trees, all converted into Flint. Not a blade of grass is to be seen around, or any symptom of vegetable life, yet here lie, half buried in sand, Trees of all sizes, and millions of Pieces, the whole resembling an immense Timber-yard. I measured one of these Petrifactions and found it nearly sixty feet long. I also observed in it marks which evidently had been made by the stroke of an axe, while yet it was in its normal condition of timber. How this Forest came into a situation so remarkable, not to mention the process of petrifaction, is profoundly mysterious.

EXCURSION TO HELIOPOLIS.

Having arranged with our donkey drivers, we set

out for the famous "City of the Sun," known in Scripture by the name of "On." It is distant from Cairo about six miles.

ARAB VILLAGE.—We had not travelled far before we came upon an Arab Village, which consisted of a number of large mud hovels, huddled together in the most indescribable confusion. They are built of unburnt brick, or lumps of mud dried in the sun, and roofed over with doura straw, plastered with mud. They are not more than five feet high, and are entered by holes about two feet square. In these wretched sties, men, women, and children, .live, apparently unconscious of their miserable state. Such mud houses probably existed in the days of Job, to which he seems to compare the human body. (Job iv. 19.) The "foundations" of these hovels are "in the dust;" for in Egypt and Arabia, in the absence of irrigation, sand everywhere prevails. Our English rains would soon wash these fabrics away; but in that dry climate they remain for years.

Onward we moved, sometimes passing along Groves of acacias, sometimes Orchards of mulberries, now under wide spreading sycamores, and occasionally through Fields of clover, barley, wheat, beans, and lentils. Peasants' Huts, Bedaween' Tents, and whitened Tombs, here and there distributed, with the fearful Desert in the distance, all tended to render the scene interesting and even picturesque, though the whole country was almost as level as a railroad.

THE LAND OF GOSHEN.—Our way to Heliopolis lay over a portion of the land of Goshen, which still answers to the ancient description of its exceeding fruitfulness. It literally teems with luxuriance. Some writers think that Rameses, the city from which the children of Israel took their departure, could not have been situated here, because the distance from the Red Sea is about seventy miles, and that 2,000,000 of people, with their flocks and herds, could not have travelled so far in three days. But the land of Goshen, anciently, must have extended much farther, for such a multitude, mostly *shepherds*, could not subsist their cattle in a confined space. Many districts which are now desert, were then, doubtless, richly cultivated. And while vast numbers of the people would assemble at Rameses, ready to start at a concerted signal, it is not improbable that those who dwelt nearer to the Red Sea would fall in and head the march. In this way they would easily reach "the wilderness of the Red Sea," for the head of the Gulf would not be more than thirty-five miles from the limits of the district of Rameses.

HELIOPOLIS.

After a most delightful ride of two hours, through

corn and clover, and Avenues of tamarisk, fig-trees, and acacia, along Causeways raised above the floods of the Summer inundations, we reached the Ruins of the ancient On. They consist simply of a wide enclosure of earthen mounds, partly planted with gardens, in which are two vestiges of the Temple of the Sun,* of which probably the father-in-law of Joseph was the Priest. (Gen. xli. 45, 50; xlvi. 20.) One is a Pool overhung with willows and aquatic vegetation, called the "Spring of the Sun," whose water probably served for the lustrations connected with the worship. The other now rising wild amidst garden shrubs, is an Obelisk which stood in front of the Temple, then in company with another, whose base alone remains. This Obelisk is a single block of granite, 66 feet high, and 6 feet 3 inches in diameter at the base. It is covered with hieroglyphics, and is said to bear the name of Osirtasen. Of this monument Dean Stanley says, "It was raised about a century before the coming of Joseph; it has looked down on his marriage with Asenath; it has seen the

---

* The Ancient Canaanites also worshipped the Solar light, and hence their *Beth-Shemesh*, or "House of the Sun-light;" and in imitation of these and other neighbouring peoples the Israelites became Sun-worshippers. Josiah "took away the Groves," and "burnt the Chariots of the Sun with fire." (2 Kings xxiii. 11.)

growth of Moses; it is mentioned by Herodotus; Plato sate under its shadow; of all the Obelisks which sprung up around, it alone has kept its position. One by one it has seen its sons and brothers depart to great destinies elsewhere. From these gardens came the Obelisks of the Lateran, of the Vatican, and of the Porta del Popolo; and this venerable pillar (for so it looks from a distance) is now almost the only landmark of the great seat of the wisdom of Egypt."

THE REFUGE OF JOSEPH AND MARY.—In a garden immediately outside the walls is an ancient Fig-Tree which, according to the Coptic belief and the tradition of the Apocryphal Gospels, marks the refuge of Mary and Joseph on their flight into Egypt. The gnarled trunk of this venerable tree is covered with the names of travellers.

Strabo says that Heliopolis stood on a slight eminence, but the country has since been so raised by the sand and Nile deposits, that the base of the Obelisk is considerably below the general level. Antiquarians fully believe that large portions of the ancient Temple and City might be discovered by removing the accumulated sand and soil.

How mutable is human greatness! Even Egypt, the first kingdom upon earth, whose Colossal Monuments, for ages defying the corrosions of the atmosphere, declare her once boundless pride and marvellous resources, stands forth a demonstration of the vanity of even Intellect without God. How admonitory those prophetic denunciations upon the iniquities of that Nation, pronounced when she was inflated with prosperity, which have since met a signal verification! "Egypt shall be the basest of the kingdoms; neither shall it exalt itself any more among the nations: for I will diminish them, that they shall no more rule over the nations." (Eze. xxix. 15.)

CHAPTER V.

THE DESERT OF SINAI.

JOURNEY FROM CAIRO.

WHILE I was engaged in studying the Manners and Customs of the Egyptians, with a view to the elucidation of various passages of Scripture, my Companions were luxuriating in a six weeks' ramble upon the Banks of the Nile. After visiting the Tombs of Beni Hassan, of the Sheykhs or Hermits, the Colossal Statues of Thebes, the Ruins of Karnac and the Royal Tombs, with the other objects of interest in which that wonderful region abounds, they returned to Cairo on the evening of the 16th of Jan., 1863. The next day we set about making preparations for the Desert, in anticipation of which, I had already contracted with a Dragoman for a party of three. It is customary for all agreements between Travellers and Dragomans to be formally drawn and signed by the Consul of the nation to which the former may belong. The annexed is a copy of our Contract, which is written in Arabic :—

بسم الله الرحمن الرحیم

در خصوص مشکلات موجود در رابطه با این جانب گزارشی تهیه و خدمتتان ارسال میگردد.

۱۳/۱۵/م
امضاء نامشخص

ورق عثمان وشروط وشاد وما اشبه ذلك
من ارنداءت الاقلام من دفع مبلغ
ثمنها ثلاثة غروش

انه كان يوم الاثنين ١٩ شهر جنذاري سنة ١٨٦٣ موافقه ٢٩ رجب سنه ١٢٧٩ حابنا المضا جوتا بير وكلباتكك وارغام المتنبه كيما علي ثلثه خطها وبنه السيد احمد ابو نبوت كمايلة السيد احمد ابو نبوت الترجمان شرحه باخذ البلغة يصور هذا المذكوره من النفوس ابو طورسنا ومعود ديلم بانيان متتاجط مبلغ وقدرة ستون جنيه انكليزي عن كامل السفن ما فيه ابن العامل والابن الذين يكونون موديه بالسفر والخيم النظيف والمرعي والفلاش للزاد والحم وما يوجد به كا من المصاريف من كل نوع والهدايا والجامش الع الماج المرب والانفار وسبج الم الحوابات المذكوره باقامة للذة ايام بو طورسنا وبعض ما الترجمان المذكور التاريخين وكلما بلغ لحيث حوث عليه المحلوجت وانه الله ذا اخذ زبت ارقام اكتر من ذلك خاصية السيد احمد ابو نبوت ارجعات الاقلام سيتولا مهم قيمه جنيزة كل يوم ودخل المحفظه ايابو وبصاريف ذلك والجامش اللازم في كوته الحيمه على يد السيد احمد ابو نبوت ارتباعك جنيه من اصل مبلغ المقاوله المذكور. تمنع ليلا الترجمان الموقع مقتنا ابني علم نزول والعيادون من جنيه الباقيه حنه عودتهم لهذا المحل. وقدة شرواقر السيد احمد ابو نبوت بان. وصل الاربعون جنيه المذكوره مقدمة قبل الموحي ما بذا وصار الاتفاق بان اذا حصل نزاع ببنهم فيها ارتكب على حكام فضلي لاكلترا وحكم ذكوونا القاطع للفصل نذاع بينهم ومليا زم بكله وقرار الرضا والتوافقه وتورحل حتم السيد احمد ابو نبوت ونظيره بالعظم الذكليز. يا بقيا اخباع جوت بر وكلبا نك وارغام غور. في شفر جنذاري سنة ١٨٦٣

المترجم فيصحي
السيد احمد ابو نبوت

For attestation of the above affixed
seal of Sayed Ahmed Abou Nabbout
H. B. M. Consulate
Cairo 20th January 1863

J. W. Drummond Hay
Consul

The elder Mr. Plummer deemed it necessary to return to England immediately; but his place was supplied by Mr. Verhaeghe, a Belgian gentleman. Everything arranged, our Caravan, consisting of a Dragoman, Sheikh, Cook, Waiter, and a number of Bedaween Muleteers, all armed, six Camels, carrying tents, bedding, canteen, provisions, and water, and four Dromedaries, started off. Four days after, we took the Train for Suez, where we were to join the Caravan, and thence proceeded in true Oriental style.

SUEZ is a miserable Town, which, within the last three centuries, has sprung up. The Houses are of stone, but its dark colour, together with the clumsiness of the erections, so far deceived me that, in one of my "Letters from the East," I described them as composed of mud. The Population is about 1,600, 150 or 200 of whom are Christians of the Greek and Latin types, whilst the rest are Muslems. The office of British Vice-Consul is filled by an Agent of the "Transit Company." There is here a most convenient and respectable Hotel, kept principally for the accommodation of Travellers by the Overland Route to India. All the appointments of this establishment are of the very highest order.

THE OVERLAND ROUTE TO INDIA.—By this Route travellers can reach their destination within a month from the time of starting, whereas to go round by the Cape of Good Hope takes two or three months. They leave Southampton in the Steamers of the Peninsular and Oriental Company, cross the Bay of Biscay, call at Gibralter and Malta (or they may reach Malta by way of France), and proceed to Alexandria, whence they run down by rail to Cairo, where they remain one night, and thence proceed to Suez. Here they embark on board a steamer, descend the Red Sea to Aden, and pass out into the Indian Ocean through the Sea of Babel-Mandeb. A glance at a map will shew that the Land passed over is trifling compared with the distance traversed by Sea, insomuch that the term "Overland" seems almost a misnomer.

THE SUEZ CANAL.—In an hour and a half we reached the Isthmus of Suez, which separates the Mediterranean and the Red Sea. These Seas were anciently connected by a Canal, of which great engineering work traces are still visible, banks in some places remaining which are five feet high, and from ninety to one hundred-and-twenty feet apart. Workmen are now busily engaged in cutting a new Canal in the same direction, which, when completed, will still further diminish, if not entirely remove, the land from the so called "Overland Route."

THE WELLS OF MOSES *(Ayûn Mûsa.)*—After a six hours' journey—sufficiently long for a first lesson in Camel riding—we came to a strange place, in which there are Seventeen Wells of brackish water, surrounded by gardens and shaded with tamarisks and palms. These Fountains have their name, according to the Muslem tradition, from the circumstance that Moses, wanting water for his followers, struck the ground here with his wand, upon which the Springs appeared. It is usually thought that there is no allusion to these Wells in the history of the Exodus, and it must be confessed there is no *direct* reference. The following words, however, are worthy of note:—"So Moses brought Israel from the Red Sea, and they went out into the Wilderness of Shur; and they went three days in the Wilderness, and found no water." (Exod. xv. 22.) Now it is evidently implied in these expressions that the People of God found water by the Red Sea before they entered the Wilderness of Shur, and these Wells exactly answer to that description. They are on the borders of the Wilderness and within sight of the Sea, which lies about a mile to the West. It is even probable that the Gulf of Suez was formerly nearer to these Springs than at present, for the ground lying between them is a kind of sandy warp, presenting the appearance of having been once laid under water. The brackishness of these Fountains also suggests that they are still connected in some way with the waters of the Gulf. At this interesting place we spread our tents for the night, and while dinner was being prepared, walked to the shores of the Sea.

THE RED SEA, according to some, derives its name

from its proximity to the country of Esau or Edom, for *Edom* signifies "Red." But to this it is objected that the Mountains of Edom hardly reach the shores of the Gulf of 'Akaba, certainly not to the shores of the Ocean. The appellation, as applied distinctively to the Gulfs of Suez and 'Akaba, is comparatively modern. It seems to have been applied to them only as continuations of the Indian Ocean, at a time when the two Gulfs were known to the Hebrews as the "Sea of Weeds," and to the Greeks as the "Bays of Arabia and Elath." This makes it probable that the name of "Red" was derived from the Corals of the Indian Ocean. It is also noteworthy that huge trunks of coral-trees are thrown up on the shores of the Gulf of 'Akaba in particular, and the rocks and sand upon those shores are also of a deep red colour. Everything here brings before us the mighty mass of the Red or Erythræan Sea, the coral strands of the Indian Archipelago, of which these two Gulfs, with their peculiar products, are the Northern Offshoots. In describing his visit to the Mountain of Nakûs, near Tûr, Captain Newbold writes :—" As we emerged from the mouth of a small defile, the waters of this sacred Gulf burst upon our view; the surface marked with annular, crescent-shaped, and irregular blotches of a *purplish red*, extending as far as the eye could reach. They were curiously contrasted with the beautiful *aqua-marina* of the water lying over the white coral reefs. This red colour I ascertained to be caused by the adjacent red-sandstone and reddish coral reefs. A similar phenomenon is observed in the Straits of Babel-Mandeb, and also near Suez, particularly when the rays of the sun fall on the water at a small angle."

THE PASSAGE OF THE CHILDREN OF ISRAEL.—We came to the spot assigned by tradition as the Landing-Place of the Children of Israel, after their fearful night's journey through the Channel miraculously opened in the Gulf. I was convinced that the landing-place could not be far from where I stood; and had the satisfaction afterwards to find that my judgment had the sanction of respectable authorities. The Arm of the Sea is here ten miles across. We are assured that the day before their passage, the Children of Israel "encamped beside Pi-hahiroth, between Migdol and the Sea, over against Baal-Zephon." (Exod. xiv. 2; Num. xxxiii. 7.) Now *Pi-hahiroth* signifies "The Mouth of the Ridge," obviously, of the Mountains, which line the Western Coast or Egyptian side of the Sea, where a Gap or Opening, seven miles wide, forms the extremity of the Valley of Bedea. The shore here is called *Attaka* or "Deliverance." I could distinctly see the Opening in the chain of Mountains, whose peaks were lit by the rays of the evening sun, and endeavoured to realise the position of the People of God, hemmed in with the Host of Pharaoh closing upon their rear. Such reflections as the following also passed through my mind:—Did Miriam, with her timbrel, stand upon this spot? Did Moses praise the God of Abraham here? Here at least the people saw their enemies dead upon the shore. But was it not strange that the Lord should have piled the waters into walls one hundred and eighty feet in height, as they must have been in this place, when, by a journey of twelve or fifteen miles Northward, the armies of Israel might have rounded the Head of the Gulf? Thus, however, it pleased Him to make His power known, and to get Him honour upon Pharaoh and upon his Host.

LIFE IN THE DESERT.

On the 30th we left the shores of the Red Sea and plunged fairly into the Desert of Arabia, where we began to taste the sweets and privations of a wild life. After a ride of about two hours we dismounted, and established ourselves under a sand-hill to take luncheon, but the repast was rendered uncomfortable by clouds of sand careering in the wind. We were soon upon our Camels again, and in a short time lost sight of everything but sand—moving, burning sand.

THE CAMEL.—I have often heard and read that the Camel and Dromedary are distinct animals, the difference being that the former has two humps, while the latter has only one. The Bactrian Camel, indeed, which however is confined to Central Asia and Chinese Tartary, has two humps; but the African animal, like the Dromedary, has only one. There is really no more difference between these creatures than exists between the Cart-horse and the Racer. The Camel, like the Cart-horse, is heavy, and adapted to bearing burdens; while the Dromedary, like the Racer, is light, and trained for running. The Dromedary will trot at the rate of eight or ten miles an hour, and some of them will keep up this speed night and day without resting for several days in succession. No horse could perform such a feat. They may therefore well be characterized as "Swift Dromedaries." (Est. viii. 10; Jer. ii. 23.) They have also been distinguished as "Patient," "Toil-enduring," "Hunger-supporting," and "Thirst-defying."

While being loaded, as also when their riders are preparing to mount, these most tractable creatures lie on their bellies, with their legs doubled up under them like a carpenter's rule. When ready to start, they raise themselves on their knees, and then, if the rider is not on the alert, he will infallibly go over the tail. Next, they spring from their hocks, when, if the rider does not "look out," he goes over the head. The third act is rising upon their fore feet. In this operation they abruptly swing their bodies back, and give the rider a furious jerk. This has to be endured every time you mount, and the reverse motions when you alight. On either occasion it behoves you to hold fast by the pommel.

The foot of the Camel is half divided, so as to spread out upon the sand, and support the weight of the creature with its burden, as it glides like a ship over the Desert-sea. It is amongst the animals forbidden to the Israelites to be eaten, (Lev. xi. 4,) but the Arabs make no scruple of this.

PITCHING THE TENTS.—About half-past four in the afternoon we arrived at the Wady Sudr, where, in the midst of a wide desert-plain, we "Pitched our Tents." This process is described in the terms—*Benona al beiout*, which is, literally, "They have built their Houses." Thus may be explained why the term "Houses," occurs so frequently in Scripture, in places where it is probable *Tents* were intended.

The Furniture of our parlour consisted of a fold-up table with tressels, and three camp stools.

In about an hour and a quarter after pitching the tents, dinner was cooked and on the table. Our usual fare was soup, hot dishes of fowl, and mutton, sometimes roast, and sometimes boiled. We had also some kind of fruit-pudding. For dessert we had oranges, dates, figs, &c., and, in true Oriental style, coffee after all. We carried our fowl with us alive, to serve as occasion might require. For Breakfast we had tea or coffee, bread and buffalo-butter, omelet and eggs, and sometimes bacon. The Mahometans, like the Jews, refuse bacon, but we had no difficulty in getting it cooked. We carried charcoal with us to serve as fuel for culinary purposes.

Soon after dinner, being weary, we prepared for a night's rest. Our beds were mattresses thrown upon the sand which was as dry as a chip. Upon these we covered ourselves with thick flock quilts. But no sooner had we lain down, than the night came on with rain and storm. Our men had, therefore, to "lengthen the cords and strengthen the stakes." (Isa. liv. 2.) For if the pegs, to which the strands are fastened, are too near the canvas, the tents are liable to be torn up by the wind. It is also especially important that the stakes be strengthened, that is to say, that iron stakes be substituted for the usual wooden pegs. All being made secure, we felt very thankful for our shelter, slept soundly, and awoke next morning greatly refreshed.

Soon after six I set out before breakfast for a short walk. Being alone, I bowed myself before the Great Being whose presence is in the wild Desert as truly as in the crowded City, and rejoiced in the blessedness of a saving interest in the infinite merits of Christ.

Upon a subsequent occasion, rising before day, I saw the manner of the Encampment of our Caravan.

The Camels were all laid down in a circle, having each one leg doubled up and tied. This was to prevent them from wandering away. Within the circle, the Arabs slept upon the sand with no other covering than their cloaks.

BAKING IN THE DESERT.—Our Arabs had new bread every morning, which they procured in the following fashion. They carried with them a stock of doura and barley meal. Some of this they mix with water, and add a little salt which they collect from the rocks, where it lies in patches, as if left there by the evaporization of sea-water. The salt is not pungent, as, by exposure to atmospheric action, it loses much of its savour. (Matt. v. 13.) The dough thus formed, they press into flat cakes. They use strong wooden bowls as kneading-troughs, which are probably similar to those anciently used by the Children of Israel. (Exod. xii. 34.) Next they make a hole in the sand, into which they put a few sticks with some dry camels' dung, which they pick up on their way. When this fuel is burnt almost to a charcoal, they rake out the embers, and supply the place with more, to be treated in a similar way. The cakes are then placed upon these, and the embers first named are put over them, so that they are surrounded with burning charcoal. In about ten minutes the bread is ready. Probably the cakes baked by Sarah were prepared in a similar manner.

But the most amusing part remains to be described. The cakes are next broken into the trough, and water is poured upon the fragments. Now the poor fellows all kneel round the bowl, and fish out the sops with their fingers. In five minutes the bowl is polished. When I saw this I was reminded of our Lord's words, "He that dippeth his hand with Me in the dish,"—"He it is to whom I shall give a sop." (Matt. xxvi. 23; Jno. xiii. 26.)

THE WATERS OF MARAH.

After breakfast we were again on our Camels and bade farewell to the *Wady Sudr*. Onward we moved until we came to the famous Waters of Marah, whose bitterness was miraculously removed by Moses. These Waters are bitter still. The miracle therefore was of temporary duration,—continued only long enough to serve the specific purpose for which it was wrought.

THE WADY GHURUNDEL.

At half-past five in the afternoon we came to the Wady Ghurundel, which is a choice spot for an encampment in the Desert, contrasting most refreshingly with the naked wilderness around. It is fringed with trees and shrubs in various forms of beauty. Here palms throw out dishevelled branches from their hairy trunks; feathery tamarisks with knarled boughs unfold leaves dripping with a gum which the Arabs call *Manna;* the acacias grey foliage and bright blossoms tangling to a thicket in its desert growth. But pleasant as the acacia is to the sight, wearied by the glare of an ocean of burning sand, it has a higher and holier interest, considered as the kind of "Bush" which Moses saw in flames yet unconsumed, and the "Shittim Wood" of which the Tabernacle of Witness was constructed. Nothing is provided for the poor Camels beyond what they can gather in the Wilderness, except a little barley with which they are fed night and morning. Here they had a rich treat in the abundance of verdure and an overflowing supply of water. This the Camel occasionally requires, though it can travel for days without drinking.

THE WELLS AND THE PALM-TREES OF ELIM.—The Fountains and Wells of Ghurundel are about half an hour further down the Wady, and may be safely identified as those of Elim mentioned in the Exodus. Accordingly we started early in the morning that we might view them. Moses speaks of "Twelve Wells of Water;" but some are now closed up. He also mentions "Three Score and Ten Palm-Trees." (Exod. xv. 27.) It is scarcely to be supposed that the number of these should still remain the same, therefore I did not attempt to count them; but the successors of the "Three Score and Ten" are very numerous.

THE WILDERNESS.

Those who imagine, as I once did, that the Desert is all a sandy Plain, are greatly mistaken; the sand is intermingled with large quantities of gravel, and the rugged mountains of granite, sand-stone, and lime-stone, are immense. Hitherto indeed, while skirting the Gulf of Suez, our journey lay through vast tracts of sand; but, about two hours after leaving the Wells of Elim, we came to the Wady Useit, and then enter upon a very different country. This is a valley embosomed in wild mountains, rendered comparatively fertile in the midst of rugged desolation, by the presence of a few brackish springs. One Writer speaks of the Mountains of the Wilderness as "The Alps stripped naked." Hence, among the sufferings of the Children of Israel, we have no mention of Sand-drifts such as those encountered by the Armies of Cambyses in the African Desert, for these are unknown in the Desert of Sinai, though they are occasionally encountered in the Wilderness of Shur.

Pursuing our journey in the same direction for four hours, we came to an open space among the low rock-ridges, where a road branches off leading to the Convent of Sinai by another route from that we were pursuing. Two hours more brought us to a large Plain lying between the mountains and the sea, called the Wady Taiyibeh.

THE ENCAMPMENT BY THE SEA.

This valley opens upon the deep blue waters of the Gulf, bright with foam, and was, doubtless, the place where, after removing from Elim, the Children of Israel "Encamped by the Sea." It was delightful to pass down through vast cliffs, white on the one side and on the other of a black calcined colour, and come upon the "shell-strewn, weed-strewn shore," into whose waves, promontory after promontory, right and left, broke, and to reflect that this very view burst upon the Israelites, in which they saw their old enemy and friend, and had a glimpse once more of the hills of Egypt in the dim and shadowy distance. For an hour we proceeded by the margin of the Sea, and then, following the example of the people of Israel, " encamped " there ourselves. The next morning we still continued skirting the Sea for about four hours and a half, and at length turned off into the Wady Shellal, or Plain of Murkhah, which is, probably, the " Wilderness of Sin." Here, it being exceedingly hot, we dismounted, and sat down to luncheon, "under the shadow of a great rock in a weary land." (Isa. xxxii. 2.)

THE STAIR-ROCK.

Onward we pushed again, and after two hours of constant climbing, we came to a splendid Gorge, out of which rises a Mountain Stair-case, called *Nukb*

Baderch, "The Pass of the Sword's Point." It is said that the Arabs describe this, as called up by Moses, to enable the Israelites to get out of the Valley below. By an effort of a full half-hour, we managed to scale this wild Flight, and thence for an hour, we followed a road which winds down through a Wady of the same name.

THE WADY MUKATTEB.

From the Wady Badereh we pass into the Wady Mukatteb, or "Valley of Writing," upon whose rocks are those celebrated Inscriptions, which many have supposed to have been the work of the Hebrews. Most of them are cut upon sand-stone, and these are deep, but some are on granite, and are slightly and rudely scratched. Some are in Greek, some in Latin, and some in Arabic characters, while others are hieroglyphs difficult to decipher. The intelligible Inscriptions are without doubt comparatively modern, and there is no certainty that a high antiquity should be assigned to the others. Any of them might be cut by an artist standing upon the shoulders of a man, and they generally occur in the public routes. The highest are proper names in Greek. There are many representations of animals which are so rude and ludicrous that it seems difficult to assign to them any serious signification. Everyway they appear to be the work of Travellers of various nations passing, at different intervals, through this Valley.

THE WADY FEIRAN.

After spending a night in the Valley of Writing, we started again, and in a few hours entered the Wady Feiran, the Paradise of the Bedaween. Wandering in the Desert, they sleep in the open air, but here they have a local habitation; and their little ones, nearly naked, may be seen issuing from tents " wild as the untaught Indian's brood." Along this valley we moved for an hour or two, refreshed by the sight of bushy palms and verdant gardens, watered from a Well at a place called Husseyah. About a mile further to the left are the Ruins of an ancient Village, after passing which, in about half-an-hour, we plunge into a much larger Palm-grove, through a streamlet which wends its way by the Ruins of an ancient city called Feiran. Amongst these are Towers, Aqueducts, Sepulchral Excavations, and the Remains of a Church, which Ruppell assigns to the fifth century. From these Ruins a wild picturesque glen—the Wady Aleiyat—winds away Southward to the base of Serbal, whose jagged peaks tower above all intervening cliffs, and is, next to Sinai, the most interesting mountain in the Peninsula. Serbal is a mass of granite pushing five grand snow-capped peaks high into the heavens, and presenting an outline even more striking and sublime than its honoured rival.

Some have endeavoured to identify this part of Feiran with Rephidim, where Israel fought with Amalek, and where "Moses smote the rock." But this place is a considerable distance from Sinai, whereas Rephidim was only a day's march from the "Mount of God." This difficulty is, indeed, obviated upon the assumption that Serbal and not Jebel Mûsa was the true Sinai. But the abundance of water naturally flowing in the Wady Feiran would render the miracle of bringing water out of the rock unnecessary in this place. This objection is also of value against the hypothesis respecting Serbal. It seems probable that Feiran is the Paran referred to in the valedictory address of Moses :—"The Lord came from Sinai, and rose up from Seir unto them; He shined forth from Mount Paran, and He came with ten thousands of His saints; from His right hand went a fiery law for them." (Deut. xxxiii. 2.)

The morning being somewhat frosty, we preferred walking a few miles through the palm-groves of this Desert Paradise. Leaving the tamarisks upon its skirts, we found the way dry and hot, and when we moved out amidst the burnt tufts of the open Desert, the heat became insufferable. There was scarcely a breath of air as we winded through the narrow passes at the foot of the Mountains. I was never given to quarrel with heat; but when the fire of this Desert burnt the skin of my nose, it was far from agreeable. Onward, however, we pushed over the scorching waste, longing for our destination. From the time of starting we had not tasted fresh bread, and what we brought with us was now so hard and dry, as to be scarcely edible. The Arabs, indeed, had new bread every morning; but I had seen them kneading and baking their cakes in a manner so dirty, that I had little inclination to share with them.

THE PLAIN OF RAHAH.

On the morning of the 31st, though way-worn and weary, we arose in good spirits, anticipating that a few hours more would bring us to the end of our journey. As the way lay over crags, we preferred travelling on foot. After an hour's march, we entered a defile, called *Nukb Hawy*, or "The Windy Pass," leading over this mountain-wall to the recess of Sinai. From the summit of this Pass to the Convent is a journey of two hours. Leaving the "Windy Pass," or "Pass of the Wind," we enter upon a broad plain, called "The Plain of Rahah," or *Rest*, probably from the fact that the children of Israel halted here, after their weary journey through the Desert. Here also, it is probable, Aaron made the Golden Calf, before which the people danced in idolatrous glee. From the centre of this Plain the dark front of Sufsafeh, otherwise called the Peak of Sinai, rises so as to conceal from the vision the "Mount of God." To the left of Sufsafeh, there is a deep narrow valley running up S.S.E., between walls of rock, as if in continuation of the S.E. corner of the Plain. About a mile up this Gorge the Convent is seen embosomed in verdure—an Oasis of beauty amid scenes of sternest desolation. At the S.W. corner also, the Cliffs retreat so as to allow an extension of the Plain in a Westerly direction, in which stands the deserted Convent of *El-Arb'aim*. It will be obvious then, that when Moses was commanded to "set bounds round the Mount," to prevent the people from touching it, or gazing upon the Glory which enveloped it, he only needed to barricade the Entrances of these Passes, for we have already seen that the Peak of Sufsafeh, concealed the "Hill of God." (Exo. xix. 12, 21.) To have surrounded the Base of a gigantic mountain with Bounds, would have been a Herculean undertaking. The topographical peculiarity upon which we have now remarked, is in itself a powerful argument in favour of the claims of Jebel Mûsa to be the Sinai of Scripture, in opposition to those of Serbal. The Dean of Westminster observes, that "Whatever may have been the scene of the events in Exodus, he could not imagine any human being to pass up this Plain, and not feel that he was entering a place, above all others, suited to the most august sights of Earth."

THE CONVENT OF ST. CATHERINE.

About noon we reached the Greek Convent of Sinai. Coming to a lofty wall, we looked up at a kind of trap-door some thirty feet overhead, and saw the faces of two or three Monks reconnoitering us. We had obtained a letter of introduction from the Branch Convent at Cairo, which any traveller can readily procure upon application. The Monks let down a cord for this letter. The heavy doors were then opened to us, and some refreshment was placed before us.

THE CHURCH OF THE TRANSFIGURATION.—After we had rested, one of the Monks conducted us through a building supposed to have been erected in the Sixth Century, when the Convent was founded. It is called the Church of the Transfiguration, from a representation of that scene, wrought in mosaics, in the central part of the vaulted roof. Christ is depicted in radiance,—Moses and Elias on either side, and the three Apostles—" eye-witnesses of His Majesty," in the foreground, Peter being in a prostrate position. Round the grand centre-piece is a border, consisting of a series of oval or circular Tablets, upon which are Busts of Prophets, Apostles, and Saints, the name of each being indicated in Greek characters. On the wall, over the apse, are Portraits of the Emperor Justinian and his Wife, Theodora. Above the former there is a representation of Moses on his knees before the Burning Bush. On the opposite side of the window, over the Empress, he appears again, receiving the Tables of the Law. The floor of the Church is tesselated marble. In the Chancel behind the Altar there is a Skull, and also a Hand, which are set in gold and ornamented with jewels. These are said to be Relics of St. Catherine, whose body, according to tradition, was miraculously transported from Alexandria to the summit of the Mountain in the Sinai range, which bears her name. On Sunday, February 1st, we rose at three in the morning to attend "High Mass" in this Church. It was a dull, lifeless affair!

THE CHAPEL OF HELENA.—The Monks also conducted us to a Chapel said to have been erected by the Empress Helena, over the place where the Bush "flourished," under the gaze of Moses, "unconsumed in fire." Hence, it is called "The Chapel of Helena," and also "The Chapel of the Burning Bush." The identical spot upon which the Bush grew, however it was discovered, is now indicated by a Silver Plate. Rich carpets are spread round it, and all who approach are expected to take off their shoes as Moses did, upon that "Holy Ground." On one day in the year a "Sun-beam" streams into this

Chapel, which is of course "miraculous" (!) but the philosophy of the miracle may be readily traced by the ascent of Jebel Ed-Deir. For there is a deep narrow Cleft in that Mountain which opens straight down upon the Convent, so that in the Sun's annual course, upon a certain day, he comes into conjunction with this Cleft and a Window of the Chapel. Superstition has ever found in Ignorance not only the Mother of Devotion, but also a Progeny of Miracles.

THE CHARNEL HOUSE, in connection with the Convent, is a place of ghastly interest. When a member of the Brotherhood dies, his remains are removed to one of the chambers, and exposed there until the flesh has wasted from the bones. The Skeleton is then conveyed to another chamber, and placed among the skeletons of his predecessors. The various bones are distributed into distinct heaps. Thus, Skulls are piled together, and near them, in grim symmetry, are heaps of Femurs, Ribs, Arm-bones, &c., so that the Skeleton of the Monk whose memory lives with the survivors, is mixed with those of Members of the Order whose history is known only to Omniscience.

THE MOSQUE.—Within the Walls of the Convent is a Mahometan Temple, with its characteristic Minaret. The Monks are obliged to tolerate this. It is attended by a few poor Arabs, who are employed to clean it out every Thursday evening.

MOUNT SINAI.

Accompanied by a Monk and a Bedouin, we started to ascend the Holy Mount. We found a winding Pathway, which was constructed by one of the Pashas, leading nearly half way to the top, up which even a horse might travel. We came to the end of this in an hour and five minutes; but now commenced a rugged and difficult ascent, rendered more dangerous by the snow, on an average eight inches thick, and in some places knee-deep. Added to this, the steeps upon which the snow could not rest were coated with sheets of ice. Upward we went, notwithstanding, and came to a low rude building containing the Chapels of Elijah and Elisha; and a narrow Grot, said to be the place in which the former, after the driving storm, heard the "still small voice." (1 Kings xix. 8—12.) From this point the ascent becomes steeper; but blocks of stone have been so laid as to form a rude Staircase, upon which the observant [Muslim] traveller will not fail to discover the Footprints of Mahomet's Camel. These greatly aided our progress, and in an hour and a quarter more, we were upon the summit—a Platform of about thirty paces in diameter, partly covered with Ruins, and still standing at the Eastern end, a Greek Chapel and a Mosque; for Moses is a Mahometan, as well as a Christian, Saint! The View from this Platform is grand, but not extensive, as it is obstructed by the loftier ridges of Tiniah, St. Catherine, and other surrounding Mountains.

In reading the Scriptures, Sinai and Horeb seem to be interchangeable expressions, though they are not exact synonyms. "Horeb" is the general term for the whole Range, of which "Sinai" is a particular Elevation; just as "Pisgah" is a part of "Nebo"—probably the highest peak of that chain.

Having gleaned all the information we could relative to this most interesting and sacred spot, we set about returning to the Convent. I found the descent far the more difficult, and I think decidedly the most perilous adventure of my life. Nothing but the associations of Sinai would have induced me to encounter such hazard. When we regained the Convent in safety, we were unfeignedly thankful to the Great Being who "giveth His angels charge concerning us that in their hands they might bear us up, lest we should dash our foot against a stone." Being greatly fatigued, we slept soundly that night.

Next morning, after breakfast, accompanied by one of the Monks, we went again through the Convent, in which are various ancient Chapels, and a Library, containing several very antique books. Our Guide also conducted us through the Gardens of the establishment, which are neatly kept, and adorned with cypress, date, fig, and various fruit-trees. Every way this Retreat had great attractions, particularly as being associated with Horeb and Sinai. And in the afternoon I walked out to the Plain of Rahah, fronting the Mount, to take a final view of the noble Theatre of so many glorious events. Then, after a three days' sojourn with the Monks, who were exceedingly kind, and to the utmost of their power made us comfortable, we began to prepare for our journey back.

We might have proceeded to Jerusalem by way of Petra and Beersheba. In that case we should have passed through the beautiful Valley of Hazeroth, where, after the departure from Sinai, the people of Israel "abode for seven days" while "Miriam was shut out from the Camp." (Num. xii. 15, 16.) Here also the Quails visited the hungry multitude; and it is noteworthy that Stanley "saw the sky literally darkened by the flight of innumerable birds, which proved to be the same Red-legged Cranes, three feet high, with black and white wings, measuring seven feet from tip to tip, seen in like numbers at the First Cataract of the Nile." We might have ridden along the Gulf of Akaba by Elath and Ezion-Geber, where the Fleets of Solomon passed and repassed in their voyages to Ophir and back. We should also have moved along the Valley of Arabah, down which the Israelites came through a Gap in the Eastern Hills, when the Valleys of Edom were closed against them.

Mount Hor—the Burial-place of Aaron, with its double top rising like a huge castle, from whose ramparts the first High Priest had a view corresponding to that vouchsafed to his brother from the crown of Pisgah.

But, passing beyond Horeb, we get into Arabia Petra, which is a region infested with robbers, and through which the inhabitants will allow no one to pass without exacting a heavy fine. We therefore deemed it wisest to return, however desirable it might have been to view the objects of interest already alluded to, as well as Kadesh, where, during the absence of the Spies, Israel "abode forty days," and in whose neighbourhood the first battle was fought with the Southern Canaanites. (Num. xiii. 25; xiv. 45.) — A place remarkable also as the scene of Moses' sin in striking the Rock to bring forth Water, whence it obtained the new name of *Meribah-Kadesh*, or "Strife at the Holy Place." (Deut. xxxii. 51.)—And a place further notable as the scene of the Rebellion of Korah, and the death of the brother and sister of Moses. We might linger in thought also upon the difficult high Pass of Sâfeh, thought to be that through which the Israelites were repulsed by the Amorites, or Amalekites, and the Wilderness of Beersheba, in which you imperceptibly pass within the domains of David and Solomon; but we must make our way back to Egypt.

RETURN TO ALEXANDRIA.

Our route back to Cairo was somewhat different from that by which we came, but it was performed in the same time. The distance from Suez to Sinai is about one hundred and sixty miles, which we accomplished in seven days and a half. From Cairo to Suez is ninety miles by Rail. The double journey of five hundred miles, reckoning also the time we spent at the Convent, required nineteen days. We were highly delighted with our Excursion, and truly thankful for the mercies which tracked our path. From Cairo we took the Train for Alexandria, and went to our favourite Hotel Abbatt. We witnessed many foolish and disgusting Processions in the streets, it being the time of Carnival. These scenes were to be repeated on the following day; but we went to the Office of the Messageries Imperials, and took our passage for Joppa. At the Landing, we bade farewell to our accomplished and amiable companion, Mr. Verhaeghe, and received a Gentleman from London into our party in his place.

After passing through the Scenes of the most stupendous events of antiquity, thoughts naturally crowd upon the mind. How strange the Providence by which two millions of persons should have been conducted into a region so wild, and subsisted there for forty years! But how appropriate a representation of the journey of life in the wilderness of this world, with the dispensations by which we are humbled, proved, and made to see what is in our heart! How truly was the miraculous preservation of that people in circumstances so untoward, foreshown in the Miracle in which their Leader received his high commission! The Bush was in flames, but was unconsumed, not because the wood was incombustible or that the fire was inactive, but because the Angel of the Lord was in the midst, as the Presence of the Most High in the Fiery Cloud was the secret of the preservation of His servants. How deeply instructive is the wondrous history! How assuring to the soul reliant upon the support, guidance, and defence of that stupendous Arm by which irresistible forces were so marvellously wielded. How withering to the child of rebellion the thought that his puny resources are brought into competition with those of a Being at whose Presence the very Mountains of the Desert trembled.

CHAPTER VI.

PALESTINE—JERUSALEM.

ALEXANDRIA TO JERUSALEM.

JOPPA, *from the Bay.*—After a sail of thirty hours, we ran into the Bay of Joppa, Japho, Jaffa or Yafa, as it is variously pronounced. The Town is beautifully situated on the bulge of a hill which dips into the waters of the Mediterranean; and this situation probably suggested its name, which expresses the idea of *beauty.* Thus in Cant. vi. 4, "Thou art *beautiful,* O my love, as Tirzah." The Hebrew word for "beautiful" is *jafeh,*—the same which gives its name to this place. The lovely effect is heightened by its Orchards of oranges, lemons, citrons, apricots, pomegranates, whose fruit is scarcely to be surpassed in any part of the world. Here fragrant blossoms are in perfection seen encircling golden fruit in March and April, when the Jaffa Gardens are enchanting. The air is then overloaded with the mingled spicery of oranges, apples, quinces, plums, and other fruit-trees, and the people frequent the grateful shade of the luxuriant Groves.

The Landing.—At eight in the morning, we attempted to land upon the Soil of that Country, which, of all others, is fraught with thrilling interest, as the Theatre of the most stupendous events. The Landing at Jaffa is certainly the most dangerous I ever saw. After being tossed on the waves in a small boat, and bounced against the rocks for about a quarter of an hour, we were at length dragged up by the arms on to a miserable Platform. On our return to this Port, after our rambles in the Holy Land and Syria, we learnt that two poor Monks had lost their lives at this most dangerous place. Steamers often pass without being able to land either a mail or a passenger; and yet this Port is honoured with the Residence of an English Consul. One can scarcely reflect without astonishment, that this should have been the Harbour to which the Cedars of Lebanon and Pines for the building of Solomon's Temple, were floated. (2 Chron. ii. 16; see also Ezra iii. 7.) But this was a necessity, for Joppa is one of only Three Harbours—all of which are bad, to be found along this inhospitable Coast,—the others being Acre and Hhaipha. Therefore Joppa was a common place of embarkation; so Jonah repaired to this place when he would take ship for Tarshish, and evade the Divine commission respecting Nineveh. (Jon. i. 3.)

The Town.—Tradition would make Joppa the most ancient City in existence; for Pliny says it was reputed to have been there before the Flood. History, however, assigns to it a high antiquity, as "Japho" is amongst the Maratime Towns allotted by Joshua to the Tribe of Dan. (Jos. xix. 46.) It owes its existence to a low ledge of rocks which extends into the Sea from the extremity of a Cape, forming a little Harbour. It is seated on this Cape. Like most Oriental towns it looks best at a distance. When approached, the Houses are found to be huddled together without regard to convenience or taste, and the Thoroughfares are a labyrinth of blind alleys and narrow, crooked, filthy lanes. The whole place is so crowded along the sides of the hill, that the rickety houses above seem to be toppling over the flat roofs beneath. The Population is about 10,000, and the trade is so brisk that the one principal street, is glutted with a motley crowd of Citizens, Wild Arabs, Foreign Pilgrims, Camels, Mules, Horses, and Donkeys. Nevertheless, the wretchedly poor are so numerous that if Dorcas were again raised from the dead she might find full employment for her benevolence.

The Grave of Dorcas.—The British Consul at Joppa found a Sarcophagus in one of his Gardens, which he presented to the Armenian Convent at Jerusalem. No doubt this was the Grave of Dorcas, for nobody can prove that it was not, and that is sufficient to satisfy the Monks that it was! Perhaps some successor of the Empress Helena will one day be erecting in the Consul's Garden a "Church of the Sepulchre of St. Dorcas."

The House of Simon the Tanner, or that which is shewn to the Faithful as such, is a comparatively modern building, which may, nevertheless, have been placed upon the true Site. It is close "on the sea-shore," for the waves beat against the low wall of its court-yard, in which yard also there is a Spring of fresh water, such as would be indispensable to the business of a Tanner. The house is entered from the street in which stand the Latin and Armenian Convents, and is occupied by Mussulmans, who regard the place as sacred, and have a small Mosque, or praying place, in one of the rooms, to commemorate the fact that "the Lord Jesus here asked God for a meal, and a table came down at once." This is manifestly a confusion of the history of the Sheet let down to Peter.

It will be admitted that there was a remarkable propriety in the revelation of this Vision to Peter at Joppa, seeing it had special reference to the Opening of the Gospel to the Gentiles. For here the Apostle looked out upon the Western World from the edge of the Mediterranean, in which direction Providence has ordered that the Tide of Evangelization should roll. And it is further remarkable that Cornelius, the first-fruits of the Gentile harvest, should hear the Gospel at Cæsarea, a place similarly situated, and founded by Herod with a special view to intercourse with the West.

THE PLAIN OF SHARON.—We were waited on at the Hotel by a Dragoman, who proposed to supply us with horses for our journey to Jerusalem. A party of five of us agreed with him for ten francs each, and two francs each additional for a mule to carry our baggage. The distance is thirty-six miles. I selected the horses, and chose a very quiet animal for my young friend, who was not accustomed to horse-exercise, while for myself I found a genuine Arabian, very frisky at first, but gentle enough as we advanced in our journey. Leaving Joppa, we were soon on our way across the vast Plain of Sharon, which is much larger than the Plain of Tyre, Acre, or even Esdraelon. For it is bounded on the North by Carmel, and stretches away Southward, so as to include the whole territory of the Philistines. It was the great Pasture-land West of the Jordan, as "The Mishor" was on the East. As its name indicates, it is comparatively *Smooth*, or apparently free from rocks; but it is far from being level, for it is agreeably varied by long swells. In riding over these for four hours, we found the comfort of English saddles we took precaution to purchase when at Malta. The "Rose of Sharon," of which Solomon sings so sweetly, Dr. Thompson seems inclined to identify with a kind of *Marsh Mallow*, which grows into a stout bush, and bears thousands of beautiful flowers. These abound in the Plain, but at present, at least, there are no Roses there, except the wild kind, which are occasionally found in their ever accompanying thorny thickets. That curious optical phenomenon, called the *Mirage*, also, is frequently seen upon this Plain, giving the inexperienced traveller the most profound persuasion that he is approaching a Lake of transparent water. Dr. Wilson tells us that the Sanscrit name for Mirage means, "The Thirst of the Antelope," which, it will be admitted, is beautifully poetic. The Arab name is *Scrab;* and, perhaps, Isaiah refers to this deceitful phenomenon, where he promises that the Scrab shall become a real Lake. Thus, not "the parched ground," but "the *Mirage* shall become a Pool." (Isa. xxxv. 7.)

LYDDA, now called "Lydd," or as it is written in the Old Testament, in our version, "Lod," (1 Chro. viii. 12; Ezra ii. 33;) lay slightly to the North of our road. In the Acts of the Apostles, it is said to be "nigh unto Joppa." It is interesting to the Christian Traveller as the scene of the curing of Eneas, and the place whence Peter was fetched to Joppa, upon the death of Dorcas. (Acts ix. 32—39.) It is now a flourishing Village of some 2,000 inhabitants, and is embosomed in noble Orchards of olive, fig, pomegranate, mulberry, sycamore, and other trees, and surrounded by a very fertile neighbourhood. But, like most of the towns in this country, it has seen better days. There are remains of large well constructed buildings mingled with the modern huts, and several extensive Soap Factories are now deserted and falling into decay. To the English traveller Lydda has the peculiar interest of being the reputed birth place and place of burial of St. George, the Patron Saint of his Country! According to the Calendars he was born here; towards the close of the Third Century suffered martyrdom in the Diocletian Persecution at Nicomedia, after which his body was conveyed to his native place. To his honour the Church of St. George was erected, the remains of which are still standing, and prove it to have been a superior structure. The material, a pale yellow rock, cut from the Quarries on the road to Jerusalem, is very hard and takes a good polish.

RAMLEH.—After a very pleasant ride across the Plain of Sharon, we arrived at Ramleh, probably the "Ramah," or "*Ramathaim*" (1 Sam. i. 1, Heb. and LXX.), where Samuel was born, resided, and was buried. It is also the "Arimathea" of the New Testament, which is manifestly a name formed upon Ramathaim. Here, therefore, the "Honourable Councillor" lived who "begged the body of Jesus," and, with Nicodemus, had it embalmed and laid in the Sepulchre. Upon the site assigned to the House of Joseph, a Christian Church was built, which in time became a ruin, and furnished materials for a Mosque, that still stands upon the ground. The site of the House of

Nicodemus is covered with a Latin Convent, said to be the largest in Syria; but this is a mistake, and possibly it is also a mistake respecting the site. This Convent is one of several belonging to the Romanists and Greeks, whose inmates consider themselves bound to "entertain strangers," providing them for a given time with bread and water, without charge. It is usual, however, to make them a present, unless the traveller is poor, and to omit this is considered unhandsome. We remained here one night, and were provided not with bread and water merely, but also with wine, soup, eggs, and other delicacies. The chief architectural attraction of Ramleh, is the Tower, which stands on high ground about a quarter of a mile West of the town, and rising 120 feet from the ground. Every traveller should ascend this beautiful erection, as from its gallery there is a most interesting view of the plain. The Town, (whose population is 3,000, two-thirds of whom are Muslems and the rest Christians,) is embosomed in olive-groves and orchards, with palms, sycamores, and carobs, the pods of which are the "husks" mentioned in the parable of the Prodigal Son. Few of its buildings, or even ruins, are earlier than the time of the Crusades. The vegetable gardens, fields of grain, and hedges of cactus, as well as the groves and orchards, invest it with an air of luxuriance.

THE ARABIAN STEED.—The next morning we rose

before day, took coffee in the Convent, and by six o'clock were again on the road. After riding several hours, we came to a Café, where we took refreshment, and saw a woman so unmercifully beat her servant, that the poor creature fell down apparently in a dying state, but sprinkling her face with cold water, she revived. Leaving this place, we began to ascend the Mountains of Judea, which run up to Jerusalem. The way became so rugged now, that no English-trained horse could keep his feet; but we travelled safely, not even fearing danger. The Arabian nags are certainly the best I have ever ridden. They are not more than fourteen hands high; but their action is very superior. Providence seems especially to have adapted them for their work, as there are no carriage roads in this country, and the saddle is consequently the only mode of travelling. In these rugged and romantic passes there are few smiths to replace the shoes or flat round plates when they fall from the horses' feet; but the hoofs of the creatures are so hard that they can go well without shoes, and are scarcely ever foot-sore. Some of the mountains over which these animals travel are so rugged, that it is like going up and down flights of steps, yet so strong are their sinews, that they seldom flounder, which is a mercy, as they sometimes pass along very narrow ridges overhanging frightful precipices. It is customary to ride with a slack rein.

APPROACH TO JERUSALEM. — Onward we moved until within half-an-hour's ride of Jerusalem, without getting a glimpse of the Holy City. The Mount of Olives was the first object which burst upon our gaze; next, what is called New Jerusalem, consisting of a Greek Convent, Schools, a Patriarch's House, and other erections, altogether a cluster of very fine buildings, put up by the Russians. Every fresh object in succession came upon my vision with a charm which still raised my anticipations—the moments were of breathless interest. At length, at a little past 3 P.M., we arrived at the Jaffa Gate. But action and reaction are reciprocal. As I rode into the City, I felt greatly disappointed, and soliloquised, "Is this Jerusalem, beautiful for situation, the joy of the whole earth"!—Is this the centre of so much attraction, the ancient "City of the Great King"!—Is this the renowned Metropolis of Christendom! But I checked these musings, and resolved to judge nothing before the time.

THE PRUSSIAN HOSPICE.—Hotels in Jerusalem present but a choice of evils. The "Mediterranean," or "English Hotel," is the best, but is capable of decided improvement in cleanliness and order. At this place we dismissed our horses, sat down to a Table d'Hote, and after resting a little, took a porter with our baggage and went to the "Prussian Hospice." This had been recommended to us in preference to the Latin Convent, to which strangers usually resort, as connected with the English Church, and open more especially for the reception of Protestants. It is justly noted for order and cleanliness; and as a limited number only can be accommodated, the company is select. We were domiciled with a Clergyman from Bagdad, a Graduate of one of our Universities from London, and a Vice Consul. These were all gentlemen of agreeable manners; and with such society in such a place, we were of course very comfortable.

JERUSALEM.

Before rising in the morning, my mind mused upon the associations of the City of God, which, notwithstanding the unfavourable impression I had received, filled me with joyous anticipation. Breakfast ended, we applied to our Host to procure us a Guide whom he could recommend as trustworthy, having a good knowledge of the place, and able to speak a little English. He introduced a young man named Hanna Habesh, a Romanist, whom we liked much, and accordingly engaged. In attempting a description of the Holy City, I shall not follow the order in which our Guide conducted us, but range the various matters of interest under distinct heads.

VIEW OF THE CITY FROM THE MOUNT OF OLIVES.

The best general view of Jerusalem is obtained from the Mount of Olives. So commanding is the situation, that the eye roams over the streets and around the walls as if in the survey of a Plan or Model of the place. A spectator standing here is at once convinced that the City is seated on the brow of one large hill, divided by name into several smaller ones, the whole gently sloping from the West. It forms an irregular square, with its shortest side facing the East, and in this is the supposed Gate of the ancient Temple, now closed up, and the Projecting Stone on which Mahomet is to sit when the world is judged in the Vale of Jehoshaphat below! The Southern side is exceedingly irregular, taking quite a zigzag direction; the South-West extreme being terminated by the Mosque built over the supposed Sepulchre of David, on the summit of Mount Zion. The place has the appearance of a great Fortification, being surrounded by Walls forty feet high, flanked at irregular distances by square Towers with Battlements and Loopholes for arrows or musketry, close to the top. These Walls, which are about two miles and a half in circumference, are entered by five Gates, viz., The Jaffa, The Damascus, St. Stephen's, Dung Gate, and Zion Gate; besides the Gate of

Herod and the Golden Gate, now walled up. The most conspicuous object is the Mosque of Omar, erected upon the site and foundations of the Temple. This is esteemed the finest specimen of Saracen architecture. On the South are some Gardens and Vineyards, with the long red Mosque El-Aksa, having two tiers of windows, a sloping roof, and a dark dome at one end. The Mosque of Sion and the Sepulchre of David are still further to the South. On the West is seen the high square Castle and Palace of the same monarch, near the Jaffa Gate. In the centre rise the two Cupolas, of unequal form and size; the one blue and the other white, covering the Church of the Holy Sepulchre, which stands on the Hill of Calvary. Around, in different directions, are seen the Minarets of eight or ten Mosques, amid an assemblage of about two thousand dwellings, with cupolas rising from their flat roofs. The scene altogether was so imposing, that my disappointment on first riding into the City from the opposite quarter was succeeded by the feeling that it was one of the grandest spectacles in the world. Well might the Psalmist have exclaimed, when Jerusalem was in her ancient pride, " Glorious things are spoken of thee, O City of God !" (Psa. lxxxvii. 3.)

THE HILLS OF JERUSALEM.

The Eminences which undulate upon the Great

Hill on which Jerusalem is built, are five, viz., Zion, Moriah, Calvary, Akra, and Bezetha.

MOUNT ZION, the largest of these hills, was the first occupied by buildings. This also was the famous Stronghold of the Jebusites, which so long defied the armies of Israel, and at length yielded to the military genius of David. (Num. xiii. 29; Jos. xv. 63; 2 Sam. v. 5—8.) Here that monarch built a Palace and a City, which was called after him "The City of David," and in which, for more than a thousand years, his successors ruled. (2 Sam. v. 9.) To the heights of Zion David also transported the Ark of God, and prepared a Tabernacle for its reception, upon which account Zion is oftentimes in the Psalms styled the "Holy Hill." It is also by synecdoche, because of its importance, put for the whole City of Jerusalem. Here David and fourteen of his successors were buried in the Family Tomb. (1 Kings ii. 10; xi. 43; xiv. 31.) Upon the slopes of Zion on the South-East, there is a series of Terraces under cultivation, extending to the King's Gardens, where Hinnom, the Tyropœan, and the Kedron unite. When one looks upon these, and upon the declivities round to the South, and contemplates the olives distributed amongst the narrow strips of corn, the words of Micah the Morasthite, spoken twenty-six centuries since, recur upon the memory,—"Zion shall be ploughed like a field." (Jer. xxvi. 18.) This Stronghold, which so stoutly stood out against the arms of Israel, was also the last to yield when Jerusalem was besieged by the Romans under Titus.

MOUNT MORIAH is memorable as the place upon which Ornan the Jebusite had his Threshing-floor, when "The Angel of the Lord, having a drawn sword in His hand, stretched out from Jerusalem," appeared, from whom Ornan and his sons hid themselves in terror. Perhaps in the Cave we still see below the sacred rock, David also saw Him from the opposite hill of Zion, when he and the elders of Israel interceded for the threatened city. Upon the Threshing-floor of Ornan the monarch offered those sacrifices which were consumed by elemental fire, whereupon the plague was stayed. It is not certain that Abraham offered up Isaac upon this eminence; possibly the hill afterwards called Calvary was the scene of that triumph of faith. The Patriarchal history simply specifies a particular mountain or hill in the "Land of Moriah," which "Land" comprehended the whole group of hills upon which Jerusalem is built. *Moriah* signifies "Vision,"—a name which may have been given to that group of eminences as the frequent Theatre of Divine Revelations. Here the magnificent Temple of Solomon stood, and here the Oracle was established.

MOUNT CALVARY, which we have already hinted as the probable eminence upon which Isaac was offered in sacrifice "in a figure," is the acknowledged site of our Lord's crucifixion. Had not Abraham a reference to the identity of the Hill upon which Isaac had been offered with that upon which the Lamb was to be offered, whom God was to "provide Himself," when he called the name of the place *Jehovah-Jireh*, viz., "the Lord will see or provide"? In this view there would have been good reason for the saying which dated from that event, "In the Mount of the Lord it shall be seen," viz., in Calvary where the Lamb of God was to suffer instead of Isaac, as foreshadowed by the "Ram." (Com. Gen. xxii.) Some writers have questioned whether the hill now called Calvary is indeed the place where Jesus was crucified; but no other place appears to me so completely to correspond to the Evangelists. They tell us that the rocks were rent; and here is shewn a Rift, whose sides so exactly agree, that it could not possibly be the work of the Priests. Here also is a Cave, which evidently had been a Sepulchre. Other Sepulchres hard by, are reputed to have been those of the family of Joseph of Arimathea. (Com. John xix. 41, and Matt. xxvii. 60.) Truly our Lord was crucified "*without* the Gate," and "nigh to the City" (Heb. xiii. 12; John. xix. 20), whereas Calvary, as now shown, is *within* the walls; but it is known that the City has considerably moved in that direction. The determination of the locality, however, is a matter of secondary consequence; the Sacred Writings attach less to physical circumstances than to moral truths. That the Son of God died for our redemption is the grand thing with which we are most deeply concerned; and may His blessed Spirit evermore enable us to realise this glorious truth by the faith of a contrite heart.

MOUNT AKRA is an eminence which is separated from Zion by the Tyropœan, and the hills so front each other that the rows of houses terminate in the same lines, separated only by the ravine. Anciently there was a broad valley here which was filled up by the Asmoneans, and thus joined to the "Lower City," as the buildings upon Akra are called by Josephus. The valley sweeps round to the opposite side, and there running in between this and the Temple Mount, and extends as far as Siloam. This is called by Josephus the "Valley of the Cheesemongers." Across this Valley Solomon appears to have raised a Bridge, leading from the Royal Palace on Mount Zion to the Temple on Moriah, which was "the ascent by which Solomon went up to the House of the Lord." (1 Kin. x. 5.)

MOUNT BAZETHA lies over against the Tower of Antonia, but is divided from it by a deep artificial valley. This Eminence is not mentioned in the Bible, but a full account of it is given in Josephus, who writes thus: "The City, overflowing with inhabitants, gradually crept beyond the walls, and the people incorporating with the City, the quarter North of the Temple close to the hill, made a considerable advance, insomuch that another hill, which is called Bazetha, was also surrounded with habitations." From these new erections the name Bezetha, which signifies "The New City," was transferred to the Mount on which they were reared. The time at which this hill began to be occupied by buildings is not precisely given; but there can be little doubt that under Herod the Great the City increased in extent as well as splendour, and that the increase then took this direction. Eight years after the death of Christ, Herod Agrippa surrounded these buildings with a wall.

THE MOUNTAINS AROUND JERUSALEM.

THE MOUNT OF OLIVES, now called *Jebel-el-Tûr*, or the "Mountain of Tûr," so named from the Village of Tûr which reposes on its summit, rises on the East of Jerusalem, in three Peaks, stretching about a mile from North to South. (1 Kings xi. 7.) Attaining an elevation of 160 feet above the City, and 416 above the Valley of Jehoshaphat, it is ever before the eyes an object of striking interest. Leaving Gethsemane on the right, and the Virgin's Tomb on the left, we began to ascend the Mount, and as we advanced observed steps and cuttings in the limestone rock, which proved the antiquity of the path. In his flight from Absalom, David ascended these. He went "over the Brook Kedron towards the way of the Wilderness . . . and went up by the ascent of Olives, and wept as he went up, and had his head covered; and he went up barefoot; and all the people that were with him covered every man his head; and they went up weeping as they went up." (2 Sam. xv. 23, 30.) On reaching the summit by the Village of Tûr, we must have been near where the King had been wont to worship God, and where he now met Hushai the Archite (verse 32). The View of Jerusalem from the Mount of Olives has been described; but there are also other Noble Prospects. Towards the South appears the Lake Asphaltites—a grand expanse of water, seeming within a short ride from the City, but in reality a considerable distance. Lofty mountains enclose it with prodigious grandeur; and resembling by their position the shores of the Lake of Geneva opposite Lausanne. To the North of the Lake are seen the verdant pastures of Jericho, watered by the Jordan, whose course may be distinctly discerned. For the rest nothing appears of the surrounding country but hills, whose undulating surface resembles the waves of the sea; bleak, destitute of wood, and seemingly without cultivation.

THE GALILEE HILL. — The Northernmost of the three Eminences of Olivet is called "The Galilee," from the supposition that there the Angels stood and said, "Ye men of Galilee, why stand ye gazing up into heaven?" This is the loftiest point of the Mount.

THE HILL OF ASCENSION. — The second Peak is called "The Ascension," and is covered with the Mosque and Church of Jebel-el-Tûr, on the supposed scene of that event—a supposition, however, which is manifestly at variance with Scripture. The reasons upon which this remark is founded will appear when we come to speak of Bethany.

THE HILL OF OFFENCE.—On the South summit, Solomon is said to have built Temples to the Idols worshipped by his Wives, whence this is called the "Hill of Offence," and also the "Mount of Corruption."

MOUNT SCOPUS.—To the North of the Mount of Olives is an elevation, in modern times usually called "Mount Scopus," on the supposition of its identity with the hill so called in the account of the Siege of Titus.

THE HILL OF EVIL COUNSEL. — To the South of the Mount of Olives there is another eminence, called the "Hill of Evil Counsel," because, as the Monks say, Caiaphas had a Country House there, at which the Consultation took place when the Priests and Rulers resolved upon the expediency of putting Christ to death. Upon this elevation there is a single wind-driven tree, called the "Tree of Judas," as it is assumed to mark the spot upon which the Traitor hanged himself. As these flank the East, there are also other Hills on the West, North, and South. To these collectively the Psalmist refers in the well known words: "As the mountains are round about Jerusalem, so the Lord is round about His people." (Psa. cxxv. 2.)

THE RAVINES.

THE VALLEY OF HINNOM.—A deep Ravine, or rather a series of Ravines, surrounds Jerusalem, except on the North-West. From the Jaffa Gate a portion of this series deepens, and forms the Valley of Gihon, which skirts the South of Zion. This is also called "The Valley of the Son of Hinnom" and "Tophet." Bate and Parkhurst construe the latter word to denote a *Fire-Stove*. Anciently a Fire was kept constantly burning in this place to consume the carcases and other offal of the City. From this Isaiah borrows his figure, when, speaking of the defeat of Sennacherib, he says, "Tophet is ordained of old; yea, for the king it is prepared; He hath made it deep and large. The pile thereof is fire and much wood; the breath of the Lord like a stream of brimstone doth kindle it." (Isa. xxx. 33.) It also supplies the usual figures by which the Place of Final Perdition is described in Scripture, which is therefore called *Gehenna*, from

"Ge" and "Hinnom," or the *Valley of Hinnom.* Others think the name "Tophet" is given to this gorge because of the sacrifices offered to Moloch there by beat of *drum,* which in Hebrew is called "Toph." The Statue of Moloch was of brass, hollow within, with its arms extended and stooping forward. A fire was lighted within the Statue and another before it. The Votaries put upon its arms, the Child they intended to sacrifice, which soon fell into the fire at its foot, whereupon a great rattling of *drums* and other instruments were made to stifle the cries of the Victim.

THE POTTERS' FIELD.—Upon the Southern side of the Valley of Hinnom, is the field now shown as the *Aceldama,* or "Field of Blood," as it is supposed to be the identical "Potters' Field," purchased with the thirty pieces of silver in consideration of which Judas sold the life of his Lord. (Matt. xxvii. 7, 8; Acts i. 19.) A square Pit, or Charnel House, sunk in the earth, is still shown here, probably one of the Tombs in which the "Strangers" were buried, for whose sepulture the Field was purchased. Some travellers assert that the earth is of such a peculiar chemical composition that bodies laid in it decay in twenty-four hours. This, however, is not authentic. A medical gentleman, some time since, examined a sepulchre here and found a number of skulls.

THE VALLEY OF JEHOSHAPHAT skirts the North of the City, winds round to the East, and runs Southward as far as the Pool of Siloam. The slopes of Olivet, on the Eastern side of this Valley, are covered with Tombs. The Jews have a singular belief that wherever they are buried, they will have to pass underground to this Valley to meet Messiah at the last Judgment, which they hold will take place here. Hence the fervid desire of every Son of Israel to lay his bones in this Vale, insomuch that the Tombs here are more numerous than the houses in the City. The famous Brook Kedron flows through the Valley of Jehoshaphat from North to South, and receives the waters of Gihon, as it turns off to the South-East through the Valley of Kedron, and seeks the Dead Sea. This Brook is generally dry, and only flows after the heavy rains.

THE GARDEN OF GETHSEMANE is a little quadrangular Inclosure, situate in the Valley of Jehoshaphat, on the slope of the Mount of Olives, opposite the Gate of St. Stephen. It is surrounded by high limestone walls, and kept by an old Latin Monk, to whom a small fee is paid by those who desire to enter. We reckoned eight venerable Olives, whose decayed trunks were supported by stones, though their branches are still flourishing. Naturalists say that these trees are more than two thousand years old, so that they must have witnessed the agony of our

P

Lord, and His betrayal by Judas. Along that winding path, by which we had come, was the Man of Sorrows led bound as a Malefactor, when His Disciples forsook Him and fled. Outside the Gate leading into the Garden is a rocky Bank, worn smooth by the kisses of Pilgrims, who hold it sacred as the place upon which the Disciples slept while their Master prayed. Perhaps the Stone would not be so sacred had the Disciples been vigilant!

The Tyropœan, or Cheesemongers' Valley, separates Ophel from Zion, and connects the Valleys of Hinnom and Jehoshaphat.

THE POOLS.

The Pools of Gihon.—A short distance from the Jaffa Gate, in the Fuller's Field, is the Upper Pool of Gihon. There Solomon was anointed King over Israel by Zadok and Nathan. (1 Kings i. 33, 34.) Here also Rabshakeh stood with his great army and defied the living God. (Isa. xxxvi. 2—13.) And here Isaiah uttered his remarkable prophecy respecting the Supernatural Birth of Messiah. (Isa. vii. 3, 14.) There is now a Mahometan Cemetery near the Pool, and from the rising ground above it there is a commanding view of the rich Plains of Rephaim, in which David twice defeated the Philistines. The "Lower Pool of Gihon" is opposite the South-West of Zion. (Isa. xxii. 9, 11.)

THE POOL OF SILOAM, or Shiloah, whose position is indicated by Josephus, is situate at the mouth of the Tyropœan Valley, and there accordingly we find a Fountain. Jerome, who is even more precise than Josephus, speaks of its Fluctuations,—a very remarkable circumstance observed by most Travellers. The water issues from a small artificial Basin under the cliff, the entrance to which is excavated in the form of an arch, and is immediately received into a larger Reservoir, 53 feet in length by 18 in width. A flight of steps leads down to the bottom of this reservoir, which is 19 feet deep. The large receptacle is faced with a wall of stone, (probably that rebuilt by Nehemiah,) now somewhat out of repair. Several columns stand out of the side walls, extending from the top downwards to the cistern, the design of which it is difficult to conjecture. Here the Blind Man, in obedience to the direction of Christ, washed and received sight. (Jno. ix. 7, 11.) The water passes out of this reservoir through a channel cut in the rock, which is covered for a short distance, but subsequently opens and discloses a stream, which is copious or scanty, as regulated by the ebb and flow of the spring. But we look in vain here for the inspiration of Milton (who, however, never visited the Holy Land), when he penned his famous Invocation—

> "If Sion's hill
> Delight thee more, and Siloa's brook, that flowed
> Fast by the Oracle of God, I thence
> Invoke thine aid to my adventurous song."

To the North of this Pool is the Village of Siloam, in which was the Tower that, in the time of Christ, fell, and killed eighteen persons. (Luke xiii. 4.)

THE FOUNTAIN OF THE VIRGIN.—The small upper basin in the Pool of Siloam is merely the termination of a long narrow subterranean passage, by which the water is supplied from the Fountain of the Virgin. This has been established beyond dispute by Dr. Robinson, who, with his companion, had the hardihood to crawl through the passage. They found it 1,750 feet in length, which, owing to its windings, is several hundred feet more than the direct distance above ground. The water of Siloam and that of the Fountain of the Virgin being the same, the latter is characterised by the remarkable tidal flow of which we have spoken in relation to the former. Dr. Robinson observed the water in the Fountain of the Virgin to rise one foot in the reservoir within the space of five minutes, and in another five minutes fell back to its old level. It is not unlikely that this phenomenon, however it is to be explained, suggested the imagery of Ezekiel's River, which, in other points also, corresponds. Thus, in its *Source*—" Behold, the waters issued out from under the threshold of the House, and came down from under, at the South side of the Altar." In its *Course*,—for issuing from the "South side of the altar," it must, by a topographical necessity, flow down the Valley of Jehoshaphat, along the bed of the Kedron Eastward into the Desert, and thus into the Dead Sea by the *Wady en Nar*. In its *Effects*—" Every thing shall live whither the river cometh." (Ezek. xlvii.) This water now, when it passes out of the Pool of Siloam, irrigates the "King's Gardens," which are in a flourishing condition.

EN-ROGEL, otherwise called "The Well of Joab," is fed by the only other Spring in Jerusalem beside that of the Fountain of the Virgin. It is situate at the juncture of the Mount of Olives and the Hill of Evil Counsel, and in ancient times marked the boundary line which divided the allotments of Judah and Benjamin. (Josh. xviii. 16.) By this Well Adonijah made a feast when he aspired to the Throne of David ; and forasmuch as he was in this assisted by Joab, hence possibly the name "Well of Joab." (See 1 Kings i. 7—9.) *En-Rogel* means the "Foot-Fountain," and it is construed by the Targum into "Fuller's Fountain," because the Fullers trod clothes there. Dr. Robinson found a depth of 50 feet of water in this Well in the middle of April; and in the rainy season it overflows the mouth, when there is a depth of 125 feet. Usually, however, the water runs off under the surface of the ground, and finds an outlet some 120 feet below the Well, whence, for sixty or seventy days in Winter, it is said to flow. The Water is of excellent quality, but not very cold.

THE POOL OF BETHESDA.—Leading to St. Stephen's Gate is a large reservoir, about 360 feet by 130, and 75 feet deep, which our Guide informed us was the Pool of Bethesda. Travellers differ respecting the identity of this Pool, but I see no reason to doubt it. The Pool of Bethesda, we know, was within the City "nigh unto the Sheep-Market," or *Gate*, as the margin reads it, and St. Stephen's Gate is admitted to be where the Sheep-Gate formerly stood. *Bethesda* denotes "The House of Mercy," and the Well had this name probably from its healing properties. It had Five Porches or Porticos, in which the Sick waited until the "waters were troubled by an Angel," upon which the first person who stepped in was healed of his malady. (Jno. v. 1—7.) Tertullian says this miraculous virtue ceased after the Jews had rejected and crucified Messiah.

THE POOL OF BATHSHEBA.—Within the Jaffa Gate, on the left as you enter, over against the Castle of David, is a vacant field, enclosed by a rugged stone wall, in which is a Cistern, supposed to be that in which Bathsheba bathed when she was seen by the King. (2 Sam. xi. 2.)

THE BUILDINGS OF JERUSALEM.

THE MOSQUE OF OMAR unquestionably stands upon the site of the Temple, and is partly constructed with materials of its ruins. It is an octagonal building, the lower part being composed of white marble, and the upper part faced with glazed porcelain of various colours. From the octagonal elevation rises its grand Dome with enamelled tiles wrought into patterns of wondrous intricacy and grace, in which all the hues of the rainbow glitter in the sunbeams like a bright and gorgeous vision of a fairy-land. Thus, "the Mountain of the House is become as the High Place of the forest," by the substitution of the Mahometan superstition for the ancient worship of Israel. (Mic. iii. 12.) It was formerly forbidden to any but a Mussulman to enter this building. Sir Sidney Smith is reported to have presented himself at the head of his followers, and when asked to produce the *firman* for his admission, replied that he himself was Sultan and required no firman! Dr. Richardson also contrived to enter the Mosque, and gives a minute description of it in his Travels. There is, however, at present, no difficulty of obtaining admission—a fee being a sufficient passport.

THE MOSQUE EL-AKSA, next to the Mosque of Omar, is the finest building in Jerusalem. Its graceful proportions and noble Dome crown the very summit of Moriah, standing, as it does, close to the South-West corner of the Harem. Oriental Christians and Gallic Catholics agree in regarding this as having been once the Church of the Virgin. Travellers, artists, and architects, generally concur in this opinion.

The Harem, or Temple Enclosure, which is almost equal in extent to one-eighth of the City, and beautiful as it is extensive, surrounds these Mosques. The Walls are at once massive and lofty. The spaces are covered with fresh green grass, dotted with dusky olives, tapering cypresses, and other forms of vegetation. Marble Fountains also adorn the place. And there is a broad elevated Platform encircled by airy Arches, and diversified with richly-carved Pulpits, Prayer-Niches, and graceful miniature Cupolas. This splendid Enclosure, with its Buildings and general arrangements, is the chief ornament of the City.

The Church of the Holy Sepulchre is composed of three Churches; that of the Holy Sepulchre properly so called; that of Calvary; and the Church of the Discovery of the Holy Cross. The first is built in the Valley at the foot of Calvary, on the spot where it is believed the body of Christ was deposited. This Church is in the form of a cross, the Chapel of the Holy Sepulchre constituting, in fact, the Nave of the edifice. It is circular like the Pantheon at Rome, and is lighted only by a Dome, underneath which is the Sepulchre. Sixteen marble Columns adorn the circumference of this Rotunda; they are connected by seventeen Arches, and support an upper Gallery, likewise composed of sixteen Columns and seventeen Arches, of smaller dimensions than those of the lower range. Niches, corresponding with the Arches, appear above the Frieze of the second Gallery, and the Dome springs from the Arch of these Niches. The latter were formerly decorated with mosaics, representing the Twelve Apostles, St. Helena, the Emperor Constantine, and three other portraits unknown. The Choir is to the East of the Nave of the Tomb; it is double as in the ancient Cathedrals, that is to say, it has first a place with Stalls for the Priests, and beyond that a Sanctuary raised two steps above it. Round this double Sanctuary run the Aisles of the Choir, and in these Aisles are situated the Chapels. In the Aisle on the right, behind the Choir, are two Flights of Steps, leading, the one to the Church of Calvary, the other to the Church of the Discovery of the Holy Cross. The first ascends to the top of Calvary, the second conducts you underneath it; for the Cross was erected on the summit of Golgotha, and said to be found under that hill.

THE SEPULCHRE, or Tomb of our Lord, is in the centre of the Rotunda, and resembles a small closet hewn out of the solid rock. The Entrance, which faces the East, is only four feet high, and two feet and a quarter broad, so that you are obliged to stoop low when you go in. The interior of the Sepulchre is nearly square. It is six feet, wanting an inch, in length; six feet, wanting two inches, in breadth; and eight feet one inch from the floor to the roof. A solid Block of the same stone, which was left in excavating the other part, two feet four inches and a half high, occupies half of the Sepulchre. On this Table the body of our Lord was laid, with the head towards the West; but, on account of the superstitious devotion of the Orientals, who imagine that if they leave their hair upon this stone, God will never forsake them, and also because pilgrims broke off pieces, it has received a covering of white marble. This now serves as an Altar for the celebration of Mass. Forty-four lamps are constantly burning in this sacred place, and three holes have been made in the roof for the emission of smoke. The exterior of the Sepulchre is also faced with slabs of marble, and adorned with several columns, having a dome above.

At the entrance of the Sepulchre there is a Stone about a foot and a half square, and a foot thick, which is of the same rock, and served to support the Large Stone which closed the access. Upon this stone was seated the Angel who spake to the two Marys:

And as well on account of this mystery, as to prevent the Sepulchre from being entered, the early Christians erected before it a little Chapel, which is called "The Angel's Chapel."

Twelve paces from the Holy Sepulchre, turning towards the North, you come to a large Block of grey Marble, about four feet in diameter, placed there to mark the spot where our Lord appeared to Mary Magdalene. Here also is the "Chapel of the Apparition," where the Franciscans perform their devotions, and to which they retire, passing into chambers with which there is no other communication.

As you leave the Tomb you come to the Stone of Unction, on which the body of our Lord was anointed with myrrh and aloes, before it was laid in the Sepulchre. Some say this is of the same rock as Mount Calvary; and others assert that it was brought to this place by Joseph and Nicodemus. This also is covered with white marble because of the indiscretion of Pilgrims in breaking pieces off; and it is surrounded with iron railings lest people should walk over it. The stone is 8 feet wanting 3 inches in length, and 2 feet less 1 inch in breadth; and above it there used to be eight lamps kept continually burning; but these are now replaced by six tapers standing inside the rails, each of which is nearly as large as a human body.

In another place there is a Stone which, we are solemnly assured, was that rolled away from the door of the Sepulchre. In another there is a Pillar affirmed to be that to which Jesus was bound when scourged. They likewise shew the Hole into which the Saviour's feet were placed during that part of His humiliation; the Prison into which He was thrust when brought from the House of Caiaphas; the Place in which the Crown of Thorns was put upon His head; and that where the soldiers parted His garments. Before these Relics, imaginary or real, Pilgrims in scores bow down; and they kiss them with ecstasy.

THE CHAPEL OF HELENA.—Descending a few steps we reach the Chapel of Helena, mother of Constantine the first Christian Emperor, built over the Place, where, during that lady's visit to Palestine, the "True Cross" was discovered. That a Cross was found there, is not doubted; but it is not clear that the Priests had not first buried it, and then, in Helena's presence, dug it up. They had a strong inducement to perpetrate this "pious fraud" as she had promised to build a Church upon whatever spot the Cross upon which the Redeemer suffered, might be discovered.

They have likewise found the Manger in which the Infant Jesus was laid; the Table upon which the Last Supper was celebrated, with a variety of things beside by which they wrought miracles upon the credulity of that Lady.

Ascending from the Chapel, a Hole in the rock is shewn, in which they say the Cross was fixed; and about a yard and a half distant is a Rent in the Rock, which extends downwards out of sight, but may be examined in the Vault below. Certainly this was not artificially produced, for the sides fit like tallies, and yet run in such intricate windings as art could not counterfeit; and there is no reason why the tradition, that it was caused by the Earthquake which happened at our Lord's passion, should not be believed. But God in His infinite wisdom has concealed the exact spot as He concealed the body of Moses. No one will deny that the Apostles and Disciples of our Lord who dwelt at Jerusalem, knew the place of their Master's crucifixion, and the Sepulchre of His burial; but there is no evidence in the New Testament that these Places were in any way honoured. On the contrary, the whole spirit of the Gospel of Christ tended to withdraw men from an attachment to Times, Places, and Physical Objects, and to lead them to a Spiritual Worship. The theme of Paul's preaching was the Death and Resurrection of our Lord; but though he laboured and wrote for some five and thirty years after these events, and though he visited Jerusalem more than once during that time, he makes no allusion to the Scenes or Instruments of the Saviour's passion. It is pretty clearly established that the Apostle John wrote his Gospel towards the close of the First Century, or from sixty to seventy years after the Crucifixion, yet he only alludes to the Sepulchre in general terms. It is thus sufficiently apparent that in the Apostolic Age, no importance was attached, no honour given, to Holy Places. Whether the Redeemer died here or was buried there are things of secondary consequence; the grand question is *Did He suffer death and rise again* FOR ME?

> "Alas! and did my Saviour bleed?
> And did my Saviour die?
> Would He devote that sacred head
> For such a worm as I?
>
> "Was it for crimes that I had done
> He groaned upon the tree?
> Amazing pity! grace unknown!
> And love beyond degree.
>
> "Well might the sun in darkness hide,
> And shut his glory in,
> When God the mighty Maker died
> For man, His creatures' sin.
>
> "Thus might I hide my blushing face,
> While His dear Cross appears;
> Dissolve my heart in thankfulness,
> And melt my eyes in tears."

The Church of the Holy Sepulchre is now occupied by Latin, Greek, Armenian, Coptic, Abyssinian, and other Christian Sects, who hate each other with a perfect aversion; and is the common centre of devotion, imposture, and superstition.

THE CONVENT OF ST. JAMES *(St. Giacomo)*, belonging to the Armenians, stands on that part of Mount Zion which is still within the Walls. It is of vast circumference, and is esteemed the most wealthy in the Levant. We are assured that it stands upon the spot where James was martyred, and the Ashes of the Apostle are amongst the various curiosities it contains. The Walls are pannelled with porcelain; and one of the Side Chapels has two doors covered with Mother-of-Pearl. It is a prevailing custom to adorn the Walls of Churches with white and blue China Plates, which are far from prepossessing; but the appearance of the Mother-of-Pearl inlays on a dark ground, is effective. Dozens of Ostrich-eggs are suspended from various parts of this building; and there are many Paintings upon the Walls.

I was domiciled with a young gentleman from London, the son of a widow, and of a Protestant family, who had earned a Fellowship worth £200 a year, but, to the great grief of his friends, sacrificed all in order to embrace the faith of Rome. This young gentleman was with me in the Armenian Church, and, wishing to engage him in argument, I pointed to a remarkable work of art, and asked—

"Who do those figures in that picture represent?"

"Our Lord and our Lady," was the response.

"Why do you give the Mother a title equal to that of her Divine Son?"

"It is the Lord Himself who does that!"

"When and where?"

"On the Cross, when He said, 'Woman, behold thy Son'—then referring to the Virgin and St. John. The term for 'woman' in the original signifies 'Lady, or Queen'—the Queen of Heaven."

"You must know better. It signifies nothing of the kind. Did He not give the same title to the woman taken in adultery?—'*Woman*, where are thine accusers?' Why, then, do you not Crown the latter as well as the former, and place them side by side upon the Throne of Heaven?"

To this he made no reply, so I proceeded:—

"Do you never reflect that the Saviour constantly addresses the Virgin by this term 'Woman,' as He would address any ordinary female, and that she is but seldom mentioned either by Him or His Apostles; as if to protest against the idolatry of which you and many others are guilty?"

Unable to release himself by fair reasoning, he fell back upon the old refuge, "No Scripture is of private interpretation," and "We must *believe the Church!*"

THE TOWER OF DAVID now forms a portion of a Castle, upon whose ramparts there are a few rusty guns.

It has its name probably from the fact that David built a Tower here, upon the Site of which Herod erected the present Structure. It is hence also denominated the Tower of Hippicus. The name of David may have been associated with it because of its position on the Stronghold of Zion, which that Monarch took from the Jebusites. (2 Sam. v. 7.) For some are of opinion that the predecessor of the present structure was a Tower built by Solomon.

THE CŒNACULUM.—On the brow of the hill now called Mount Zion, a conspicuous minaret marks the Mosque of the Tomb of David. Within the precincts of that Mosque is a vaulted Gothic chamber, with which are associated a greater confluence of traditions than with any other place of like dimensions in Palestine. It is startling to hear that this is the Scene of the Last Supper, of the Meeting after the Resurrection, of the Miracle of Pentecost, of the Residence and Death of the Virgin, and of the Burial of Stephen. Upon this Stanley remarks, "If one might hazard a conjecture respecting the cause of such a concentration of traditions, some of them dating as far back as the fourth century, it would be this:—We know from Cyril and Epiphanius that a building existed on this spot claiming to be the only edifice which had survived the overthrow of the City by Titus. This building of unknown origin would naturally serve as an appropriate receptacle for all recollections which could not otherwise be attached to any fixed locality."

THE STREETS OF THE CITY.

The Streets of Jerusalem are mostly narrow, and the paving-stones uneven, hard as marble, and when rain falls, the paths are as if composed of bits of soap, so that a person walking is obliged to be careful as though he moved on ice. In the Jewish Quarter, which lies on the East of Zion, the lanes are particularly filthy and miserable—everywhere the Jews seem to bear the brand of the curse. Indeed that unfortunate people are the Low Irish of the wide-world. Though in the principal Bazaars there was activity, there seemed an air of deathliness over everything—no hilarity or vivacity, so that the words of the Prophet came to me with peculiar force.— "Then will I cause to cease from the Cities of Judah, and from the Streets of Jerusalem, the voice of mirth and the voice of gladness." (Jer. vii. 34.) Neither in Jerusalem, nor yet elsewhere in Palestine, have I seen or heard of a Carriage; in fact there are no roads upon which carriages could travel. The Houses are stone, irregularly built, and having cupolas upon the roofs—sometimes three or four upon a single residence. These invest the City with a picturesque appearance, at the same time that they serve to break the force of the Elements which are violent in the

Rainy Season. The flat roofs are weak, owing to a scarcity of timber, so these cupolas are thrown up from them. The rain-water which is collected from the roofs runs into deep chambers cut in the limestone rock, somewhat after the fashion of the reservoirs at Malta, and upon this supply the people mainly depend.

THE VIA DOLOROSO.—In returning from Gethsemane, at the corner of the Temple Enclosure, is a building, said to be erected on the site of Pilate's House, from which the Redeemer was led to Crucifixion. The Street leading from this place to Mount Calvary is called *Via Doloroso*, or, "Dolorous Way." It first rises gradually, but afterwards becomes much steeper, and runs through the City in a zigzag course. Near Pilate's House the lane is spanned by an ancient Arch, which is called "*Ecce Homo*," as from a window over this archway, the Priests say, Pilate exclaimed, "Behold the Man!" Another station is pointed out in which place Jesus sank under the weight of His Cross, whereupon it was transferred to the shoulders of Simon. In all there are *Eight Stations* in this Way, with each of which some legend is associated.

THE PLACE OF WAILING.—There is a small paved area between the low houses on the South-East of the Harem and the ancient Temple Wall. Here the Jews have for centuries been permitted to approach the precincts of the House of the Lord in which their ancestors worshipped. The remains of the Wall is in a fine state of preservation, though in some places it is much worn by the Kisses and Tears of many generations. A touching scene presents itself to the eye of a Stranger every Friday, when Jews of both sexes and of all ages, from all quarters of the Globe, raise a lamentation in melancholy concert over the desolations of their dishonoured Sanctuary. Old men may be seen tottering up to the massive stones, kissing them with fond rapture; burying their faces in the joints and cavities, while tears stream down their cheeks, and accents of deep sorrow burst from their trembling lips. Most feelingly do they repeat the pathetic words of the Psalmist: "O God, the Heathen are come into Thine Inheritance; Thy Holy Temple have they defiled; they have laid Jerusalem on heaps. We are become a reproach to our neighbours, a scorn and a derision to them that are round about us. How long, Lord? Wilt Thou be angry for ever? Shall Thy jealousy burn like fire?" (Psa. lxxix. 1, 4, 5.)

LEPERS.—It is generally believed that Lepers are excluded from the City; but they reside together in a few mud hovels just within the Zion Gate. They are, however, strictly confined to their own district. Those I saw, and I met many, were most deplorable objects—half-starved, wasted, and often deformed by disease. They have no means of subsistence but begging; and hence their cravings are irresistible. They marry amongst themselves, and their children, at from ten to fourteen, begin to shew symptoms of the plague. Lepers suffer little pain; but they are said to die by inches, though sometimes they attain the ages of 45 and 50 years.

Our Guide conducted us to a Chapel belonging to the Syrian Christians, said to occupy the site of the House of Mary, the mother of Mark. We were also shewn the House of Thomas; the House of Annas, the High Priest; the Prison of Peter—a Cave in the Rock; the House of Simon the Pharisee; the House of John, in which he and the Virgin resided after the Crucifixion, and many other places of Legendary interest.

POPULATION.—The Population of Jerusalem has been variously estimated; there being no authentic census; but the following numbers may be accepted as an approximation:—

Jews	6,400
Muslems	4,300
Greeks	2,000
Latins	1,100
Armenians	320
Protestants	300
Greek Catholics	300
Syrians, Copts, and Abyssinians	280
	15,000

THE TOMBS.

THE TOMB OF DAVID.—There is nothing more historically certain than that David and most of his successors upon the Throne of Israel were buried in Zion. Peter further states that the Sepulchre of that Monarch was identified in his days. (Acts ii. 29.) It is, therefore, not impossible that the place still shewn as the Tomb of David may be correctly indicated, particularly as Christians, Jews, and Mussulmans agree upon the point. The Mosque called the "Cœnaculum" is built over it, and it is strictly guarded by the Turks, so that we were not able to enter. A few years since, however, Sir Moses Montefiore, a wealthy Israelite, and Mr. Nicholayson, obtained admission by unsparingly bribing the Guard.

THE TOMB OF ZACHARIAS.—This Monument is said to have been constructed in honour of Zachariah, who was stoned in the Court of the Temple, in the reign of Joash. (2 Chron. xxiv. 21.) Our Lord speaks of the same Zacharias as having been slain "between the Temple and the Altar." (Matt. xxiii. 35.)

THE TOMB OF ST. JAMES lies a few paces North of that of Zacharias. Tradition says that the Apostle sought refuge here during the interval between the Crucifixion and Resurrection of our Lord.

THE TOMB OF ABSOLOM.—In the full belief that Absolom is buried in this Tomb, which lies in the Valley of Jehoshaphat, the Jews in passing cast stones upon it. This is to express their indignation against him for his unnatural rebellion against David. But did they reflect upon the words of our Lord, they might spare themselves this trouble, "He that is without sin among you let him first cast a stone." (John viii. 7.)

THE TOMB OF JEHOSHAPHAT is in the North-East angle of the excavated area round the Pillar of Absolom. Owing to the accumulation of rubbish, the pediment alone is visible. But Jehoshaphat "was buried with his fathers in the City of David" (1 Kings xxii. 50), from which place it is by no means probable that his remains should have been removed.

TOMBS OF THE PROPHETS.—Ascending the terraced side of Olivet for about a quarter of a mile in a South-East direction, we reach the "Tombs of the Prophets." They are situated between the foot path and the main road to Bethany. Their plan and style differ from all other tombs yet known in the vicinity of Jerusalem. They have no traces of inscriptions, sarcophagi, or remains of any kind, tending to throw the least ray of light upon their history or antiquity. Christ reminded the Pharisees that they "*Built* the Tombs of the Prophets" (Matt. xxiii. 29); but these relics are excavations.

THE TOMBS OF THE KINGS.—Travellers are generally agreed that this name is fictitious, and that the

Sepulchres, or rather Sepulchre, was the Tomb of Helena; but what authority they have for the latter assumption does not appear.

TOMBS OF THE JUDGES.—These are at the head of the Valley of Jehoshaphat. The Judges were not all buried in this region, for Jeptha, Ibzan, Elon, Samson, and others, were certainly buried elsewhere. It is questionable whether a single individual of that ancient line of worthies found his last resting place here. Fully to examine these tombs, it is necessary to be provided with candles or torches.

THE GROTTO OF JEREMIAH is situated on the Southern side of the rocky hill, a short distance to the North-East of the Damascus Gate. It is a huge rude Cave, and has the appearance of an old quarry.

THE TOMB OF THE VIRGIN is not mentioned by Jerome amongst the Sacred Places visited by Paula; and, if the authority of Convocations is to be respected, it ought not to be found at Jerusalem, but at Ephesus, where it was placed by the Third General Council. The Legend which connects the burial with this place, though of later origin than the Decree, has had more respect. The Tomb of the Virgin, then, is situate at the foot of the Mount of Olives opposite the Garden of Gethsemane, and is covered by a Greek building, called "The Chapel of the Tomb of the Virgin."

THE TOMB OF ST. STEPHEN.—We have seen under

the head of *The Cœnaculum*, that amongst the many wonderful things shewn there, is a "Tomb of St. Stephen." But there is another "Tomb of St. Stephen" shewn to all who wish to believe it, outside St. Stephen's Gate. This Gate also has its name from the tradition that it was here the protomartyr was stoned. The precise spot on which he suffered is accordingly shewn, and that upon which Saul of Tarsus stood when he held the clothes of the young men.

THE PROTESTANT MISSION.

A brief account of the rise and progress of the Protestant Mission at Jerusalem may not be out of place here.

In 1814, an agreement was signed by the English and Prussian Governments to establish a Bishopric of the Anglical Church at Jerusalem, with a Diocese embracing Mesopotamia, Chaldea, Syria, Palestine, Egypt, and Abyssinia. It was stipulated that the Bishop should be alternately nominated by the Crowns of England and Prussia—the Archbishop of Canterbury having a *Veto* upon the nomination of the latter. It was agreed that special care should be taken not to disturb or divide the Churches already represented at Jerusalem, and that all Lutheran congregations should be supervised by a Clergyman ordained by the Bishop, and under his jurisdiction.

The King of Prussia gave the large sum of £15,000, the annual interest of which, £600, together with £600 raised in England, was to constitute the Episcopal revenue.

In pursuance of these arrangements, Michael Solomon Alexander, a Jewish Proselyte, was consecrated first Bishop of the United Church of England, Ireland, and Jerusalem, in the Autumn of 1841. In 1842, he laid the foundation of a neat Gothic Church, which now stands near to the Tower of David, on Mount Zion. While this edifice was in progress, in January, 1843, the Turkish authorities interfered, and would only consent to its completion upon condition that it should be attached to, and dependent upon, the Consulate. Such was the gratitude of the Sultan, who, but two years before, was indebted to the British arms for his possession of Syria. The Church is accordingly considered as an appendage of the Consulate.

Bishop Alexander died in 1845, and was succeeded by a Prussian Nominee, the present Prelate, Samuel Gobat, who was formerly a Missionary in Abyssinia.

The Services of this Church are as follow:—On Sunday there is, first at 7 A.M., a Service in Judæo-Spanish. At 10 A.M., another in English. And at 3 in the afternoon there is a Service in German, which alternates with that of the Luthern Church.

On Mondays, Wednesdays, and Fridays, at 6 P.M., the Service of the Church of England is read in Hebrew. There are also two public Prayer-Meetings held weekly in the adjoining School-Room, in which, during my sojourn, I had the privilege and happiness to take a part.

In connection with the Mission, there is an Hospital for Jews, containing thirty-six beds, under the management of a House-Steward and a Matron, together with two Surgeons—a Dispenser and an Assistant. This Institution has been of incalculable benefit to the poor suffering Israelites. There is also a Diocesan School, which was founded by Bishop Alexander, in 1845, and is supported partly by the London Jews' Society, and partly by private subscriptions. The Boys' School is on that part of Zion now outside the Walls, in a building lately erected. Here are from twenty to thirty boarders, and a number of day-scholars. There are under the Head Master, an Assistant English Master, and an Arab Teacher. The Girls' School is within the Walls, and contains a good number of day-scholars. There is likewise a House of Industry for Converts and Inquirers. Further, there is a School of Industry for Jewesses, under the management of Miss Cooper, which appears to be an excellent Institution. And there is a Prussian Hospital and Girls' School under the charge of four

Deaconesses, beside the Hospice for Travellers, of which we were so happy as to avail ourselves.

The number of Protestants in Jerusalem presided over by Bishop Gobat, who is a truly good man, is about 300. He is assisted by three Clergymen, Missionaries of the "Jews' Society," two Representatives of the "Church of England Missionary Society," and a Prussian Chaplain.

During my sojourn in Jerusalem, I repeatedly visited the Memorials of events the most intensely interesting to humanity which the universe presents, not to idolize, thank God, as many do, alas, but to admire and reflect with gratitude upon the Events. Pilgrims too commonly worship the "*Holy Places*," and "seek the living among the dead;" but in the final Conflagration these Relics are destined to be consumed, as of no intrinsic worth. Salvation is by Faith. Here "we see through a glass darkly." Even from the sacred enclosure of Gethsemane, or from the brow of Calvary, the spiritual vision is obscure. But once within the glorious walls of the New Jerusalem, I shall see "the King in His beauty"—I shall "see Him as He is"—

> "I'll view the Lamb in His own light,
>   Whom angels dimly see;
> And gaze transported at the sight
>   To all eternity."

CHAPTER VII.

PALESTINE—CONTINUED.

As in the Desert of Arabia, so in travelling through the interior of Palestine, it is necessary to have a written agreement with the Dragoman, signed and sealed by the Consul. The following is a copy of the document drawn between us and our worthy Guide :—

"*Agreement between John Brocklebank and John E. Plummer and Hanna Habesh.*

"Hanna Habesh undertakes to conduct John Brocklebank and John E. Plummer to Jericho, the Jordan, the Dead Sea, Hebron, Bethlehem, and back to Jerusalem.—Then to Samaria, Nazareth, Mount Tabor, Tiberias, and on to Mount Carmel, the Journey extending over eleven days, said Hanna Habesh paying all expenses, including Horses to ride upon, a Tent, with Sheikh, Cook, Board and Lodging, Buckshcesh, &c. In consideration of which, John Brocklebank and John E. Plummer engage to pay the sum of £33, one half at the time of starting, and the remainder on reaching Carmel.

"JOHN BROCKLEBANK,
"JOHN E. PLUMMER."

"Signed by the respective Parties in my presence, in Her Britannic Majesty's Consulate of Jerusalem.—This 26th day of February, 1863.
"JAMES FINN,
"H. B. M. Consul."

JERUSALEM TO JERICHO.

In the journey from Jerusalem to Jericho, an Escort is still necessary, lest the Traveller should "fall among Thieves," and need the services of some "Good Samaritan." Accordingly, in addition to our Dragoman, Cook, Waiter, Muleteers, and other travelling attendants, the Consul sent with us a Sheikh, mounted upon a splendid Arab Mare, and two Armed Men under his command.

ROADS TO BETHANY.—From Jerusalem to Bethany there are three Roads. The first takes a long circuit over the Northern Shoulder of the Mount of Olives, and down the Valley which parts it from Scopus. The second is a steep Footpath over the summit. The third winds round the base of the mountain by the Southern shoulder, and is the continuation of the Road from Jericho. Our Dragoman recommended us to issue by the first, and return by the last, that we might go out with David in his flight from Absolom, and return with the Saviour in his Triumphal Entry. Accordingly, we passed over the Brook Kedron, by Gethsemane, up the hill, and by the little Village of Tûr. The face of the hill is horizontally streaked with green and grey, viz., by the terraces of corn and ledges of limestone rock supporting them; and the whole is dotted with trim-looking olives, the successors of those from which the Mount derives its name.

BETHANY—HOME OF LAZARUS.

BETHANY.—About three quarters of a mile from the Village of Tûr, on the Eastern slope of Olivet, is a Hamlet, containing about twenty Mahometan families, called *El Azaricth*. This rests upon the site of the ancient Bethany, a place which has derived immortal interest from the fact that Jesus found a Home there during His visits to Jerusalem. For what Capernaum was to Him in Galilee, Bethany was in Judea. Hither He retired in the quiet evening after His arduous, though unappreciated, toil in the City, and found in the Family of Lazarus a congenial retreat —a fact expressing the highest commendation of that worthy person and his sisters. The place is beautifully situated on the slope of the Mount, surrounded by rocky ground once carefully terraced, and still containing a few Orchards of fig-trees. In the days of its glory the foliage of this neighbourhood must have been profuse. In the time of Ezra they "went forth unto the Mount, to fetch for the Feast of Tabernacles, Olive-branches and Pine-branches and Myrtle-branches, and Palm-branches, and branches of Thick-trees." (Neh. viii. 15.) Myrtle-trees also flourished in the same region. (Zech. i. 8—11.) From the profusion of its Palms it had its name, which signifies, "The House of Dates." There can be no difficulty therefore in determining whence the crowd obtained the Branches of Palm-trees" with which they went forth to meet Jesus, when "they cried, Hosanna,

Blessed is the King of Israel that cometh in the name of the Lord." (Jno. xii. 3.)

The House of Martha and Mary. — The Guide pointed out a Ruin not unlike the Castle at Scarbro', but considerably smaller, which he said was the "Castle of Lazarus." Whether this is indeed the remains of the Mansion in which Jesus was entertained it would be as difficult to prove. One can have little faith in stones and mortar professing an antiquity of two thousand years.

The Tomb of Lazarus.—At the bottom of a descent, not far from the "Castle," is shewn the "Sepulchre of Lazarus." It is a deep Vault, partly excavated in the rock, and partly lined with masonry. The entrance is low, and opens into a long winding series of steps, now in a dilapidated condition. Below is a small Chamber, out of which, by the descent of a few steps more, we are conducted to a Vault, in which the Body of Lazarus is supposed to have lain. It is not improbable that this is the identical Tomb.

On the further side of a deep Valley, away among the blue mountains, Jesus abode when the sisters sent to inform Him that Lazarus was sick. Along that dreary descent they looked with anxious expectation of His coming. On the old road outside the Village, Martha met Him, with the despairing, almost reproachful words, "Lord, if Thou hadst been here, my brother had not died."

The House of Simon the Leper, in which the grateful Mary anointed the feet of Jesus with precious ointment, and wiped them with the hair of her head, is pointed out for the edification of the credulous.

BETHPHAGE.—I inquired for the site of Bethphage; but no trace of it appears to have been discovered. A certain writer suggests that the way in which the names of "Bethany" and "Bethphage" are associated in the Evangelical Narrative, renders it probable that they designated different Quarters of the same Town. Thus the latter was called by a name signifying "The House of Figs," from the abundance of the Figs in the Orchards at that end, as the former had its name from its proximity to the Groves of Palms. (Com. Mark xi. 1; Luke xix. 29.)

THE SCENE OF OUR LORD'S ASCENSION certainly was not on the broad top of Olivet, in sight of Jerusalem, where Helena has built her Church to commemorate the event. It was in the vicinity of Bethany. Luke distinctly says, "He led His disciples out as far as Bethany, and was parted from them and carried up into heaven," after which, "they returned to Jerusalem." (Luke xxiv. 50—52.) They returned probably by the direct road over the summit, which fact may have suggested the idea that the Ascension took place there. (Acts i. 12.)

THE FOUNTAIN OF THE APOSTLES.—On leaving

Bethany, we cross a rocky ridge, and dive into a bleak glen, at the bottom of which is a fountain, called *Ain el Haud*. This was probably the *En-Shemesh* mentioned by Joshua, (Jos. xv. 7,) for the Valley is called by that name. The Spring is now styled "The Fountain of the Apostles," through a tradition that Christ and His Apostles often retired there to drink.

As our "Guard" had not yet joined us, we dismounted here to wait, not feeling very comfortable in so lonely a situation. But the Sheikh, with his men, soon came up, the former flourishing his old matlock with all the consequence of a Field Marshal. Confident in the protection of so redoubtable a personage, the cavalcade moved on.

The Way-Side Inn.—Passing down the glen, the road winds for an hour or more, and then leaving it to the right, opens into a broken country, and reaches an extensive ruined *Khan*, or Caravansary. This is supposed to be the wreck of the "Way-side Inn" alluded to in our Lord's parable of the Good Samaritan. (Luke x. 30—37.) In 1820, Sir F. Henniker was assaulted, stripped, wounded, and left for dead at this very place. Here we halted to take our luncheon; but our Arab Sheikh refused to eat, as it was then *Ramadan*, or the Ninth Month in the Mahometan year, during which all good Muslems so strictly fast, as not even to taste a drop of water from sunrise to sunset. They also refrain from smoking their pipes, which is to them, perhaps, a still greater self-denial.

THE WILDERNESS OF TEMPTATION.—On leaving the Khan, we enter a region even wilder than that through which we had just passed, supposed to have been the Wilderness into which Christ was "driven by the Spirit to be tempted of the devil." (Mark i. 12, 13.) All here is death-like desolation. Limestone mountains rise one above another without the slightest symptom of vegetation. Towering cliffs, overhanging crags, and yawning ravines, fill the mind with sentiments of awe. Often we were upon ledges so narrow, steep, and rugged, that a single slip of the horses' feet to the extent of a few inches would be sufficient to have dashed us headlong into a gaping chasm. Such roads could never be passed in safety by an English-trained horse; but former experience of the character of our animals relieved us from alarm. An ever watchful Providence protected us.

Maniacs wander in these wild passes, who are sometimes so "exceeding fierce that no man can pass" them. (Matt. viii. 28.) But such is the madness of superstition, that these poor creatures are regarded as Saints, and, therefore, permitted to be at large. It is an interesting fact that there should still exist in these desolate regions representatives of those

Lunatics so notorious in the history of the sojourn of Christ.

THE WADY EL KELT.—At length we came to the brink of one of the sublimest ravines in the Holy Land—a glen from four to five hundred feet deep between perpendicular walls of rock, through whose sides springs issue and flow into the dell. The sides of these steep cliffs are pierced with grottos, apparently inaccessible except to the eagles, which are seen hovering round them. Yet history declares that these were once the abodes of Hermits. The Brook in this Wady is supposed to have been the "Cherith" where Elijah was "fed by the ravens" when famine desolated the land of Israel. (1 Kings xvii. 1—7.) The Wady itself is unquestionably the Valley of Achor, stated to have been on the Northern border of Judah, in which Achan was stoned. (Jos. vii.)

THE PLAIN OF JERICHO.—As we proceed, the Great Plain suddenly opens, the green banks of the Jordan sloping into a kind of fissure, and the waters of the Dead Sea gleaming in the sunshine from the bosom of a cliff-bound coast, away on the right. Travelling through the Wilderness of Judea, the heat is intensified by the reflection of the solar rays from the limestone cliffs and soil; but on entering the Plain, the air seems like the blast of a furnace. We were painfully reminded that we were now 1,300 feet below the level of the Sea. The descent into the Plain is rapid and rough, and in some places would be dangerous but for stone fences thrown up on the brows of the cliffs.

JERICHO.

After crossing many foundations of buildings, fording streams, passing two aqueducts with pointed arches, and leaving the mountains at a distance of about two miles and a half, we pitched our tents at *Rihah*, a Village said to mark the site of the ancient Jericho. We ascended a Tower dignified by the name of the "House of Zacchæus," from the summit of which we had a full view of a place indescribably wretched. The cottages are roofed simply with branches and dried leaves, which serve to exclude sunshine, but afford no protection against a heavy shower. The hovels have no windows, the only aperture being a hole, about the size of the entrance to a moderate pig-sty, while the little yards outside are dens of filth and fleas. The population is entirely Mahometan, and is governed by a Sheikh. Their habits are those of Bedaween, and plunder is their chief and most gainful occupation. In the evening a number of them turned out to dance before our tent, and assumed such an air and attitude of wildness as one would expect to see amongst the savages of the South Pacific.

THE JERICHO OF THE CANAANITES is by Moses spoken of as the "City of Palm Trees;" and in our Lord's time the Palm-Grove of this region was seven miles long and nearly three broad. This, together with its famous Gardens of Balsamum, were given by Anthony to Cleopatra, for whom they were farmed by Herod the Great. This monarch also made the place one of his princely residences. The solitary relic of that Palm-Forest, seen as recently as 1838, has now disappeared. But such is the richness of the soil, and such the warmth of the climate, this district being about 1,500 or 2,000 feet below the mountains, that cotton, indigo, sugar, tobacco, everything in short which grows in Egypt, would flourish here. The City anciently seated in the midst of this fertile region, was the first taken by the Israelites after passing the Jordan. But Joshua demolished it, and then pronounced the following malediction:—
"Cursed be the man before the Lord that riseth up and buildeth this city Jericho: he shall lay the foundation thereof in his firstborn, and in his youngest son shall he set up the gates of it." (Jos. vi. 26.)

THE JERICHO OF HIEL.—The prediction of Joshua was literally accomplished 534 years after. In the days of Ahab "Hiel the Bethelite did build Jericho; and he laid the foundation thereof in Abiram, his firstborn, and set up the gates thereof in his youngest son Segub, according to the word of the Lord, which He spake by Joshua the son of Nun." (1 Kings xvi. 34.) This is the city mentioned in the Gospel history in connection with the ministry of our Lord; but it rested probably upon a different site from that upon which the village of Rihah stands. Mr. Buckingham has shewn out of Josephus that Jericho was a hundred and fifty furlongs (about nineteen miles) from Jerusalem, and sixty furlongs (seven miles and a half) from Jordan. But Rihah is full twenty-three miles from Jerusalem, and not more than three from the Jordan. The same intelligent traveller found a large square area, enclosed by regular mounds, uniform in height, breadth, and angle of slope, about four miles higher up the Valley, at least seven miles from the Jordan, which corresponds with the description of the Jewish historian. Upon that place, therefore, he has fixed as the site of the City of Hiel, in which conclusion he was confirmed by foundations of walls in detached pieces, portions of ruined buildings, several large *tumuli*, shafts of columns, and a capital of the Corinthian order, lying promiscuously about.

THE MODERN JERICHO.—Eusebius says that the city built by Hiel was destroyed by the Romans during the Siege of Jerusalem; and that standing in his time was a third, erected subsequently to the

Jewish war, and occupying a position different from either of its predecessors, for he states that the Ruins of the two former were then still shewn. It is probable that the Village of Rihah stands upon the site of this last city; and, therefore, there is some propriety in the statement of the Guides, viz., that it marks the place where Jericho stood.

THE QUARANTANIA.

Behind the "City of Palms" is the mountain range, to one of whose peaks the Spies fled, and concealed themselves from the vigilance of their pursuers, probably in one of the caverns with which its sides are perforated. (Jos. ii. 16, 22.) In later years these caves have afforded shelter to Hermits, who took up their abode there under the belief that it was the mountain of the "Forty Days of the Temptation"—the "Quarantania," from which it still derives its name. (Luke iv. 5.)

THE FOUNTAIN OF ELISHA flows at the base of the Quarantania, and contributes nourishment to the rich vegetation of the plain which opens so gratefully upon the vision. This remarkable Spring has its name from the belief that it was the same whose waters were healed by Elisha in connection with the casting in of salt. (2 Kings ii. 21.) Josephus says these waters "afford a sweeter nourishment than any others;" and they are certainly excellent.

JORDAN AND THE DEAD SEA.

THE JORDAN.—Leaving the meadows of the Plain of Jericho, and crossing the sandy Desert, which, by cultivation, might be speedily transformed into a "fruitful field," as there is an abundance of water, in about an hour, we came to the principal river of Palestine. Though narrow, it is a noble stream. It rises in the mountains of Anti-Lebanon, about twelve miles North of Cesaraea-Philippi, passes through the Lake of Gennesareth, and after a course of 160 miles, empties itself into the Dead Sea, at the rate of about seven millions of tons per day. The Jordan has an upper and a lower Bank, the latter of which is subject to inundation about the time of the harvest, after the latter rains. In this limited sense we are to understand the Biblical expression that the "Jordan overflowed its banks." (Jos. iii. 15; iv. 18; 1 Chro. xii. 15.) The water is turbid, but sweet and good. The Banks are lined with willows, tamarisks, oleanders, and other trees, and green bushes fill the spaces so as to form a jungle. Here wild boars, leopards and Bedaween robbers, harbour; and our Sheikh accordingly warned us to keep very near to him.

The part of the stream upon which we descended is supposed to be the place where Jesus was baptized. It is also believed to have been the place at which the Israelites crossed when the waters were driven back and stood on a heap. Perhaps here, likewise, Elijah divided the stream, and passed over to the bank from which he stepped into the Chariot of Fire, and rode into Heaven upon the wheels of a whirlwind. Here, therefore, Pilgrims who visit Jerusalem at Easter, come in a body to bathe, and rush in promiscuously, men and women. Upon these occasions many are carried away by the force of the current and drowned. The river was not flushed when I visited it, nevertheless the current was then very great. The Pilgrims generally bring with them white bathing dresses, using the same from year to year, and finally serve as their winding sheets. The stream at this point is from 80 to 100 feet across, and the depth from 10 to 12 feet; higher up, in some places, it is full 150 feet broad.

The Mountains of Moab and Ammon, with Pisgah, upon which Moses stood to view the Land of Promise, and Peor, on which Balaam was solicited by the King of Moab to curse the people of God, stretch away in the distance beyond.

THE DEAD SEA.—To gain the Dead Sea by following the course of the Jordan would be circuitous, so we passed over sands and sand-banks through a country totally destitute of verdure, and in about an hour and a half reached the Mysterious Lake. It is perhaps the most remarkable sheet of water in the world. Its length is forty miles; its greatest breadth is eight and a half, and it gradually narrows to about five miles at the Northern extremity. Its waters are very nauseous, as they hold in solution vast quantities of muriate of lime, magnesia, and soda. These elements so increase the specific gravity of the waters, that it is impossible to sink in them. Mr. Plummer tested this. Upon coming out his body was covered with a white precipitate of salt. The water itself, however, is clear as crystal. Fish are never found alive in this Lake; but they are often seen dead near the mouth of the Jordan, by whose current they had been forced into this uncongenial element. The statements are unfounded that animals cannot live upon the borders of this Lake, and that birds flying over it will fall dead into its waters. We observed many birds flying over it and about its banks without appearing to suffer the slightest injury. There is no outlet from the Dead Sea, so that the quantity of water evaporated from its surface must be equal to that received from the Jordan, the Arnon, and other streams that fall into it.

The Soil of the Vale of Siddim, which is now covered with the Dead Sea, or Lake Asphaltites, as, on account of the vast quantities of bitumen with which its water are impregnated, it is designated by Josephus and the Greek and Roman Writers, was anciently "full of slime pits," or, more properly, pits of *bitumen*, for such is the sense of the word in the original. (Gen. xiv. 10.) That the soil was also in a state of combustion is suggested by the fact that when Abraham "looked toward Sodom and Gomorrah and toward all the land of the Plain, and behold and lo, the smoke of the country *went up* as the smoke of a furnace." (Gen. xix. 28.) Josephus also speaks of occasional eruptions of flame and smoke from the soil of that neighbourhood in his days; and Volney, Burkhardt, Buckingham, and other travellers, speak of hot springs and volcanic substances, consisting of lava, sulphur, and basalt, still in the vicinity of the Lake. By volcanic means, then, it is highly probable the whole Vale of Siddim, with its cities, viz., Sodom, Gomorrah, Admah, and Zeboim, were sunk and destroyed, while fiery meteors from heaven were rained upon them. Bannister thinks that this depression of the land diverted the Jordan from its original course which he supposes to have been through an opening, still visible, leading into the Valley *El Ghor*, which descends uninterruptedly through *El Araba*, to the Elanitic Gulf of the Red Sea.

Josephus, employing a poetic expression, says, that he saw on the banks of the Lake the shades of the overwhelmed Cities. The Ruins of Sodom are mentioned by Tacitus and Strabo, the latter of whom gives them a circumference of sixty *Stadia*—about seven miles. Father Nau, the Guardian, and the

Procurator of Jerusalem, both men in years, and to Maundrell "seemingly not destitute either, of sense or probity," informed him that they had once actually seen one of these Ruins. They say that the waters were then so low, that they, together with some Frenchmen, went to it, and found there several Pillars and other fragments of buildings. But the height of the waters prevents travellers in general from seeing these Ruins. Those who have seen them were favoured with seasons of peculiar drought, when the depth and volume of the waters are diminished by copious evaporation. Saline waters do not decompose and destroy, but, on the contrary, harden and preserve organic bodies. If the branch of a tree, or the bone of an animal fall into this Lake, it becomes petrified. The testimony of these weighty authorities, therefore, need not be despised.

This "deep caldron,"—150 feet below the level of the Mediterranean,—is in the Bible variously called the "Salt Sea," the "East Sea," and the "Sea of the Plain;" while the Arabs style it *Bahhr Lout*, or the "Sea of Lot." Its shores are completely sterile, surrounded as they are by high limestone cliffs, with a burning sun above, and a bitter flood beneath. On the South is a hill called the "Salt Mountain," which is composed of rock-salt, but too bitter to be used. Indeed all the hills are more or less incrusted with crystals of salt and sulphur, which sparkle under the beam of the sun.

Most travellers remain a night at the Greek Convent of *San Saba;* but the English Vice-Consul having been murdered in that vicinity a few days before, the inhabitants were in such a state of excitement, that our Sheikh said it would not be safe to venture that way. We, therefore, made a detour to the West, in order to return to Jerusalem. Our way lay through another portion of the "Wilderness of Temptation," over limestone hills, during which, from the eminences, ever and anon, we caught sight of the Dead Sea, which, with the increasing distance, gradually appeared less until it disappeared. Onward we moved up and down the mountains, like ships upon the stormy waves, and at length we came to Bethany, which we entered at the Northern side.

THE TRIUMPHAL WAY.

Passing out of Bethany, we were reminded that the road upon which we travelled was rendered sacred by the fact that upon it Christ had ridden in triumph to Jerusalem. The crowds who had assembled at the Village on the previous night to satisfy their curiosity respecting the miracle of raising Lazarus, naturally flocked into this road, which was the main thoroughfare round the Southern shoulder of Olivet.

In passing along this road, we soon lose sight of Bethany, and circumambulating the little Valley that furrows the hill, we cross a ridge on the Western side, where the first glimpse of Jerusalem is seen. Here probably "as He drew near, at the descent of the Mount of Olives," the shout was raised by the multitude, "Hosannah to the Son of David! Blessed is He that cometh in the name of the Lord." (Matt. xxi. 9.) As we proceeded, the road declines, and the City is concealed behind the ridge of the Mount; but the path rises again, and after a rugged acclivity, crowns the ledge of a smooth rock. In an instant the whole City bursts into full view. Historians, with great probability, say that here the multitude paused, and "He, when He beheld the City, wept over it." (Luke xix. 41.) It is impossible to describe the feelings which came over my mind as I trode those hallowed pathways, which had been repeatedly traversed by Prophets and Apostles, and by the ONE infinitely greater.

We dropped down the hill by a shelving path, having on our left a vast multitude of Jewish Tombs paving the declivity; and near the foot of the descent we skirted the wall of Gethsemane, then passing over the Kedron, ascended to St. Stephen's Gate, and thence, winding round the City Walls, came to an open space, where we spread our tents for the night.

When on the point of leaving Bethany, our Lord directed two of His disciples to "Go into a Village over against them." (Matt. xxi. 2, 3.) The question arises—Where was this Village situate? Some identify it with a poor Hamlet upon a rocky height, about a mile South of Bethany. But a quarter of a mile from Bethany, on the way to Jerusalem, there is a projecting point, some 200 yards below the road, upon which the site of an ancient village is marked by scarped rocks, cisterns, and stones. The claims of this seem preferable, as it lies more in the Saviour's route, and answers more truly to the expression "over against you." Besides, being close to the road, the inhabitants would already have seen the multitudes flocking from the City to meet Jesus, and the owners of the ass and colt would understand the disciple's words, "The Lord hath need of them."

JERUSALEM TO HEBRON.

The Clergyman with whom we had been domiciled at the Hospice breakfasted with us in our tent on the morning of the 11th, and joined us in praising God for His gracious care over us in a foreign land. At half-past eight we struck our tents, and were on our way to Hebron.

THE PLAIN OF REPHAIM.—Leaving the frowning walls of the Citadel, we crossed the opposite bank, skirted the "Hill of Evil Counsel," and entered a well cultivated plain, about a mile in length. This is the "Plain of Rephaim," in which David vanquished the Philistines, and which is also called "The Valley of the Giants." (2 Sam. v. 18—25; Jos. xv. 8.)

MAR ELIAS.—The Plain opens into the well cultivated fields of the Greek Christians, in which stands the Convent of Elias,—a large gray pile surrounded by a high wall. Here, according to tradition, the Prophet reclined beneath the shade of an olive, careworn, hungry, and weary, as he fled from the fury of Jezebel, and was comforted and nourished by the ministry of Angels. The Bible says that he rested under a juniper in the Wilderness South of Beersheba, at least fifty or sixty miles distant from this place; but of course the Monks know best!

THE SEPULCHRE OF RACHEL.—Passing down a steep hill on the side of the road, about a half-hour's journey from the Convent, a small white square building, surmounted by a cupola, was pointed out to us as the "Sepulchre of Rachel." The present structure is comparatively modern, but there can be no doubt respecting the site, since it is one of the few things upon which the traditions of Jews, Muslems, and Christians agree. The Tomb, as Jacob left it, remained in the time of Moses, who speaks of it in the following terms: "And Rachel died, and was buried in the way to Ephrath, which is Bethlehem, and Jacob set a pillar upon her grave: that is the pillar of Rachel's grave unto this day." (Gen. xxxv. 19, 20.) That pillar has given place to other monumental forms; but the roll of thirty centuries has not oblivioned the site so dear to the memory of the posterity of Rachel. Bethlehem is seen at a distance of about a mile,—a fact which enhances the beautifully poetic description of the Shade of Rachel rising from the Sepulchre to wail over the Massacred Innocents. (Jer. xxxi. 15; Matt. ii. 17, 18.)

SOLOMON'S POOLS.—Leaving Bethlehem on the left, in about an hour and a half, we next come to three deep Reservoirs, supplied by very powerful springs of excellent water, which is thence conveyed by Aqueducts to Bethlehem and Jerusalem. Dr. Robinson measured these Reservoirs, and describes the lower one as 582 feet by 207 at one end, and 148 at the other. Its companions are not quite so large. They are constructed of stone, covered with cement, and bear unmistakeable evidence of a high antiquity. Few doubt that they are the works of Solomon, who probably refers to these and the Gardens surrounding them in the following expressions:—"I made me Gardens and Orchards, and I planted Trees in them of all kinds of fruits; and I made me Pools of Water, to water therewith the wood that bringeth forth trees." (Ecc. ii. 5, 6.) The water flows into the upper Pool from the Springs, and thence the middle and lower Pools are successively supplied.

This place, together with a little Village below, is supposed to be the *Elam* referred to in Judg. xv. 8, 11; and *Tekoa* (2 Chro. xi. 6) is not far off. Many places and things of minor interest lay in our way which I have omitted to notice, not wishing to be too minute.

HEBRON.

ENCAMPMENT.—After being seven hours and a half on the Saddle, we reached the usual place of encampment, outside the walls of Hebron. It is an open plot of ground near to which are two Wells, that nearest the Town being approached by a flight of steps from each corner of a square opening. Both Wells are evidently very ancient, and doubtless one of them was that over which David hung the bodies of Rechab and Baanah who had slain Ish-bosheth the son of Saul. (2 Sam. iv. 12.) Soon after we had pitched our tents here, the Governor, accompanied by one of his friends, politely waited upon us, and conversed freely with our Interpreter respecting the Strangers under his guidance.

HISTORY OF HEBRON.—The most ancient name of Hebron was *Kirjath-Arba*, or the "City of Arba," from ARBA the father of Anak and of the Anakim who dwelt in that district. (Gen. xxiii. 2.) It appears also to have been called *Mamre*, probably from the name of Abraham's Amoritish ally. It was one of the most ancient cities, having been built "seven years before Zoan in Egypt." (Num. xiii. 22.) The Hebrew Patriarchs spent much of their time in this neighbourhood; were all entombed here, and from this place the patriarchal family departed for Egypt. After the return of the Israelites. the city was taken by Joshua and given over to Caleb, who expelled the Anakim. It was subsequently made one of the Cities of Refuge, and assigned to the Priests and Levites. David on becoming king made Hebron his royal residence. Here he reigned seven years and a half over the tribe of Judah, and thence removed to Jerusalem when his kingdom extended over all Israel. In process of time this city fell under the power of the Edomites, who had taken possession of the South of Judah, but was recovered from them by Judas Maccabæus. (1 Macc. v. 65.) John the Baptist is supposed to have been born here. Soon after the Crusaders had taken Jerusalem, Hebron also appears to have passed into their hands, in 1100, and was bestowed as a fief upon Gerhard of Avennes; but two years after it is described as being in ruins. In 1167, it was made a Bishopric, and the title of "Bishop of Hebron" is found in the records of the Romish Church as late as 1365, though, it was merely nominal, for after the capture of Jerusalem by Saladin in 1187, Hebron reverted to the Muslems, and has ever since remained in their possession.

The Town lies low down on the sloping sides of the narrow Valley of Mamre. The Houses are stone, high and well built, with windows and flat roofs, and on these roofs small domes, sometimes two or three to each house. The streets are narrow, seldom more than six or eight feet in width, dark, dirty, and difficult. The Bazaars are to a considerable extent covered, either by some kind of awning, or by arches springing from the tops of the houses. The Shops are well furnished with commodities similar to those exposed in Egypt, the only display of local manufacture being the produce of the Glass Works, for which the place has long been celebrated in these parts. Gates are placed, not only at the entrance, but in different parts of the interior of the City, and are closed at night to prevent communication between the different quarters. There are nine Mosques in Hebron, none of which possesses any architectural or antiquarian interest, with the exception of the massive structure built over the Tombs of the Patriarchs.

The Cave of Machpelah, containing the Tombs of Abraham, Isaac, and Jacob, with those of Sarah, Rebecca, and Leah, according to a tradition amongst the Jews, was surrounded by a building, the foundations of which still remain. Upon these Helena erected a Church, about the year 326, which afterwards was converted into the present famous Mosque of Hebron, and is one of the Four Sanctuaries of the Mahometan World. It is a long black building, having two stately domes. Ali Bey, a Spaniard, who travelled as a Muslem, and Giovanni Finati, the Italian servant of Mr. Banks, contrived to gain access to the Mosque, from which Christians have been rigorously excluded. The Prince of Wales, however, has lately been permitted to enter. The Rev. V. Monro furnishes an account of the interior, without, however, stating the means by which he obtained his information. He says "the dimensions within are about forty paces by twenty-five. Immediately on the right of the door is the Tomb of Sarah, and beyond it is that of Abraham, with a passage between them. Corresponding with these, on the opposite side of the Mosque, are those of Isaac and Rebecca, and behind them is a Recess for Prayer, and a Pulpit. These Tombs resemble small huts, with a window on each side, and folding-doors in front, the lower parts of which are wood, and the upper of iron or bronze bars plated. Within each of these is an imitation of the Sarcophagus, which lies in the Cave below the Mosque, which no one is allowed to enter. Those seen above resemble Coffins, with pyramidal tops, and are covered with green silk, lettered with verses from the Koran. In the Mosque is a Baldacchin, supported by four columns, over an octagonal figure of black and white marble, inlaid round a small hole in the pavement, through which a chain passes from the top of the canopy to a lamp continually burning to give light in the Cave of Machpelah, where the actual Sarcophagi rest. At the upper end of the court is the chief Place of Prayer; and at the opposite side of the Mosque are two larger Tombs, where are deposited the bodies of Jacob and Leah."

The Tomb of Esau is behind the Mosque, he not being privileged to lie among his relatives. It is covered with a small cupola, having eight or ten windows.

The Population of Hebron is probably about 8,000. There are no resident Christians. The Jews amount to about one hundred families, mostly natives of European countries, who have immigrated for the purpose of laying their bones near the Sepulchres of their illustrious ancestors. They have two Synagogues and several Schools. As usual, they have a "Quarter" of the City to themselves, where the streets are narrow and filthy, and the houses mean.

HEBRON TO BETHLEHEM.

Eshcol.—Vineyards abound in Judea more than elsewhere in Palestine. Hence the propriety of the blessing pronounced by Jacob upon his favoured son. "Binding his foal to the vine, and his ass's colt to the choice vine, he washed his garments in wine, and his clothes in the blood of grapes." (Gen. xlix. 11.)

It was from the Valley of Eshcol that the spies cut down the gigantic bunch; and this Valley is still remarkable for the quality of its vines. (Num. xiii. 23, 24.)

ABRAHAM'S OAK.—After riding along this fruitful Valley for about twenty-five minutes, we came up to to the so-called "Abraham's Oak." It stands alone in the midst of vineyards; the ground is smooth and clean beneath it, and close by is a well, but now filled with brushwood. This splendid tree measures 23 feet round the lower part of the trunk, and its foliage covers a space of nearly 90 feet in diameter. Though evidently of great age, it is sound and flourishing, and there are few trees in Syria to be compared with it. The great Plane-tree of Damascus is nearly double its girth; but it has suffered much, both from the hand of man and the tooth of time. Though we have no history of this venerable tree, it is a fine representative of the "Oaks of Mamre," under whose shade Abraham communed with his Creator and entertained Angels.

Following that ancient road to Jerusalem, though rugged and rough, the ground was holy as having been traversed by Patriarchs and Prophets. Abraham passed over it in his journey to Moriah to sacrifice his Isaac in faithful obedience to the voice of God. David led his veterans over it when he

BETHLEHEM

advanced to storm and take the strongholds of Zion. And probably the infant Jesus was borne over this road in the Virgin's arms in flight to Egypt from the cruelty of Herod. To English eyes the country may look wild, yet the prospects are beautiful, as they are varied by hills and dales, craggs and sheltered nooks, rugged glens and level plains. Every prospect of beauty opened once to the eyes of the Hebrew Patriarchs, to Samuel, to David, and to Solomon. The cities in which they sojourned are indeed heaps of ruins; but the broad features of nature remain. Onward we moved, until at length Bethlehem hove in sight, and appeared a very pretty town; but experience led us to presume that

"'Tis distance lends enchantment to the view."

BETHLEHEM.

BETHLEHEM, or the "House of Bread," was probably so called on account of the fertility of the District in which it stood. It was also called *Ephrath* or *Ephrata*, that is, "The fruitful," after Caleb's wife; and "The City of David," because that Monarch was born there; also "Bethlehem of Judea," to distinguish it from another Bethlehem in the Tribe of Zebulun. (Gen. xlviii. 7; Mic. v. 2; Lu. ii. 4; Matt. ii. 1, 5.) Here David spent his early years in the humble occupation of a Shepherd; until his encounter with Goliath opened to him a more glorious career. Here also were born Abijam, Elimelech, Obed, Jesse, Boaz, and Matthias; and here is the Scene of the beautiful Eclogue of Ruth. But that which gives this place preeminence, Jerusalem excepted, is, that here the Son of the Highest condescended to be born in humbleness and poverty.— "And thou Bethlehem-Ephratah, though thou be little among the thousands of Judah, yet out of thee shall He come forth unto Me, that is to be Ruler in Israel, whose goings forth have been from of old, from Everlasting." (Mic. v. 2.)

The Church of the Nativity has been built over the place where this stupendous event is supposed to have transpired. It is built in the form of a Cross; the Nave being adorned with forty-eight Corinthian Pillars in four rows, each column being two feet six inches in diameter, and eighteen feet high, including the base and the capital. The Nave is separated from the three other branches of the Cross by a Wall, so that the Unity of the Edifice is destroyed. The top of the Cross is occupied by the Choir. Here is an Altar dedicated to the Wise Men of the East, at the foot of which is a marble Star, corresponding, as the Monks say, to the point of the heavens where the miraculous Meteor became stationary, and directly over the spot where the Saviour was born.

The Grotto of the Nativity.—A flight of fifteen

steps, and a long narrow passage conduct to the sacred Crypt or "Grotto of the Nativity," which is 37½ feet long by 11¼ broad and 9 feet high. It is lined and floored with Marble, and provided on each side with five Oratories, "answering precisely to the Ten Cribs or Stalls for Horses that the Stable in which our Saviour was born contained." (!) The exact spot of the Birth is marked by a "Glory" in the floor, composed of marble and jasper encircled with silver, around which are inscribed the words, HIC DE VIRGINE MARIA JESUS CHRISTUS NATUS EST,—*Here Jesus Christ was born of the Virgin Mary.* The Vault is lighted by lamps and tapers in considerable numbers. Over the "Glory" is a Marble Table, or Altar, which rests against the side of the rock, here cut into an Arcade. The *Manger* is at the distance of seven paces from the Altar. It is in a low recess hewn out of the rock, to which you descend by two steps, and consists of a block of marble, raised about a foot and a half above the floor, and hollowed out. The Friars insist that the Infant Saviour was laid here; but this is imposing too much upon credulity. It is possible that the Stable in which the Lord was born was in a Cave, for Caves are now used for Stables in the East, and may have been so used two thousand years since; but this *Marble* Manger! Before the Manger is the Altar of the Magi.

The Grotto of St. Jerome.—In another Subterranean

Chapel, tradition places the Sepulchres of the Innocents. From this the Pilgrim is conducted to the "Grotto of St. Jerome," where the Monks shew the Tomb of that Father, who passed a great part of his life in this place; and who in the Grotto shewn as his Oratory, is said to have translated that Version of the Bible which has been adopted by the Church of Rome and is called the Vulgate.

The Convents.—Abutting upon the Church of the Nativity on its North-Eastern side is a Latin Convent; upon the South-Eastern side is another belonging to the Greeks, and the Armenians have a third which lies upon the South-West. Thus, as in the Church of the Holy Sepulchre at Jerusalem, these Sects, who inveterately detest each other, find rallying points in their superstitions. In their own way they are all sufficiently learned in historical details to be able to shew, in addition to things already described, the Corner in which Joseph stood awaiting the announcement of the "New-born Child."

The Well of Bethlehem.—Josephus makes allusion to a celebrated Well, which, both from his account of its situation and from that of the Sacred Scriptures, seems to have been the identical Fountain which stands near to the Sepulchre of Rachel. "Considered," says Dr. E. D. Clarke, "merely in point of interest, the narrative is not likely to be surpassed by any circumstance of Pagan history. David being a native of Bethlehem, calls to mind, during the sultry days of harvest, a Well near the Gate of the Town, the delicious waters of which he had often tasted; and expresses an earnest desire to assuage his thirst by drinking of that limpid spring. 'And David longed and said, O that one would give me to drink of the water of the Well of Bethlehem, which is by the Gate!' The exclamation is overheard by 'three of the mighty men whom David had,' viz., Adino, Eleazar, and Shammah. These men sallied forth, and having fought their way through the Garrison of the Philistines at Bethlehem, 'drew water from the Well that was by the Gate' on the other side of the Town, and brought it to David. Coming into his presence, they present to him the surprising testimony of their valour and affection. The aged Monarch receives from their hands a pledge they had so dearly earned, but refuses to drink of water every drop of which had been purchased with blood. He returns thanks to the Almighty, who had vouchsafed the deliverance of his warriors from the jeopardy they had encountered; and, pouring out the water as a libation on the ground, makes an offering of it to the Lord." (2 Sam. xxiii. 14—17.)

THE POPULATION of Bethlehem, or *Beit-Lahm*, as it is now called, is about 3,500, the whole of whom are Christians. The greater part of the inhabitants gain their livelihood by making beads, carving mother-of-pearl shells with sacred subjects, and manufacturing small tables and crucifixes. Such things are eagerly purchased by the Pilgrims.

RETURN TO JERUSALEM.

Having travelled twenty miles from Hebron, we had only six more to ride to regain Jerusalem. Leaving the terraced slopes and vineyards of Bethlehem, we came up to a Ruin, pointed out as the "Tower of Simeon," the aged Saint, who lifted the Infant Messiah in his arms, and, having feasted his vision, desired to die. Pursuing our way through the Plain of Rephaim, the Holy City came in sight, and awakened in my mind trains of thought relative to the wonderful history of that most interesting place. At 4.15 we arrived outside the Jaffa Gate, and a second time pitched out tents for the night.

CHAPTER VIII.

PALESTINE—CONTINUED.

JERUSALEM TO BETHEL.

About Two o'clock in the afternoon, March 13th, we were on our way to Bethel, having for the last time visited Jerusalem. After riding several miles, the road led to a lofty Mountain, from whose summit the dear old spot came full in View. The first Vision of the City was one of disappointment; but this last prospect was one of intense admiration, awakening the deepest sympathy and gratitude. "Peace be within thy walls and Prosperity within thy Palaces!" Another lingering look, and we bade Jerusalem adieu, hoping next to see that Holy City, New Jerusalem coming down from God out of heaven, and to behold the King Himself in His beauty. I could almost adopt the plaintive, passionate language of the captive Hebrews by the Streams of Babylon :—" If I forget thee, O Jerusalem, let my right hand forget her cunning. If I do not remember thee, let my tongue cleave to the roof of my mouth."

Passing over the Mountain, we enter a naked desolate track. A broad undulating plateau extends Northwards for about half-a-mile, and then passing between a bare conical peak on the right, and a bleak rounded hill on the left, declines gently into a wide vale. The trees are few and stunted; the patches cultivated, have a gray parched appearance, and are almost hidden by bald crowns of limestone rock, rugged heaps of stone, and ruins of Villages.

RAMAH OF BENJAMIN was formerly seated upon a hill a little to the East of the road we were pursuing, and is marked by a ruined Village called *Er-Ram*. From the story of the poor Levite we learn that that place was not far from Gibeah, and this desolated Village agrees to the description. (Jud. xix. 13.) It lies between Gibeon and Beeroth, with which places it is associated in the Catalogue of the Cities of Benjamin given in the Book of Joshua. (Jos. xviii. 25.)

This is set forth as one of the valuable identifications for which Biblical Geography is indebted to Dr. Robinson, as elucidating the difficult text:—" A voice was heard in Ramah . . . Rachel weeping for her children,"—which the Evangelist transfers to the Massacre at Bethlehem. This Ramah being farther South than other places of the same name, has been thought best to agree with the imagery of Jeremiah taken in connection with the Evangelical accommodation. But it is still too far North, being about twelve miles from Rachel's Sepulchre. There is, however, within four hundred yards of the Sepulchre, a heap of old rubbish, which Dr. Thompson's Guide, with far greater probability, pointed out to him as the remains of the Ramah in question.

BEEROTH.—Leaving Ramah of Benjamin, we soon reached Beeroth, or *El-Bera*, a town pleasantly situated on a large hill, numbering a Muslem population, with a few Christians among them, of about 800. It has its name from a Well or Spring at the bottom of the hill, *Beeroth*, being simply the plural of *Beer*, a Well. There are here the Ruins of a fine old Gothic Church.

BETHEL.

REMINISCENCES. — Attracted by its waters and pastures, Abraham pitched his tent at this place, while yet it was known by the name of Luz. Here Jacob, in his flight from Esau, slept upon the bare ground, as many an Arab does to this day, and had that wonderful dream of the ladder, from the Shekinah, upon whose summit the Voice came rolling forth, "In thee, and in thy Seed, shall all the families of the earth be blessed." Here, therefore, he erected a Pillar for a memorial and called the place "Bethel," or "House of God." To this place he returned after an interval of twenty, or, according to others, forty years, and wrestled with the Angel of Mercy by Whom his name was changed to "Israel." Here he buried Deborah, Rachel's nurse, under an oak. At this place, already consecrated in the time of

T

the Patriarchs, the Ark of the Covenant, and probably the Tabernacle, were for a long time deposited. It was also one of the places at which Samuel held, in rotation, his Courts of Justice. Jeroboam made it the Southern seat of the worship of the Golden Calves, whence the Prophet, in derision, calls it *Bethaven*, the "House of Vanity," or "Idols," instead of the "House of God." (Hos. iv. 15.)

THE TOWN.—Until within the last few years, Bethel and its name were believed to have perished; but the Protestant Missionaries at Jerusalem discovered that the name was preserved in the form of *Beitin*—the Arabic termination *in* for the Hebrew *el*, being a usual change. In about half an hour after leading El-Bera we came to this place, and remained there for the night. It is everywhere, except upon the South, surrounded by rising ground, and yet from its loftiest point the Dome of the great Mosque at Jerusalem is visible. The Ruins of the ancient City cover the whole surface of the ridge, and are three or four acres in extent. They consist of foundations, fragments of walls, and heaps of stones. Upon the highest ground are the remains of a square Tower. Towards the South are the walls of a Greek Church, which stands within the foundations of a much older edifice, built of large stones. About twenty huts were thrown up from the materials of the wreck. In the Western Valley there is a large Cistern, 314 feet by 217, constructed of massive stones. The Southern side is entire, but the others are in a dilapidated condition. In the bottom is a beautiful grass-plat watered by two crystal fountains, from which, doubtless, the Maidens of Sarah filled their pitchers, and the flocks of Abraham were refreshed.

SHILOH.

On leaving Bethel we had a dreary ride for three hours, through a desolate uninteresting district, and at length sighted *Seilun*, a City surrounded by hills, with an opening from a narrow valley into a plain on the South. This Robinson identifies with the ancient Shiloh. There are few places whose situation is more particularly indicated in Scripture:—
"On the North side of Bethel, on the East of the highway that goeth up from Bethel to Shechem, and on the South of Lebonah." (Jud. xxi. 19.) Here the Tabernacle and the Ark remained from the days of Joshua to the end of Eli's life. Here Abijah, the Prophet, resided. But after the removal of the Ark it sunk into insignificance, and is more than once mentioned as "accursed" and "forsaken." The Ruins at present consist chiefly of an old Tower, with walls four feet thick, and large stones and fragments of columns.

SHECHEM.

At the end of a verdant Plain, stretching away Northwards about seven miles, and varying from one to two miles in breadth, whose surface is unbroken by either village or fence, stands Shechem, sometimes in the Old Testament called "Sichem," in the New Testament, "Sychar," and in modern Arabic, *Nabulus*.

REMINISCENCES.—The history of Shechem extends over a period of nearly four thousand years. The first spot where Abraham pitched his tent in Canaan was "the place of Sichem unto the plain of Moreh." (Gen. xii. 6.) Jacob also came to this fine pastoral region immediately on his return from Mesopotamia, and pitched his tent *before*, that is, East of the City, near to Shalem. To this day there is a little village called *Salim*, on the lower slope of the hills, at a distance of about two miles. There the Patriarch bought from Hamor that " parcel of a field " still marked by his *Well* and the Tomb of his favourite son. (Gen. xxxiii. 18—20.) It was here too that Simeon and Levi so treacherously avenged the dishonour of their sister Dinah. When Jacob removed to Hebron, he retained possession of his fields, and to these he sent Joseph to seek his brethren, whence he was directed to Dothan, and there sold to the Ishmaelites. (Gen. xxxvii.) In Shechem Rehoboam was proclaimed King over Israel, and here the standard of revolt was raised against him, which seated Jeroboam upon the Throne of a rival Kingdom. The dignity of this place, however, soon paled before Tirzah, which in its turn gave place to Samaria; but it remained one of the Cities of Refuge as long as the Jewish polity was in force.

THE TOWN in all probability now occupies the site of the ancient Shechem, although its dimensions may be more contracted. The fertility and beauty of the deep and narrow Valley in which it stands have been much admired by travellers, as far exceeding what they have elsewhere seen in Palestine. This Valley is not more than five hundred yards wide at the Town, which stands directly upon its watershed, the streams on the Eastern part flowing off towards the Jordan, while the fountains on the West send off a pretty brook toward the Mediterranean. The Town is long and narrow, extending along the N.E. base of Mount Gerizim, and partly resting upon its declivity. The Streets are narrow, tortuous, and filthy, and the Houses are high, generally well built, all of stone, with domes upon the roofs, as at Jerusalem. The Bazaars are good and well supplied. There are no ruins which can be called ancient in the place, but there are remains of a Church of fine Byzantine architecture, and a handsome arched Gateway, both apparently of the time of the first Crusades. These occur in the main street, through the whole length of which a stream of clear water rushes down—a rare circumstance in the East.

EBAL AND GERIZIM.—The little Vale of Shechem is shut in on the North and South by the dark rocky sides of Ebal and Gerizim, which have the appearance of twins. Whenever a nook or projection is presented in the side of one, there is a nook or projection corresponding in the side of the other. On the summit of Ebal is a broad stony platform, with a few important Ruins; but there appears no trace of the Altar built by Joshua, on which the Law was inscribed. (Jos. viii. 30—35.) As from this mountain curses were denounced, so from Gerizim, at the opposite side of the Valley, blessings were declared. The ascent of Gerizim is steep; but it winds up a beautiful glen on the South side of the Town, which opens in charming prospects, rich in many-tinted foliage, and vocal with the warbling of birds and murmuring of streams. The summit is a broad irregular plateau, thickly strewn with stones, but cultivated in patches and terraces between them. From hence the great wall of the Trans-Jordanic mountains is seen on the East; on the North the snowy peak of Hermon appears on the horizon; the Plain of Sharon peeps through the openings of the hills, and the waters of the Mediterranean are seen stretching away on the West, while the Mountains of Ephraim close round. Our attention was directed to the place where the Samaritans annually encamp at the Feast of the Passover; and in another place are shown the Ruins of the ancient Samaritan Temple, with its "Holy of Holies," towards which that people still turn when they pray, and which they approach reverently without their shoes. Amongst the Ruins are also the remains of a Muslem Wely, a Cemetery, several deep Cisterns and Wells, with a multitude of things which to describe would require pages.

JOSEPH'S TOMB.—South of Nabulus is Joseph's Tomb; a little Muslem Wely marks the spot, which is probably identical. On his death-bed in Egypt, "Joseph took an oath of the Children of Israel, saying, God will surely visit you, and ye shall carry up my bones from hence." Accordingly, when they came out, they remembered his words, "And the bones of Joseph, which the Children of Israel brought out of Egypt, buried they in Shechem, in a parcel of ground which Jacob bought of the sons of Hamor, the father of Shechem." (Gen. L. 25; Jos. xxiv. 32.)

JACOB'S WELL.—A few hundred yards from the Tomb of Joseph is Jacob's Well, now surrounded by the Ruins of an old Greek Church. Here Jesus rested at noon, wearied with a long walk up the hot Plain, He having come from Jerusalem, as we had, and engaged the Woman of Samaria in that marvellous conversation in which He "told her all the things that ever she did."

> "At Jacob's Well a Stranger sought
> His drooping frame to cheer:
> Samaria's daughter little thought
> That Jacob's God was there."

The uninterrupted expanse of corn-fields, still in a flourishing condition, naturally reminds one of the words of Jesus to His disciples. "Lift up your eyes and look on the fields, for they are white already to harvest." He doubtless referred to the multitude of the Samaritans who by this time were flocking from Sychar to hear His words; but the image was suggested by the cultivation. (Jno. iv.)

POPULATION, &c.—Nabulus has a population of about 8,000: 500 of whom are Christians; 130, Samaritans; about 50, Jews; and the rest Muslems. The chief productions are Soap, Cotton, and Oil. The Soap-Works are large, and the trade flourishing. The Oil is considered among the best in Syria. Like every town in the district, this is embowered in Olive-groves. The trees are of slow growth, and live considerably more than one thousand years. The old ones with their great gnarled and furrowed stems have a venerable appearance. The Olive is ten or twelve years old before it yields a return for the expense of cultivation. The berries ripen in November or December, and are then beaten off the branches with long sticks. (Deut. xxiv. 20.) Women and children pick them up, and carry them upon their heads to the

Presses, where, by a rude and clumsy apparatus, the Oil is extracted, and then poured into Skins or Earthen-jars. Figs, also, and Vines, abound in this district, which still stand forth a memorial of the fruitfulness promised to the inheritance of Ephraim. (Gen. xlix. 22—26; Deut. xxxiii. 14—16.)

THE SAMARITANS. — Being Saturday evening, we found our way to the Samaritan Synagogue, whose worship appeared to us a wild irreverent rant, consisting of hackneyed recitations, interspersed with repeated undevotional prostrations. Nothing like solemnity or even decent propriety appeared throughout the Service. But "The Lord knoweth them that are His." We should remember that "In every nation he that feareth God and worketh righteousness is accepted with Him." After the ceremony, the Priest showed us their celebrated Copy of the Pentateuch, written, as they affirm, by Abishua, the Son of Phineas, the Son of Eleazar, the Son of Aaron. This would make it nearly 3,300 years old; but though tattered, patched, and stained, neither the parchment nor the writing appeared to us of great antiquity. It is a ponderous roll, kept in a cylindrical brass case, which opens upon hinges. The hatred of these Samaritans to the Jews is as bitter now as it was eighteen centuries since. They will neither eat nor pray with them, but have no objection to transact a little profitable business! (Jno. iv. 9.)

SAMARIA.

REMINISCENCES.—Samaria was the imperial City of the Ten Tribes, and Capital of the Province of the same name. It was built by Omri, the Sixth King of Israel, B.C. 921. "He bought the Hill of Shemer for two talents of silver, and built on the hill, and called the name of the City which he built after Shemer, the owner of the hill, Samaria." (1 Kings xvi. 24.) It was twice besieged by Benhadad, King of Syria, but without success, though, during the second siege, it was reduced to such an extremity, that the head of an ass was sold for eighty shekels— value about £10. In 721 B.C. it was taken after a three years' siege, by Shalmanezer, who rased it to the ground, carried the Ten Tribes captive into Assyria, and replaced them by Colonists from that country. (2 Kings xvii. 6, 24.) It was again reduced to ruins by Hyrcanus B.C. 129; after which it was rebuilt by Gabinus, and restored to magnificence by Herod, who called it *Sebaste*, in honour of Augustus (Sebastos) Cæsar. At that time it was twenty furlongs in circumference. Here Philip "preached Christ," and founded a Church. Here too Simon the Sorcerer, was baptized, and afterwards, excommunicated. (Acts viii. 5—24.) It became the Seat of a Bishop in the early days of Christianity, but in the Fifth Century sunk into ruins.

THE TOWN at present consists of about sixty houses

substantially built of the materials of its former magnificence, and occupied by about four hundred Mahometans. We came to it after a pleasant ride of six miles from Shechem. It stands on a fine large insulated hill compassed by a broad deep valley, the hills surrounding which are terraced and cultivated to the top, sown with grain and planted with fig and olive-trees. The first object seen on entering the Village is the ruined Church of St. John converted into a Mosque. We did not enter this because of the surliness of the inhabitants, who sometimes resort to violence to prevent travellers from doing so. The hill has so long been under cultivation that the stones of ruined Temples and Palaces have been carefully removed from the soil and thrown into heaps. There are still standing, however, about sixty ancient Columns, all decapitated, and deeply sunk in the soil, and many others lie among the Terraces and Olive-trees, which probably are relics of Colonnades with which Herod had adorned the City. The present state of the place recalls the words of prophecy: "I will make Samaria as a heap of the field;"—"Samaria shall become desolate, for she hath rebelled against her God." (Mic. i. 6; Hos. xiii. 16.)

FROM SAMARIA TO JENIN.

GIBEAH.—Leaving Samaria, and travelling through

a pleasant country, the hills and vales in whose course are dotted with Hamlets, we came to a large and flourishing Village picturesquely seated on the lower slope of a hill, and overlooking a rich green Valley. This is "Geba," formerly called "Gibeah," which, because it was the native place and afterwards the royal residence of Saul, is also called "Gibeah of Saul." (Isa. x. 29.)

DOTHAN.—We next enter the verdant Plain of Dothan, whose fertility was not unknown to the sons of Jacob; for having pastured their flocks for a time in the Plain of Shechem, they led them on to this more Northerly vale. The name Dothan, or *Doth-ain*, signifies "The Two Wells." Hither Joseph came after his brethren, who from the eminence could easily see him "afar off" as he descended the side of the hill. Here they conspired to throw him into one of those empty Cisterns or Pits common in this region, and afterwards agreed to sell him to the Midianitish Merchants. In later times, when the Syrian army under Benhadad invaded Israel, and marched against Samaria, the Prophet Elisha was residing at Dothan, and gave full information to his countrymen of the most secret designs of the enemy. Apprised of this the Syrian Monarch resolved upon seizing the Prophet, and surrounded the place with his warriors. The Servant of the Man of God came running in and crying, "Alas, my Master! how shall we do?" but his confidence was assured by the vision of "horses and chariots of fire round about Elisha." (2 Kin. vi. 8—23.)

JENIN.—Passing over the Plain we came to Jenin and pitched our tent for the night. It is a town of some importance, numbering from two to three thousand inhabitants, a few Christian families amongst them. An *Agha* also resides here with a force of fifty horsemen, to protect the district and keep the roads clear,—duties however, which are very indifferently performed. The place abounds in rich Gardens, hedged with the prickly-pear, and receiving an Oriental air from a few palm-trees. Jenin was the ancient *En-Gannim*.

THE PLAIN OF ESDRAELON.

Again on our way on the morning of the 16th March, we enter the Great Battle-field of Palestine, the Plain of Esdraelon, better known to the Biblical Student as the "Plain of Megiddo." Here Barak triumphed over the hosts of Sisera. Here Josiah fought in disguise against Necho, King of Egypt, and fell by the arrows of his antagonist. Jews, Saracens, Crusaders, Frenchmen, Egyptians, Persians, Druses, Turks, and Arabs—Warriors "out of every nation under heaven," have pitched their tents here. In 1799, Murat here obtained a decisive victory over the Mamelukes and Arabs, in their bold attempt to relieve Acre. This Plain is the Armageddon of the

Apocalypse. It is about thirty miles in length and twenty in breadth, enclosed on all sides by mountains; the hills of Nazareth to the North; those of Samaria to the South; to the East, Tabor and Hermon, and Carmel to the South-West. Hitherto we had little else than riding up and down rugged mountains, but here we could canter along a smooth and most fertile plain. Gilboa was full in view before us.

JEZREEL.—In two hours and a half we came to Jezreel, now called *Zer'in*, which is perched on the crest of a low spur projecting some distance into the Plain from Gilboa. This spur is only a few feet higher than the country we had crossed; but on the North side there is a descent of nearly 100 feet into the central arm of the Plain. The Modern Village is composed of about twenty wretched houses, fast falling into ruin. Such is the vestige of the once Royal Jezreel, where Ahab had a Palace and where three of his Successors resided;—the scene also of some of the bloodiest tragedies in Sacred History. Standing upon the crown of the ridge, perhaps on the site of Ahab's Palace, with the 21st Chapter of the 1 Kings open, the Story of poor Naboth is read with fresh interest. Below us in the Plain is a Vineyard, if not that of Naboth, at least a representative of the occasion of the covetous and cruel craft of Jezebel. After the house of Ahab fell, Jezreel sank into decay.

SHUNEM.—The road now leads through rich corn-fields along the Plain of Shunem, a City of Issachar, now called *Solem*. (Jos. xix. 18.) The scene of the interesting Story of the Shunamite and her Son is now before us. Here stood the Village where that noble woman built a little Chamber on the Wall for the use of the Prophet. Into one of these Corn-fields surrounding the Village the "child" of promise— the reward of piety and hospitality, "went out to his father to the reapers," and fell a victim probably to a sun-stroke. Across that great Plain to yonder ridge of blue mountains, his mother rode to the Man of God to Carmel to open to him the sad tale of her bereavement. Accompanied by the Prophet she returned over the same Plain to receive from him her Son, thus doubly now the Gift of Heaven. (2 Kings iv. 8—37.) In the present Village there is not a vestige of antiquity. It is encompassed with Gardens hedged with prickly-pears, and is evidently in a flourishing state.

From Shunem we pass round the Western base of Little Hermon, here getting our first view of Tabor; which rises like the segment of a vast Sphere, and is dotted with oaks to its very summit. It stands alone in the Plain, and presents an outline of grace surpassing expectation. Over its left shoulder, far away upon the horizon, the Snowy Peak of Hermon towers. From this aspect the Royal Poet might well sing—

"The North and the South, Thou hast created them; Tabor and Hermon shall rejoice in Thy name." (Psa. lxxxix. 12.)

NAIN.—After a ride of about fifty minutes we came to the hamlet of Nain, consisting of a few poor houses in a bleak situation, but commanding an extensive view of the Plain with the Mountains of Galilee beyond. Yet uninteresting as the place looks, it leaves a deeper impression upon the memory than many places on which Nature has lavished her choicest gifts. In imagination we see the Funeral Procession of the Widow's Son issuing from the Gate—the Men carrying the Open Bier, the Women behind grouped round the bereaved Widow, and rending the air with their wild cries as Mourners in the East do to this day. We see another Procession meeting this, headed by ONE Whose glance of compassion is more than human. To the Widow He says, in accents which thrill her soul, "Weep not," and approaches the bier. The bearers halt, awed by the mien of the mysterious Stranger! "Young man, I say unto thee, Arise." Immediately the Shawl is thrown up, and the Son of the Widow is in the midst of the crowd clasped in the embrace of his mother. (Lu. vii. 11—15.)

ENDOR.—At a distance of not more than three or four miles from Nain stands Endor, situate on the Northern slope of the lower ridge of Little Hermon. It has its name, according to some, from *En* and *Dor*, that is, the "House-Fountain;" but Mr. Bryant derives it from *En* and *Ador*, viz., "The Fountain of Light," referring to the Oracle of the God *Ador*, probably founded by the Canaanites. That many such Oracles existed in Canaan is evident from the number which Saul is said to have suppressed. At this Oracle of Endor that Monarch, on the eve of the battle in which he perished, consulted with the Sorceress, whereupon Samuel appeared, and predicted the sequel. Whether it was Samuel himself or some impersonation of him raised by legerdemain, or by Satanic agency, has been much discussed; but whatever comes of the controversy, the history has invested this place with an imperishable interest.

THE MOUNT OF PRECIPITATION.—Leaving the Plain, we ascended a barren hill that rises more abruptly than others in the ridge, to which the Monks have given the name of the "Mount of Precipitation." The reference is to the passage in the Evangelist where the Jews, filled with wrath at the words of Jesus, "rose up and thrust Him out of the City [Nazareth] and led Him unto the brow of the hill whereon their City was built, that they might cast Him down headlong." (Lu. iv. 29.) But this is justly denounced by Dr. Robinson, as the most clumsy of all the local legends of the Holy Land, since the Evangelist states that the "hill" was one "upon which the City was built," whereas this place is about two miles distant. The Monks themselves are now so pressed with the absurdity of their tale that they allege the ancient Nazareth was nearer to the Mountain than the modern. This, however, only increases their difficulties, as it destroys the credit of their own Holy Places within the present City. The Doctor has noticed several Precipices around the Western hill upon which Nazareth was seated, any of which might, with some appearance of probability, have been indicated as the spot to which the Jews led Jesus.

NAZARETH.

REMINISCENCES.—Crossing the rugged mountains of Galilee, in about an hour we arrived at Nazareth, a place intensely interesting to the Christian as the home of the Saviour until His entrance, at the age of thirty, upon His Public Ministry. Here was the scene of His domestic virtues and private life. Often in His boyhood must He have moved through those streets, and in company with His mother visited the Fountain, or sat upon the housetop in the tranquil eventide. To Him those rocky heights were all familiar, as probably He there meditated upon His grand commission and held communion with the Father. After entering upon His Great Vocation, His preaching so exasperated the citizens that they sought to destroy Him by pushing Him

over the brow of a cliff. Only one other occasion is recorded of His appearing in Nazareth, upon which violence was not offered, but bitter taunts were substituted:—" Is not this the Carpenter, the Son of Mary, the Brother of James and Joses and Judas and Simon? And are not His Sisters with us? And they were offended at Him." (Matt. xiii. 54—58; Mar. vi. 1—6.) We cannot wonder at the Satire of Nathanael upon the proverbial wickedness of the Town, " Can any good thing come out of Nazareth ?"

The Town at present is one of the neatest in Palestine. It appears not to have suffered so much from war as other places, and it has recently been restored and beautified by the erection of a number of excellent houses. It is built in the form of a Cross, and the Valley which it commands is a circular basin, encompassed by a range of fifteen mountains, which seem as if they met and united to form an enclosure for this delightful spot. A comparison of the present City with the Evangelical references to the ancient Nazareth will shew that the sites are identical. The Houses in some places seem to cling to the precipices of "the hill on which the City is built;" in others they nestle in glens, and others stand out boldly and overlook the valley. The most prominent objects are the great Franciscan Convent, and the Turkish Mosque. The Houses are of stone, and have a clean substantial appearance, and the Streets, though not so good, in comparison, are yet superior to those of most Oriental Towns. Behind is a lofty Hill, the prospect from which is certainly one of the most beautiful in Palestine, taking in the snowy peak of Hermon, the rounded summit of Tabor, the long dark ridge of Carmel, and the white strand of the Mediterranean beyond the plain of Acre, with the great battle-field of nations—the Plain of Esdraelon, spreading out upon the South. Hence also are seen in beautiful effect the verdant corn-fields, gardens enclosed with cactus-hedges, olives sprinkled in clumps, or singly, and streaks of fig-trees, wild shrubs, and other foliage, lying round the Town.

The Latin Convent stands on a spur of the hill, projecting into the green plain. It is a square of heavy buildings, encompassed by a high wall. On entering we are struck with its solemn appearance. A great part of the walls inside the Convent are covered with canvas hangings, painted in imitation of tapestry with appropriate Scripture Scenes.

The Holy Grotto in the Church of the Annunciation is under the Choir, which is raised eight or ten feet above the floor. Here Mass is celebrated by the Monks. At the entrance of this Grotto is a Marble Slab with a Cross in the centre, to mark the place where the Virgin stood during the Annunciation... This is surmounted by a fine Marble Altar.

Close by is a broken Pillar, which the Friars formerly affected to believe was miraculously suspended in the air, because there is a clear space of eighteen inches between it and the pedestal, though it is manifestly connected with the roof. But, in deference to the spirit of the times, this is no longer advanced. Behind the Cross is a little Nook, from which the Angel is said to have issued. The whole Sanctum and Vestibule are encased in marble and hung with beautiful silver Lamps. Over the Altar is a good modern painting of the Annunciation, presented by the Emperor of Austria. A little door opens into the back of this Grotto, which has been left in its original rough and irregular state. Here is another Altar back to back with the former, and a fair painting of the "Flight into Egypt." From this a narrow rock-hewn Staircase leads up to the "Virgin Mary's Kitchen," a low Cave, in which the Fire-place, Chimney, and other details, are still pointed out!

JOSEPH'S WORKSHOP.—To the North-West of the Convent is a small Church, built over "Joseph's Workshop"(!) An old "Wall of the Original Shop" is shewn. Above the Altar is a picture, presented by a noble lady, whose name and arms appear on it, representing the Carpenter at work, assisted by Jesus, a comparative youth.

THE SYNAGOGUE. — To the West of "Joseph's Workshop" there is a small arched building, which the Guides say is the Synagogue where Christ applied to Himself the language of Isaiah, upon which the Jews were so exasperated that they sought to cast Him over the brow of the hill above the Maronite Church. They further state, that the manner in which Jesus avoided this was to leap down of His own accord; and the frightful precipice shewn is called *Saltus Domini*,—"The Lord's Leap." This tradition is far more probable than that of the Monks already alluded to under the head of "The Mount of Precipitation."

THE FOUNTAIN OF THE VIRGIN.—The Greeks have a rival "Church of the Annunciation," in Nazareth, constructed near a Well at the opposite side of the Town. In the Apocryphal Gospel which bears the name of St. James, it is stated that the first Salutation of the Angel came to Mary as she was drawing water from the Spring in the neighbourhood of the Town. That Spring still remains, and bears her name. In fact there are two springs, one outside, and another under the Altar within the Church. The edifice is very plain and gloomy, and is tricked out with the characteristic tasteless finery of the Greeks.

THE POPULATION, as estimated by Dr. Robinson, numbers 1,040 Greeks, 520 Greek Catholics, 480 Latins, 400 Maronites, and 680 Muslems, being a total of 3,120; but others state the total at 4,000.

The Christians here have an air of sturdy independence that pleases the Western traveller, shewing that, if not "lords of the soil," they are at least at home. They are better dressed, fed, and mannered, than any we had met, not excepting those of Jerusalem. The following encomium is passed upon the female part of the population by a recent traveller :—" The women are famed, and justly too, for their beauty. If we go out and sit for an hour of an evening by the little Fountain, we will see many a face which Raphael might have chosen as a study when about to paint his *Madona della Seggiola*, and many a figure that Phidias might have selected as a model for Venus. Their style of dress and ornament will also attract attention;— the capacious *Shintian*, the close-fitting jacket, and the long-pointed white veil;—then the curious strings of large silver coins round the head and chin, reminding one of the massive chain of a dragoon's helmet. The Fountain here is the place for gossip and flirtation; and the young damsels of Nazareth, as they gracefully poise the pitcher of water on head or shoulder, are just as ready to give drink to a well-conditioned stranger or to give ear to a proposal of marriage, as Rebecca was at the Fountain of Mesopotamia nearly 4,000 years ago."

TABOR.

Having a long ride before us, we were on the

saddle at seven o'clock in the morning, and in two hours reached Tabor. The Mountain stands out almost isolated on the South-Eastern frontier of the Hills of Galilee, with the great Plain of Esdraelon sweeping its base. Its graceful outline, wooded slopes, and grassy glades, made it the object of universal admiration. Its beauty was proverbial, —" As Tabor is among the Mountains and Carmel by the Sea." (Jer. xlvi. 18.) Its height has been variously estimated at 1,000, 1,500, and 2,000 feet; but Mr. Stephens, who ascended it in 1836, declares its extreme elevation to be nearly 3,000 feet. In addition to the groves and clumps of trees which adorn its sides, it is beautifully enamelled, from its base to its summit, with every variety of plant and flower.

At the foot of the Mountain is the miserable Village of Deborah, supposed to be the place where Deborah, the Prophetess, who judged Israel, and Barak and " ten thousand men after him, descended upon Sisera, and discomfited him and all his chariots, even nine hundred chariots of iron, and all the people that were with him."

THE ASCENT.—After three-quarters of an hour of steep climbing, we gained the summit. The path winding round the Mountain gave us a view from all its sides, every step presenting something new, and more and more beautiful, until all was forgotten in the exceeding loveliness of the view from its elevated crown. Standing at its foot, the Mountain appears to terminate in an inaccessible point; but, on arriving at the top, the surprise is agreeable to find an oval plain about a mile in circumference, covered on the West with a bed of fertile soil, and exhibiting on the East a mass of interesting Ruins. From this elevated platform the hills and valleys extending as far as Jerusalem,—a distance of fifty miles, come into view. To the East the Valley of Jordan and the Lake of Tiberias, stretch out, the latter appearing as if inclosed within the crater of a volcano. On the North-West, in the distance, is the broad expanse of the Mediterranean. A few points to the North, appears the Mount of Beatitudes; while due North is a fine panoramic view of the Plains of Esdraelon and Galilee, skirted in the background by a chain of Mountains which sweep round and terminate the view on the Sea. Pococke, Van Egmont, Maundrell, Stephens, and Heyman, all speak of Tabor as the most beautiful Mountain they ever saw, and that which, of all others, best recompenses the toil of ascending.

THE RUINS.—If tradition be true, this was the "High Mountain" into which "Jesus took Peter, and James, and John, and was transfigured before them," so that "His face did shine as the sun, and His raiment was white as the light; and a voice out of the cloud" was heard, saying, "This is My beloved Son, in whom I am well pleased." In honour of that scene a Grotto is built, as Peter proposed, with three Altars, one for Christ, one for Moses, and one for Elias. To this, once a year, the Monks of the Convent and all the Christians of Nazareth, ascend in solemn procession. The Greeks have recently built a magnificent Church here. There are also Ruins of an old Wall built by Josephus when he was Governor of Galilee, and this strong position was occupied in earlier times as the Key of Esdraelon. The summit of Tabor appears to have been covered by a Town as early as the time of Joshua. (Jos. xix. 22.) It is said Helena built a magnificent Cathedral here, and made Mount Tabor an Episcopal See; for in her days the Town was yet upon the heights. There are several rock-hewn Cisterns among the Ruins, in one or other of which good water is always to be found. And on the side of the hill the Monks shew a Church in a Grot, where they say Christ charged His disciples not to tell what things they had seen in the Transfiguration till He was glorified.

TIBERIAS.

From Tabor to Tiberias is a journey of five hours, so that after a good day's riding—nine hours from the time of leaving Nazareth, we arrived at our destination. This was quite a modern Town when our Lord frequented this region, having been built and named by Herod about the time of His advent. Seventy years afterwards Josephus found it an important place, and no other in Galilee is so often mentioned by him. Almost every other city was destroyed by Vespasian and Titus, but this was spared, and, as a reward for its adherence to the Romans, made the Capital of the Province. These facts explain the circumstance that Tiberias is mentioned only by John, who alone wrote after these events. The present Town, which was much shattered by an Earthquake, in 1837, is upon the ancient site close to the waters of the Lake. It is of a rectangular form, surrounded by a wall with towers distributed at intervals; but the whole is now in a dilapidated state. In some places it is not difficult to ride over the ruins, while in others the shocks of the Earthquake have left such breaches as would have been produced by a battery of siege-guns. There are here a little Latin Convent inhabited by a solitary Italian Monk, and a Church connected with it, which tradition places upon the site where the Miraculous Draught of Fishes was landed! There are few towns in Syria so utterly filthy as Tiberias, and so little to be desired as a place of residence. Being six hundred feet below the level of the ocean, and overhung on the West by a high mountain, which effectually shuts off the Mediterranean breezes, it is fearfully hot in summer. And yet the population number about 2000, of whom 800 are poor Jews, who look even more squalid and sickly than those in other towns of Palestine. The Jews occupy a little "Quarter" of their own in the middle of the city, where they have several Synagogues and Schools, and keep up some smattering of Rabbinical lore.

THE SEA OF GALILEE.

The noble expanse of water, variously called the "Lake of Tiberias," "Cinnereth," or "Gennesareth," and the "Sea of Galilee," laves the Eastern coast of Lower Galilee. It is an irregular oval, with the large end to the North, about fourteen miles long, and from six to nine in breadth. In the words of Dr. Thompson, "Seen from any point of the surrounding heights it is a fine sheet of water—a burnished mirror set in a framework of rounded hills and rugged mountains, which rise and roll backward and upward to where Hermon hangs the picture against the blue vault of heaven." By these hills the Lake is in a great measure protected from storms, so that its surface is usually as smooth as that of the Dead Sea. We refreshed ourselves by bathing in the waters of this Sacred Lake. It is, however, in some seasons, visited by squalls, whirlwinds, and sudden gusts from the mountains, especially when the strong current created by the passage of the Jordan through it, is opposed by a South-Easterly wind. Its surface is then lashed into violent commotion, and, owing to the suddenness and fitful variableness of these squalls, the small craft, formerly used for fishing, were often sunk. It was in such a storm that the Disciples of Jesus awoke Him, when "He arose and rebuked the winds" so that immediately "there was a great calm." (Matt. viii. 24—26.) The boats which once crowded this Sea disappeared when the Arabians conquered the country; and at present there is but *one* which is used for the convenience of Travellers.

Almost every spot along the shores of the Sea of Galilee is sacred, since a great portion of our Lord's public ministry was spent there; but since then, everything save the broad outline of nature is completely changed. Then they teemed with life and activity, having many flourishing Towns such as Magdala, Capernaum, Chorazin, the two Bethsaidas, 'Gamala, Hippos and Tarichœa; and other large Cities as Scythopolis, Gadara and Pella, with innumerable Villages, studding the surrounding country. In Chorazin, Capernaum, and Bethsaida, the Saviour wrought many of His mighty works, and, probably standing on the beach of Gennesareth, He denounced those Cities. (Matt. xi. 21.) So irreparable and complete is their ruin that the Sites can with difficulty be recognised. Most of the Towns flourishing in the days of our Lord are now extinct, and mounds of black Ruins alone remain to attest the places where they stood. So crowded were the Streets of Capernaum in those days that those who brought a sick man to Jesus were obliged to open up the flat roof and let him down. (Mar. ii. 1—12). So closely pressed by the multitude was He when upon the shore that He was forced to enter a boat. (Matt. xiii. 1, 2.) So numerous were His followers that thousands were fed by Him in a miraculous manner. Preaching to the Fishermen of that district He compared the "Kingdom of Heaven" to a "Net;" addressing the people engaged in Commerce, His image was that of a "Merchantman seeking Goodly Pearls;" while to the Agriculturalists He spoke of "a Man which sowed Good Seed in the Field." (Matt. xiii. 24—48.) Thus the people in these coasts who "sat in darkness saw great light." From these the Apostles of Christ were chosen, and the Membership of the Infant Church came from the region of Galilee. But if the Sea of Gennesareth is sacred to the Christian from such circumstances as these, it is also sacred to the Jew, but for a reason of a fanciful kind. The Rabbins have a notion that Messiah is yet to rise out of its waters, land in Tiberias and establish His Throne at Safed!

I cannot close these remarks without quoting the beautiful lines of the sainted M'Cheyne:—

"How pleasant to me thy deep blue wave
    O Sea of Galilee!
For the glorious One who came to save
    Hath often stood by thee.

"Fair are the lakes in the land I love,
    Where pine and heather grow,
But thou hast loveliness above
    What nature can bestow.

"It is not that the wild gazelle
    Comes down to drink thy tide,
But He that was pierced to save from hell
    Oft wandered by thy side.

"Graceful around thee the mountains meet,
    Thou calm reposing sea;
But ah! far more, the beautiful feet
    Of Jesus walked o'er thee.

"Those days are past—Bethsaida, where?
    Chorazin, where art thou?
His tent the wild Arab pitches there,
    The wild reed shades thy brow.

"Tell me ye mouldering fragments, tell,
    Was the Saviour's city here?
Lifted to heaven, has it sunk to hell,
    With none to shed a tear?

"O Saviour! gone to God's right hand,
    Yet the same Saviour still,
Graved on Thy heart is this lovely strand,
    And every fragrant hill."

TIBERIAS TO CARMEL.

THE MOUNT OF BEATITUDES.—Leaving Gennesareth

we soon enter the Plain, from which a Hill rises to an elevation of from 200 to 300 feet. This is supposed to have been the "Mount" from which our Lord delivered that sublime Discourse recorded in the fifth, sixth, and seventh chapters of Matthew's Gospel. Hence it is called the "Mount of Beatitudes." In the Plain at the foot of this hill it is also assumed that Jesus fed the multitude with a few loaves and fishes.

CANA OF GALILEE.—About noon we reached Cana of Galilee, so called to distinguish it from another Cana or Kanah, not far from Sidon, in the tribe of Asher. (Jos. xix. 28.) It rests on a gentle eminence in the midst of a fine valley, and in its position agrees with the language employed by the Evangelist, and shows the geographical accuracy of the Writer. This was the birth-place of Nathanael. Here also the first Christian Marriage was solemnised, Jesus and His Disciples being amongst the Guests, upon which memorable occasion—

"The modest water saw its Lord and blushed."

The present Village is in a half-ruined condition. Some of the Olives in its neighbourhood are so ancient as, probably, to have witnessed the Miracle which has rendered this place so famous. The inhabitants of Cana are Greek Christians principally, if not exclusively.

About eight miles to the South lay Nazareth, which we reached at three in the afternoon, and revived our sympathies by rambling once more through the scenes of the most hallowed association. Here we remained over the night, and then bade the dear place a last farewell.

BETHLEHEM OF ZEBULUN.—After passing Yaphia [not Yafa] on the left, we sighted *Beit-Lahm*, which is situated in the midst of an Oak-Forest. Though now but a miserable Hamlet, consisting of a few hovels, it marks the site of Bethlehem, which was once a city of the Canaanites. (Jos. xix. 15.) It is called Bethlehem of Zebulun to distinguish it from its more important namesake in the tribe of Judah.

THE BROOK KISHON.—About noon we came to the river Kishon, now styled *El Mukutta* or "The Ford," before crossing which we dismounted to take some refreshment. One of our Muleteers became suddenly ill and appeared likely to die, but happily revived. This was the Brook at which Elijah slew all the Prophets of Baal. (1 Kings xviii. 40.) Our confidence was in Elijah's God. On our noble steeds,— spirited yet docile animals, which for eleven days in succession had carried us like Zebras over rugged cloud-capped mountains as well as plains, were now belly-deep in mud and water, bearing us through the Brook. Charming creatures! Never do I expect to see the like again!

CARMEL.

Our way now lay along the base of Carmel, which is a ridge of Mountains rather than a single peak. The name signifies "The Park" or "Fruitful Field," and its wooded heights and picturesque green dells, descending on one side into the fertile Plain of Acre, and in the other to the no less fertile "Vale of Dor," give propriety to the apellative. The Copse—for so small and stunted are the trees that it scarcely deserves the name of a Wood, chiefly consists of the Prickly-Oak. This is an evergreen, and so the "Excellency of Carmel" was a type of the prosperity. The "withering" of its foliage, as in its present diminished luxuriance, represents the desolation of Israel. (Isa. xxxv. 2; Am. i. 2.) The Ridge branches off from the Northern end of the Mountains of Samaria, runs in a North-Westerly direction between the Plains of Phœnicia and Sharon, and projects far into the sea, forming a bold Promontory at the Bay of Acre. Its length is about 18 miles, its breadth nearly 5, and its greatest elevation is 1750 feet. Those who visit Carmel in the Spring of the year agree that it is a delightful region, and describe with enthusiasm the profusion of hyacinths, jonquilles, tazettos, anemones, and other odoriferous plants and flowers, and the varied foliage of the olives, laurels, pines and oaks, which adorn its sides. It abounds also with game, as partridges, hares, quails, and woodcock; and is said to be infested with jackalls, wolves, wild-bears, hyænas, and leopards.

THE CAVES.—The Mountain is compact limestone, and, as often happens in that formation, there are many Caverns. Here, it is said, are more than a thousand. In one tract, called the "Monks' Caverns," there are as many as four hundred adjacent to each other, with windows and dormitories hewn in the rock. The entrances of many of these Caves are so narrow that only a single individual can creep into them; and so crooked that a person is immediately out of sight unless closely followed. This may serve to give a clearer idea of what is intended when the Lord says to those who endeavour to escape His punishments: "Though they hide themselves in the top of Carmel, I will search and take them out thence." (Am. ix. 3.) These Grottos and Caves were resorts of Elijah and Elisha. (1 Kings xviii. 19; 2 Kings ii. 25; iv. 25.) Possibly it was in the Caves of Carmel that Obadiah hid and sustained a hundred Prophets of the Lord, during the Jezebelian persecution. (1 Kings xviii. 4; Com. ver. 13.) At the present day is shewn a Cavern called "The Cave of Elijah," a little below the "Monks' Caverns" already mentioned, and which is now a Muslem sanctuary.

THE CONVENT.—Upon the crown of the ridge is the Carmelite Convent, one of the sweetest retreats, one of the most luxurious resting-places for the weary traveller in Palestine. The House would not disgrace Royalty. The Monks are eminently hospitable; and the air is cool and refreshing, for the Convent stands upon the promontory hanging over the Mediterranean. It consists of a large block of buildings with several tiers of windows all round, and a handsome cupola springing from the centre. In front is a little terraced garden with a pyramidal Monument, placed there to the memory of some French sailors. The old Convent was destroyed by Abdallah Pasha, who converted the materials to his own use; the present Structure was built by the aid of Contributions collected in Europe. The Church in the centre is a fine Rotunda with a large recess at the East-end for the Altar, directly over the Cave where Elijah is said to have concealed himself during the persecution, and near to the Grotto of Elisha. The Carmelite Monks date their Order from Elijah, who they say, "left to Elisha not only his Mantle but his Grotto also; that the Sons of the Prophets succeeded Elisha, and that St. John was the successor of these."

Arrived at this most comfortable Retreat we had to part with our Dragoman and Suite. Though a Romanist, we found Hanna Habesh, as far as we could judge, a sincere Christian. His care and attention to us during the whole of our perilous excursions, were so constant that I felt much at parting with him. After paying him his well-earned wages, and presenting him with our English saddles, we took an affectionate leave, invoking the Divine blessing upon him as the inheritance of his life. Then I reflected with gratitude upon all the way by which God had led us in the Wilderness and in the Land of Promise, defending us from all evil, and filling our hearts with gladness.

ELIJAH'S ALTAR.—Carmel derives its chief interest from having been the scene of one of the most glorious passages in the Old Testament history—the well known defeat of the Prophets of Baal, in presence of Ahab and the people of Israel, by the descent of celestial fire upon the Sacrifice of Elijah. There is a certain part of the Mountain, about eight miles from the point of the Promontory, which the Arabs call *Mansur*, and the Europeans "The Place of Sacrifice," in commemoration of that miraculous event. Having parted with our horses we did not visit this place. It is said that Pythagoras passed some time in solitary meditation upon this spot. From the promontory he descended, entered an Egyptian Vessel which lay in the Bay, and sailed to the land of the Pharaohs, where he drank deep into the hieroglyphical lore of that ancient nation.

In travelling through Palestine I was reminded of the assurance given to Israel in Egypt, that the Land of Promise was "A good land, a land of brooks of water, of fountains and depths that spring out of valleys and hills; a land of wheat, and barley, and vines, and fig-trees, and pomegranates; a land of oil-olive and honey." (Deu. viii. 7, 8.) In the crevices of the rocks bees fix their nests, whence the honey literally flows down their sides, giving propriety to the characteristic, "a land flowing with honey." (See Deu. xxxii. 13; Psa. lxxxi. 16; 1 Sam. xiv. 25.) The words in Psa. xix. 10, and elsewhere, translated "honey-comb," literally mean *droppings*, viz., from the comb, which are always considered the sweetest of the honey. In allusion to this, the blessings of grace are frequently called the "droppings of the Sanctuary." If properly cultivated the lands would now produce plentiful crops of wheat, barley, millet, grapes, and everything for which they were anciently famous. Vegetation languishes, not because of any barrenness in the soil or imperfection in the climate, but through the barbarous rule of the Turks! Nothing is more common than the Ruins of Walls which the ancient cultivators had built to support the soil in Terraces on the declivities of mountains; or of Tanks and little Canals by which the rain-water was collected and distributed over the fields. There is no reason to doubt that well directed labour might reproduce a Paradise. The desolation we see has also been predicted about eight hundred years before the destruction of Jerusalem by Titus. In the Prophetic style which realises the future in the vividness of a present vision, Isaiah says: "Your country is desolate, your cities are burned with fire: your land, strangers devour it in your presence, and it is desolate as overthrown by strangers." This melancholy state of things he traces directly to the rebelliousness and iniquity of the people. (Isa. i., ii., iii.)

CHAPTER IX.

SYRIA AND THE MEDITERRANEAN.

HHAIFA.

AFTER remunerating the Carmelites for two days' hospitality, we left for Hhaifa, there to await the arrival of the Austrian Steamer for Beyrout. This is a small Port of the Mediterranean. The Town is built close upon the beach, and surrounded by a rickety wall. The Population is about 200. The only tolerable houses are those of the Consular Agents, who abound here, though one is at a loss to know why. There are two or three rusty old pieces of ordnance lying about, covered with filth, and half-buried in rubbish. The Bay is very fine, spreading out from a graceful sandy beach, the battlements of Acre appearing towards the horizon on the North. A solitary Vessel may occasionally be seen at anchor in the Roadstead; and, at intervals of fifteen days, the Port is visited by the Austrian Packet by which we hoped to sail.

THE EMBARKATION.—Expecting to remain all night at Hhaifa, and there being no decent Hotels in the place, by the advice of our Consul, we repaired to the Greek Convent. Scarcely had we been ten minutes in bed, however, than we were rapped up, and apprised in a loud voice that the Steamer had arrived. With all speed we were upon the beach, but had to wait there some time. At length a small boat drew to the Shore to float us to the Steamer. The night was pitch dark, and there was a heavy swell on the sea. Our little bark was crammed with passengers. In these frightful circumstances we were tossed between the winds and waves for half-an-hour, and at length, through the good providence of God, we arrived on board the Austrian. He who "holds the winds in His fists, and the waters in the hollow of His hand," restrained the deep from swallowing us. In the passage from Hhaifa in the boat I was very sick; but on board the Packet I immediately went to my berth and slept until morning.

ACRE.

The first place of importance which we passed upon the Phœnician shore was Acre, a Town and Haven within the nominal territory of the Tribe of Asher. (Jud. i. 31.) In the Septuagint it is called *Accho*; the Greek and Roman writers style it *Ace*; but it was eventually better known by the name of *Ptolemais*, which it received from the first Ptolemy, King of Egypt, by whom it was much improved. By this latter name it is mentioned in the Acts as a place at which Paul touched, on his way to Jerusalem. (Acts

xxi. 7.) The Town occupies the North-Western point of a commodious Bay called the Bay of Acre, the opposite, or South-Western point of which is formed by the Promontory of Mount Carmel. In the time of Strabo, Accho was a great City, and continued a place of importance until the Turks gained possession of it, from which time it rapidly declined. Buonaparte, in the early part of his career, besieged this place, but was compelled to raise the siege by the gallant defence of the English, who, under Sir Sidney Smith, successfully resisted twelve assaults. After that, the Fortifications were further strengthened, and it became the strongest place in Syria. In 1832 the Town was besieged for nearly six months by Ibraham Pasha, during which 35,000 shells were thrown into it, and the buildings were literally beaten to pieces. It had not recovered from this calamity when it was subjected to the operations of the English Fleet under Admiral Stopford, in pursuance of the plan for restoring Syria to the Porte. On the 3rd of November, 1840, it was bombarded for several hours, when the explosion of a powder-magazine destroyed the Garrison and laid the Town in ruins.

TYRE.

The next important place we passed in our voyage was Tyre, which is thirty-two miles North of Acre, and was one of the most celebrated Cities of antiquity for wealth, strength, population, and commerce. According to Josephus, it was founded by a colony of Sidonians, 240 years before the erection of Solomon's Temple, or about 1250 years before the Christian era. But this must be a mistake, since Joshua, defining the territory allotted to the Tribe of Asher, speaks of Tyre as a "Strong City." (Jos. xix. 29.) Such was once the strength of this place, that Nebuchadnezzar, the greatest Conqueror of his time, was detained thirteen years in the Siege before he could gain possession. At length, the City was taken by assault and utterly destroyed, verifying in the most remarkable manner, the prophecy of Isaiah. (Isa. xxiii. 1.) The Tyrians, however, had removed with their property to an Island which lay opposite to the City, about half a mile from the shore. After seventy years they built a new City on the Island, near the site of the former, of which nothing remained but a small village amongst the ruins, called Old Tyre. The new city,—Insular Tyre, in course of a few years, rivalled its predecessor, and for a period of two hundred years continued to monopolise the Commerce of the East. It was so strong, that to reduce it cost the powerful army of Alexander seven months of incredible labour. To surmount the obstacle presented by its insular position, he had to construct an artifical Isthmus, or Causeway, from the Continent to the Island. This he accomplished by means of Timber brought from Lebanon, and by throwing the rubbish and ruins of the Old City into the sea. Like the sites of Nineveh and Babylon, that of Continental Tyre, cannot now be accurately recognised. The New City also gradually declined after the building of Alexandria, which, from its superior local advantages, drew away from Tyre her vast trade with India. Its downfall was accelerated by assaults of the Ptolemies of Egypt, and the Seleucidæ of Syria; after which it fell into the hands of the Romans, then of the Saracens, Crusaders, and Mamelukes, who nearly rased it to the ground; and finally it came under the rule of the Turks.

The prophecies have been verified to the letter in relation to this once proud City, which is now as Ezekiel describes it, a mere Fishing Village,—"a place for the spreading of nets." (Eze. xxvi. 5.) Lamartine visited it in 1832, and says, "Tyre, at present called *Sour* by the Arabs, appears to rise from the waves themselves. At a distance you would call it a handsome, new, white, and lively Town, looking on the sea; but it is only a beautiful shadow which vanishes on drawing near. A few hundred crumbling, and almost deserted, houses, in which the Arabs collect at evening, the large flocks of sheep and black goats, with long hanging ears, which defile before you in the plain. Such is the

Tyre of to-day! She has no longer the Harbour in the seas, or a Road on the land. The prophecies are long ago accomplished in her. We journeyed in silence, occupied in contemplating this wreck and dust of Empire, which we trampled. . . . . I thought on the prophecies, but saw neither Eagles nor Vultures, which ought, in order to fulfil them, to descend instantly from the mountains to devour this Corpse of a Town, reproved by God and the enemy of His people. At the moment I was making this reflection, some large, strange, and motionless object appeared on our left on the top of a perpendicular rock, which advanced into the plain, even to the route of the Caravans. When we were only fifty steps from the rock, we saw one of these objects expand his wide wings, and flap them against his sides with a noise like that of a sail set to the wind. We distinguished them as five Eagles of the largest kind I had ever seen. It required an effort of my reason not to behold behind them the lofty and terrible figure of the Poet of Vengeance, Ezekiel, rising above them, and pointing out to them with his eye and finger the City which God gave them to devour, whilst the storm of Divine anger shook his snowy streaming beard, and the fire of celestial wrath shot from his eyes."

SIDON.

About twenty-five miles North of Tyre is Sidon, or Zidon, which, like Tyre, was appointed to the Tribe of Asher, but they never took possession of it. (Jud. i. 31.) According to tradition it was the second city built after the Flood, and is supposed to have been founded by Sidon, the son of Canaan and great-grandson of Noah. For a long time it was a place of great architectural beauty and commercial importance; and the Sidonians are even said to have introduced the knowledge of Alphabetical Writing into Greece. They were the first manufacturers of Glass, and the earliest Shipwrights; and Sidonian workmen were employed by Solomon to hew and carve the wood for the Temple, and also to construct and navigate his Ships. Sidon, under her own Kings, enjoyed a high degree of opulence and commercial prosperity; though sometimes tributary to the Kings of Tyre. It was taken by Nebuchadnezzar, who, however, consented to receive the submission of this people, and permitted them to retain their own Monarchs. Entering afterwards into league with Nectanebus, King of Egypt, against Darius Ochus, King of Persia, the latter laid siege to the City. Finding resistance useless they set fire to their ships and the City, in which so large a quantity of gold and silver was melted down by the fire that Ochus sold the ashes for a considerable sum of money.

Sidon, however, was soon rebuilt, as, about eighteen years after, we find it submitting to Alexander. It subsequently shared the fate of the rest of Phœnicia, being alternately oppressed by the Kings of Syria and Egypt, while its extensive and lucrative Trade was diverted to Alexandria. After the subversion of the Grecian Empire, Sidon fell into the hands of the Romans, who deprived it of freedom. Many of the Sidonians were converted by the preaching of Christ, (Mar. iii. 8.) Paul touched here in his voyage to Rome. (Acts xxvii. 3.) After the breaking up of the Roman Empire, Sidon fell successively under the Saracens, Seljukian Turks, and the Sultans of Egypt, who, in 1289, that they might never again afford shelter to Christians, destroyed both it and Tyre. But it revived, and has since remained in the hands of the Ottoman Turks. Sidon, called *Saide*, has a population of about 5,000, and was the chief mart for Damascus and Upper Syria, until superseded by Beyrout. The harbour is nearly choked with sand. Broken columns and fragments of edifices,—relics of its eclipsed and departed grandeur, are yet discoverable without the walls.

BEYROUT.

After a seven hours sail, we landed at Beyrout on Sunday Morning, enjoyed·a Sabbath's rest, and on the morning following started for Lebanon and

Damascus; but in returning we remained here a week.

Beyrout is supposed to be the "Berothai" or "Berothath" mentioned in Scripture. (2 Sam. viii. 8; Eze. xlvii. 16.) It is beautifully situated, especially as viewed from the Sea. The Promontory on which it stands is triangular, the apex projecting some three miles into the Mediterranean, and the base running along the foot of Lebanon. The South-Western side is wholly composed of loose drifting sand, and has all the appearance of a Desert. The shore-line on the North-Western side is formed of a range of deeply-indented rocks and cliffs, worn by the waves into a thousand fantastic forms;—here gloomy caverns, into which the waters surge with a roar as of distant thunder; there jagged isolated rocks and bold precipices around which the white surf plays like a thing of life, sending up showers of spray whose globules and streamers like diamonds sparkle in the sun-shine. Behind these rocks the ground rises gradually for a mile or more, where it attains a height of 200 feet. In the middle of the shore-line stands the City—first a dense nucleus of buildings surrounded by an old tottering wall; then a broad *nebula* of picturesque villas, embowered in rich foliage, running up towards the heights of Lebanon, and extending far to the right and left. Beyond these are mulberry groves covering the acclivities and variegated by graceful palms and dark cypresses interspersed. The view commanded by the higher houses is magnificent, embracing the Bay of St. George; the indented Coast, retiring promontory on promontory, till lost in the distance; and the noble Ridge of Lebanon, with its wild glens, dark pine-forests, clustering villages, castellated convents, and snow-capped peaks sleeping in the clouds.

THE TOWN.—The old Town stands so near the beach as, during the prevalence of the Northerly gales, to get more of the sea-water than is agreeable. The Streets are narrow, dirty, badly paved, and so steep and tortuous that the merchandise landed at the Port has to be carried off on the backs of men. The Houses are of stone, substantially built; and a few of the Villas in the suburbs have some pretensions to architectural taste. The narrow lanes that pass through the gardens from one villa to another, seem to have been constructed after the models of the streets, as irregular, circuitous, and inconvenient as possible. They form a complete labyrinth, which a stranger tries in vain to thread. In Summer they are filled knee-deep with sand, and shut in by tall hedges of prickly-pear, excluding every breath of air, so that in passing through them one feels as if walking amid the ashes of a half-extinct furnace. In Winter every lane becomes a torrent-bed, sometimes almost impassable to man, and even dangerous to

Y

quadrupeds. Yet through these the Merchants plod day after day from their trim Villas to their Counting-houses in the City, equipped as for an aquatic excursion. "It is amusing," says an eye-witness, "to see them, here taking a flying leap over a gulf, there making a desperate plunge, while yonder a kind of ferry is established over a little lake, at which half-a-dozen ferry-men fight, the passenger the while grasping the neck and brawny shoulders of one, and keeping the rest at bay with the point of his umbrella." In time Beyrout may have the luxury of streets and roads; but until they are formed, it is folly to talk of wheeled conveyances. The Walls of the Town were never strong, and at present serve only to interrupt traffic, for which beneficent reason the Turks seem inclined to preserve them!

THE PORT is small but crowded; it lies between a projecting Cliff and an insulated Tower, now in ruins, called *Burj Fanzar*, which bears, like the rest of the Fortifications, many a mark of British projectiles. The little Quay is full of bustle. Though Beyrout ranks only as a third-rate town in Syria, it is decidedly the most prosperous. The Warehouses, Offices, and suburban Villas, of the European Merchants give the place a Western air, and the wealth and activity of foreign enterprise seem to have infused vitality into the natives. The principal article of export is raw-silk; and the trade in this is ever increasing.

Lebanon is gradually becoming one vast Mulberry-Plantation, to meet the growing demand for silk-worms. The Mulberry-groves surrounding Beyrout are rich and highly ornamental. Vines are so trained from tree to tree, as to form beautiful festoons, laden with clusters of grapes. The importance of this Port is recognised in the residence of the Consular-General of Syria, and a Vice-Consul. In addition to the Austrian lines, there are also French packets constantly running in here; and once a month, there is likewise an English screw steamer direct from Liverpool.

POPULATION, &c.—The Population of Beyrout is now estimated at 45,000. One-third of these are Muslems, and the rest Christians and Jews. The American Presbyterians have a Mission here, and conduct a public Religious Service in their Chapel at half-past ten on the Sunday Mornings. Since the establishment of this Mission, now nearly a quarter of a century ago, Education has been stimulated. Their Schools have created a taste for letters, and the Press conducted under their guidance has done much to foster and improve it. They publish not only excellent Religious Books, but also good Elementary Treatises in the various branches of Science and Art.

LEBANON.

In passing from Beyrout to Damascus we cross

over a shoulder of the famous Mountains of Lebanon, so frequently mentioned in the Sacred Writings as an emblem of "Majesty" and "Strength." The Road over which we went was constructed at considerable cost by the French, and is traversed every alternate day by an Omnibus which is so arranged as to accommodate First, Second, and Third-Class Passengers. We found the privilege of travelling once more upon a wheeled conveyance a very agreeable change. The Omnibus was drawn by five horses, but the steeps of the mountain were such, that it consumed about nine hours before we were over the shoulder and at the base on the other side.

Lebanon is not an isolated Mountain, but rather a long Range, extending from the neighbourhood of Sidon on the West, to the vicinity of Damascus Eastward; and forming the extreme Northern boundary of the Holy Land. It is the centre, or nucleus, of the Ridges running North, South, and East, and overtops them all, its summits being capped with clouds and tipped with snow. This magnificent rampart seems to enclose the country. From its highest point, distinguished by the name of *Sannin*, the immensity of space becomes a fresh subject of admiration. On every side the horizon seems without bounds; the sight being lost over the Desert which extends to the Persian Gulf, and over the sea which washes the coasts of Europe. Surveying chains of mountains the mind is instantly transported from Antioch to Jerusalem, and is filled with fresh delight as the thunder growls beneath. On the sides of the mountain, stones, detached by the waters, rise like artificial ruins. By thaws and earthquakes these rocks have been known to lose their equilibrium, roll down on the neighbouring houses, and bury the inhabitants. About twenty years before Volney's visit, a whole Village was overwhelmed by a fragment of the mountain slipping from its base, and he notes that more recently an entire hill-side, covered with mulberries and vines, was detached by a sudden thaw, and launched like a ship from the stocks into the valley below. By cultivated terraces all these mountains have the appearance of amphitheatres, every step of which is a row of vines or mulberries; in some instances the gradations on the same acclivity being from a hundred to a hundred and twenty. The valleys which separate them are also extremely fertile, producing corn, wine, and oil, in great abundance.

THE CEDARS are famous in Sacred History as the "Trees of the Lord" and "Trees of His planting"—the emblems of majesty, grandeur and strength, and as furnishing the wood used in the Temple of Solomon. (1 Kings v. 6; Ezra iii. 7; Isa. ii. 12, 13; xxxvii. 24; Am. ii. 9; Psa. xxix. 4, 5; xcii. 12; civ. 16.) Not lying in our way, we had no opportunity of seeing the representatives of the vast forests which once, beneath the stress of the storm, made the very sides of Lebanon seem to shake. (Psa. lxxii. 16.) But we give the following descriptive passage from a recent traveller:—

"At the head of the Wady Kadesh there is a vast Recess in the Central Ridge of Lebanon, some eight miles in diameter, in the midst of which, on an irregular knoll, stands the clump of Cedars. There is scarcely a patch of verdure on the surrounding declivities. Seen at a distance, they are like a speck on that vast mountain; but on entering the grove, all feelings of disappointment vanish. Then the beautiful fan-like branches, and graceful pyramidal forms of the younger trees; the huge trunks of the patriarchs, and their great gnarled branches extending far on each side, interlacing with their brethren; and the sombre shade they make in the midst of a blaze of light—all tend to excite the highest admiration. The whole Grove is now scarcely half-a-mile in circumference, and may contain about four hundred trees of all sizes—the young ones mostly on the outskirts, and the oldest in the centre. Only about a dozen very ancient trees remain, one or two of which are upwards of 40 feet in circumference; but the trunks are much broken and disfigured partly by the snows of Winter, but chiefly by the *Vandalism* of Visitors, inscribing their names on their sides. There are thirty or forty others of respectable dimensions, some being three or four and even five feet in diameter."

In returning from Damascus over the back of Lebanon, we encountered a heavy fall of snow, in consequence of which the horses had difficult work to drag us along. The temperature of these mountains is so various, at different degrees of elevation, that the Arabian Poets say, "Lebanon bears Winter on his head, Spring upon his shoulders, and Autumn in his bosom, while Summer lies sleeping at his feet." Its Hebrew name, as well as the modern appellation of *Gibl Leban*, both signify "The White Mountain," and refer to the perpetual snows which lie upon its peaks. Judging from the position of the line of congelation, the summits must be about 11,000 feet above the level of the Sea.

DAMASCUS.

Our Royal road makers have thrown up a batch of temporary buildings Eastward of Lebanon, for the accommodation of travellers. We remained there for the night; but such a night's lodging I never had before. The apartments for man and beast are very similar. Our table was spread with abundance of provisions, and wine into the bargain, but so roughly and dirtily served that none but Arabs or Turks could relish the repast. The horses of the Company arrived from Damascus for our conveyance over the remainder of the journey, as the carriage-road had not been completed the whole length of the route. We were therefore once more on the saddles, but such saddles that the bare backs of well kept horses would have been preferable. "Over the hills and far away" we went, reached Damascus at half-past one, and put up at the Hotel El Locanda, a large aristocratic establishment, situated in the centre of the City, in the "Street which is called Straight," believed to have been the identical Street of that name in which Ananias found Saul of Tarsus in the house of Judas. (Acts ix. 11.)

REMINISCENCES. — Damascus, according to Josephus, was founded by Uz, the Son of Aram, and great-grandson of Noah—an opinion which does not appear to have been disputed by historians. The family of Aram colonised the North-Eastern portions of Syria, whence that region is in Scripture uniformly called *Aram*, in places rendered "Syria" in our Version. (Thus, Jud. x. 6; 2 Sam. viii. 6; 1 Kings x. 29; Isa. vii. 2; Eze. xvi. 57.) This particular section of the country is called *Aram Damesk*, or "Aram of Damascus," because, to use the words of Isaiah, "The Head of Syria is Damascus," and so it still remains. (2 Sam. viii. 6; 1 Chro. xviii. 6; Isa. vii. 8.) Certain it is that Damascus was already a noted place in the days of Abraham, the "Steward of whose house was

Eliezer of Damascus." (Gen. xv. 2.) Under the sovereignty of the Hadads, it was the great rival of Israel. (1 Kings xv. 18—21.) During that stormy period the little Jewish maid was carried captive, whose suggestion led to the healing of the leprosy of Naaman. (2 Kings v. 1—14.) David subdued Damascus and laid the inhabitants under tribute; but after his death one Rezon, a servant of Hadadezer King of Zobah, made himself master of the place, and "was an adversary to Israel all the days of Solomon." (1 Kings xi. 23, 24; xv. 18, 19.) After a variety of fortunes, Damascus successively fell under the power of the Assyrians, Babylonians, and Persians, from the last of whom it was taken by Alexander the Great. Then it made a part of the Kingdom of the Selucidæ, from whom it passed into the hands of the Romans. In the time of the Apostle Paul, whose miraculous conversion was so interestingly associated with this City, it belonged to the dependent Kingdom of the Arabian Prince Aretas. Christianity advanced rapidly here; and its Metropolitan, with *seven* of his Suffragans, was present at the council of Nice. About seventy years afterwards the great Temple of Damascus, in which idolatry had been practised, was converted into a Christian Church and dedicated to St. John the Baptist. For nearly three centuries Christianity was dominant; but in the year 634, Abu-Beker, the successor of Mahomet, subdued the City and substituted Islamism. It then became the Capital of the Mahometan World, till the Caliphate was removed to Bagdad, and finally came into the hands of the Turks.

The Town, by the natives called *Es Sham*, lies in a plain at the Eastern foot of Anti-Libanus. Its environs are exquisitely beautiful, to which, however, the interior does not fully correspond. Both the Plain and City are well watered by the rivers Abana and Pharpar, which Naaman favourably contrasted with the Jordan of Palestine. Damascus occupies one of those sites which nature seems to have intended for a great perennial City. It is most remarkable that under every change of Dynasty or Form of Government through which it passed, it held its station among the great Capitals of the World. It prospered alike under Persian despotism, Grecian anarchy, and Roman patronage; and prospers still despite the oppression and misrule of its Turkish Masters. It has stood for ages, surviving the decay of many cities upon whose birth it looked down as a venerable Patriarch looks upon a Child. In 1858, thousands of its Christian population were barbarously massacred and their dwellings burnt to the ground, making the Christian Quarter of the city a Ruin, in which state it still remains. A few days before we arrived two Christians had been murdered. Still, despite all the elements of strife, Damascus remains a noble Metropolis.

THE BAZAARS have long been celebrated as amongst the best in the East. Every trade has its own Quarter or Section in the immense network of business establishments. Thus, there is the Mercers' Bazaar, the Tailors' Bazaar, that of the Tobacconists, that of the Shoe-Makers, of the Silversmiths, Clogs, Books, and "Old Clo'." Before each shop turbaned heads and long-robed figures are the familiar objects. All the Costumes of Asia may be seen here pushing along the crowded thoroughfares, and struggling with panniered-donkeys, mules and camels. The Shops are well stocked; but five or six times the value of each article is ruthlessly demanded, while the Vendor assures you with an oath that only yourself could buy it for the money! Englishmen, who have not patience to bargain with these gentry, are generally "fleeced." The principal manufactures are Silk goods, which are exported to Egypt, Bagdad, and Persia; coarse woollen cloth, almost universally worn by the peasants of Syria and the Bedaween; gold and silver ornaments; and "Damascus blades."

ANTIQUITIES.—In the thoroughfare now called the "Street of Bazaars," have been recently discovered fragments of pavement and broken columns showing the course of the "Street called Straight" or *Via Recta*, which here, as in all the Syro-Greek or Syro-Roman towns—Palmyra, Gerasa, Sebaste, Philadelphia, and Antioch—intersected the City in a "straight" line, adorned on each side with Corinthian colonnades. A few steps out of the "Street of Bazaars," in an open space called "The Sheykh's Place," is the so-called "House of Judas" which contains a square room with a stone floor, one portion walled off for a Tomb, which is covered with the usual offering of shawls. In another "Quarter" is shown the "House of Ananias." Both are reverenced by Mussulmans as well as Christians. Four traditional sites are pointed out as the "Scene of the Conversion of St. Paul," which of course makes it at least three chances to one that any of them is the true place. At a distance of two miles outside the Walls of the City is the village of Hobah said to be that to which Abraham pursued the Kings. (Gen. xiv. 15.) The Synagogue there, is the only place now visited. In a corner of this is a cavity said to have been the Retreat of Elisha. It is entered by a rude Staircase now almost worn away. Sick pilgrims "come and sleep here and rise the next morning well."(!) In the centre of the building is a space enclosed within rails, formerly said to mark the place of Hazael's Coronation, but now called the "Grave of Gehazi," Elisha's Servant, said to have died here aged 120. Outside the Gate of the City is a Leper Hospital supposed to occupy the site of Naaman's House. The place where Paul was "let down in a basket from the Wall" is also pointed out by the Monks. (Acts ix. 25; 2 Cor. xi. 33.)

POPULATION, &c.—The population of Damascus last census was about 150,000, of which 129,000 were Muslems, 15,000 Christians, and 6,000 Jews. But since the Massacre of 1858 the number of the Christians will be greatly reduced. The Presbyterian Church of Ireland has a Mission Staff of three Ministers. The Associated Reformed Church of the United States has also two Missionaries, together with a Physician, and a Lady who superintends a Female School.

RETURN TO ALEXANDRIA.

As already expressed, after spending two days at Damascus, we re-crossed the shoulder of Lebanon and arrived at Beyrout where we remained a week. While here, when comfortably sheltered in the Hotel, the rain came pouring down; but during our fifteen days in the Desert, on the Dromedary and in the Tent, and during the nineteen days we spent in the Mountains and Valleys of Palestine and Syria, the weather was beautifully fine. This was to us a cause of gratitude to the Sovereign Disposer. From Beyrout, on the 5th of April, we took Ship for Marseilles, and on the third day entered the Port of Alexandria. The Sultan was in the Harbour, in honour of whose presence the vessels riding at anchor had all their colours flying, and the City was brilliantly illuminated at night.

MESSINA.

On the afternoon of the 9th we sailed out of the Harbour of Alexandria, and after a very pleasant voyage of four days, we touched at Messina. Like all Mediterranean Towns, it has a most pleasing appearance viewed from the water. The houses are lofty, stone-built, and partly covering the sides of the hills. The present town is new; for the old town was completely destroyed by an Earthquake in 1780; it has several excellent buildings, and one or two good streets. It contains about 73,000 inhabitants. They carry on a brisk Trade in spinning and weaving silk; beside the Exports of various kinds of fruits and wines, and a large quantity of kid-skins. The Harbour is more than two miles in circumference, and is one of the best in the Mediterranean. The surrounding country also opens beautiful with varied prospects of mountains and woods, in a district of uncommon fertility.

STROMBOLI.

Sailing out of Messina we had a noble view of Stromboli, which of itself constitutes one of the most Northerly of the Lipari Islands. The mountain has two summits, and is nine miles circuit at its base.

About half way up on the Northern side is the Crater, which for two thousand years has never ceased to burn, and still continues to throw up lava attended with violent detonations. Even when peaceable, the vortex is in a state of ignition, and reflects a clear light into the atmosphere above, with coruscations resembling those of the *Aurora Borealis*. At times pieces of lava of a globular form, four or five feet in diameter, are thrown to the distance of a mile from the shore, while the flames are distinguishable for ninety miles. About a thousand persons inhabit the sides of the Volcano, who make them yield Malmsey-wine and olives. The Southern side, which, from the position of the Crater and the intervening Summit, is little liable to injury, has a copious Spring of excellent water, the only one on the Island.

ETNA.

Running along the Northern Coast of Sicily, we next sighted Etna, a huge Volcano, whose base covers a circumference of sixty-three miles, and whose peaks attain an altitude of 10,954 feet above the level of the sea. No less than sixty Eruptions of this mountain are recorded. In 1693 there was a violent Earthquake in the Island, and the Cone of the mountain sank considerably. The last eruption occurred in November, 1832, when the burning lava spread for miles over the Country, desolating luxuriant gardens and cultivated fields. From the recesses of the Volcano came forth the purest streams of fire and burning torrents of smoke. Those who ascend this Mountain, pass through all gradations of Climate from the glow of Italian sunshine to the cold of the Polar regions. About a mile below the Great Crater are the Ruins of an ancient structure, called *Il Torre del Filosofo*, which some imagine to have been built by the philosopher Empedocles, and others suppose to have been a Temple of Vulcan. These Ruins are of brick, and seem to have been ornamented with marble.

SYRACUSE.

About a hundred miles South of Messina is Syracuse, where Paul spent three days, after leaving Melita, when being conveyed a prisoner to Rome. (Acts xxviii. 12.) Under its own Kings it acquired great wealth and power by means of an extensive Trade. About two hundred years B.C. it was taken by the Romans after a Siege, rendered famous by the mechanical contrivances whereby Archimedes protracted the defence. Strabo assigns to the ancient City, some of whose Ruins are still visible, a circumference equal to twenty English miles. It is still a Town of considerable importance.

CORSICA.

On the second day after leaving Messina, we passed through the Straits of Bonifaccio, which separate the Islands of Sardinia and Corsica, the latter of which is famous as the birth-place of Napoleon Buonaparte. It is about a hundred and fifty miles long, forty-five broad, and nearly three hundred and twenty in circumference. It has few natural advantages; the air is unwholesome, and the soil in general barren; but it has several excellent Harbours. In this inconsiderable place that fiery spirit first drew the vital air, whose insatiable ambition and incomparable genius carried him through seas of blood to all but the Imperial Throne of Europe. It is remarkable that Napoleon never shewed much affection for his native country; on the contrary, all his attachment was to France, as appears by his Will, which was registered at Doctors' Commons, August 5th, 1824, in which he recommended his son to do as he did—"Everything for France."

SEQUEL OF THE JOURNEY.

The Straits of Bonifaccio, through which we passed, are three miles across. The passage is considered highly dangerous. In the first year of the Crimean War, a French Ship was wrecked there, with 1000 troops on board, every man of whom perished. Leaving the Straits, we sailed before the wind until we reached Marseilles on the evening of the 15th, so that the Voyage from Alexandria was accomplished in Six Days. The same night we were on the Rails for Paris, and slept comfortably in the carriage. During the whole of the day following we travelled incessantly, and continued running until four o'clock on Friday morning, when we arrived in the French Metropolis. Here we revisited some places of interest, and the same evening booked for Dieppe, whence we embarked for Newhaven, and arrived in London before noon on the next day. The following morning (Sunday) I was melted to tears under a rich discourse by Dr. Cumming, from 1 John iii. 1. In the Afternoon I heard a useful Sermon in St. Paul's Cathedral on the "Eleventh Hour Labourer." (Matt. xx. 1—16.) And in the Evening I was edified by a heart-searching address by the Hon. and Rev. Baptist W. Noel, on the "Virgins." (Matt. xxv. 1—13.) How remarkable the contrast with Popish Superstition and Christless Mahometanism! By the first train on Monday morning we were off for Leeds, and arrived safely in the afternoon. But O! the sight of dear old friendly faces! It is impossible to describe the heartfelt gratitude and blissful emotions which can only be excelled by those of our anticipated arrival at the Heavenly Home! The Climate of Egypt is beautiful; the Sights of the Holy Land are wondrous; but my sympathies are with the sentiment of Cowper:—

"England with all thy faults I love thee still."

What can compensate the loss of Civil and Religious Liberty; the banishment of the Gospel, and the privation of Christian Friendships?

In conclusion, I would devoutly record my deep gratitude to the God of my life for His gracious goodness evermore resting upon me "in journeyings often, in perils of waters, in perils of robbers, in perils by the heathen, in perils in the city, in perils in the wilderness, in perils in the sea." During our Excursion two Shipwrecks occurred in the seas over which we sailed, yet no storm invaded us. Three Murders were perpetrated in localities through which we journeyed, yet no weapon was lifted against us. I thank God I have do disposition to assign these things to the play of chances; I acknowledge no chance, but adoringly confess a Supreme and Universal Providence. To the Living God I would devote the remnant of my days, and I would fain join in the immortal song which shall celebrate His Glorious Praise in a superior clime. To His approbation, above all others, I commend the present attempt to possess my Friends with the information elucidatory of various passages in the Volume of Inspiration, collected particularly in connection with my Excursions into the Lands of the East.

www.ingramcontent.com/pod-product-compliance
Lightning Source LLC
Chambersburg PA
CBHW030257240426
43673CB00040B/989